GLOBAL ECOPOLITICS REVISITED

Faced with worsening environmental indicators, cooperation hurdles, and the limited effectiveness of current institutions, reforming international environmental governance has proven elusive, despite various diplomatic initiatives at the United Nations level over the last two decades. Overcoming the current dead end, however, may rest less in devising new arrangements than in challenging how the problem has been approached.

Presenting a multifaceted exploration of some of the key issues and questions in global ecopolitics, this book brings together recent advances in research on global environmental governance in order to identify new avenues of inquiry and action. Each chapter questions elements of the current wisdom and covers a topic that lies at the heart of global environmental governance, including the reasons for engagement, the evolving relationship between science and policy, the potential and limits of the European Union as a key actor, the role of developing and emergent countries, and the contours of a complex governance of international environmental issues.

Laying the foundation for rethinking at a time of great transformation in global ecopolitics, this book will be important reading for students of environmental politics and governance. It will also be of relevance to policy makers with an interest in going beyond the prevailing discourse on this crucial topic.

Philippe Le Prestre is a professor of political science at Laval University (Quebec, Canada) where he specializes in international environmental politics. He was the founding director of Laval University's Sustainable Development Institute (2005–11) and between 1995 and 1999 he chaired the environmental studies section of the International Studies Association.

"Le Prestre provides a refreshing exposé of the convenient fictions which underlie the largely US-centric study of global ecopolitics, and how they distract attention from the complex nature of global challenges more generally. He calls for a more comprehensive and interlinked approach to the study of global environmental politics, and IR more generally; borrowing from and applying complexity theory."

Peter Haas, Professor of Political Science, University of Massachusetts Amherst, USA

"A seasoned observer of global environmental politics, Le Prestre goes far beyond conventional wisdom to offer refreshingly alternative insights into the evolution of the field in this well-crafted treatise. This is an impressive work that captures multiple perspectives and channels them into a robust agenda for future scholarship."

Peter Stoett, Director, Loyola Sustainability Research Centre and Professor of Political Science/International Relations, Concordia University, Canada

"By questioning some apparently strong assumptions that structure the field of global environmental governance, *Global Ecopolitics Revisited* brings a clear added value and a welcome complement to existing textbooks. The author not only deconstructs common understandings of global environmental politics, but also proposes new thinking, tackling recent issues of global environmental governance with an innovative perspective based on complex systems and fractal governance."

Amandine Orsini, Professor of International Relations, Université Saint-Louis – Bruxelles, Belgium

GLOBAL ECOPOLITICS REVISITED

Toward a Complex Governance of Global Environmental Problems

Philippe Le Prestre

First published 2017
by Routledge
2 Park Square, Milton Park, Abingdon, Oxon OX14 4RN

and by Routledge
711 Third Avenue, New York, NY 10017

Routledge is an imprint of the Taylor & Francis Group, an informa business

© 2017 Philippe Le Prestre

The right of Philippe Le Prestre to be identified as author of this work has been asserted by him in accordance with sections 77 and 78 of the Copyright, Designs and Patents Act 1988.

All rights reserved. No part of this book may be reprinted or reproduced or utilized in any form or by any electronic, mechanical, or other means, now known or hereafter invented, including photocopying and recording, or in any information storage or retrieval system, without permission in writing from the publishers.

Trademark notice: Product or corporate names may be trademarks or registered trademarks, and are used only for identification and explanation without intent to infringe.

British Library Cataloguing in Publication Data
A catalogue record for this book is available from the British Library

Library of Congress Cataloging in Publication Data
Names: Le Prestre, Philippe G., author.
Title: Global ecopolitics revisited : towards a complex governance of global environmental problems / Philippe Le Prestre.
Description: Abingdon, Oxon ; New York, NY : Routledge, 2017.
Identifiers: LCCN 2016041404 | ISBN 9781138680180 (hb) | ISBN 9781138680203 (pb) | ISBN 9781315563695 (ebk)
Subjects: LCSH: Environmental policy--International cooperation. | Environmental management--International cooperation. | Global environmental change--International cooperation. | Globalization--Environmental aspects.
Classification: LCC GE170 .L424 2017 | DDC 363.7/056--dc23
LC record available at https://lccn.loc.gov/2016041404

ISBN: 978-1-138-68018-0 (hbk)
ISBN: 978-1-138-68020-3 (pbk)
ISBN: 978-1-315-56369-5 (ebk)

Typeset in Bembo
by Taylor & Francis Books

CONTENTS

List of acronyms   vi
Acknowledgments   x

Introduction: challenging the doxa of global ecopolitics   1

1   The injunction of the ecological crises   8

2   International environmental governance: beyond cosmopolitanism   27

3   Bridging the science-policy divide   53

4   The European Union and global environmental diplomacy   73

5   The power of the weak: developing countries in the global governance of climate change and biodiversity   104

6   Toward fractal governance   129

Index   *159*

LIST OF ACRONYMS

ABM	Agent-Based Models
AILAC	Asociación Independiente de América Latina y el Caribe
AOSIS	Association of Small Island States
ASEAN	Association of South-East Asian Nations
BASIC	Brazil, South Africa, India, China
BRICS	Brazil, Russia, India, China, South Africa
CBD	Convention on Biological Diversity
CCD	See UNCCD
CDM	Clean Development Mechanism
CFC	Chlorofluorocarbon
CGIAR	Consultative Group on International Agricultural Research
CI	Conservation International
CITES	Convention on International Trade in Endangered Species of Wild Fauna and Flora
CMS	Convention on Migratory Species
COP	Conference of the Parties
CSD	Commission on Sustainable Development
DDT	Dichlorodiphenyltrichloroethane
EEZ	Exclusive Economic Zone
ENGO	Environmental Nongovernmental Organization
ESCAP	Economic and Social Commission for Asia and the Pacific
FAO	Food and Agriculture Organization
FIELD	Foundation for International Environment Law and Development
FSC	Forest Stewardship Council
GBA	Global Biodiversity Assessment
GEF	Global Environment Facility
GEG	Global Environmental Governance

GEOBON	Group on Earth Observation Biodiversity Observation Network
GHG	Greenhouse Gas
GMOs	Genetically Modified Organisms
IAASTD	International Assessment of Agricultural Knowledge Science and Technology for Development
IAC	InterAcademy Council
ICLEI	International Council for Local Environmental Initiatives
ICSU	International Council for Science [International Council of Scientific Unions]
IEG	International Environmental Governance
IGO	Intergovernmental Organization
IMO	International Maritime Organization
INDC	Intended Nationally Determined Contribution
IPBES	Intergovernmental Platform on Biodiversity and Ecosystems Services
IPCC	Intergovernmental Panel on Climate Change
IR	International Relations
ITPGRFA	International Treaty on Plant Genetic Resources for Food and Agriculture
IUCN	International Union for Conservation of Nature
IWC	International Whaling Commission
LDCs	Least Developed Countries
MA	Millennium Ecosystem Assessment
MARPOL	International Convention for the Prevention of Pollution from Ships
MEA	Multilateral Environmental Agreement
MSC	Marine Stewardship Council
NGO	Nongovernmental Organization
NIEO	New International Economic Order
NRC	National Role Conception
OECD	Organisation for Economic Co-operation and Development
OPEC	Organization of Petroleum Exporting Countries
PCDR	Principle of Common but Differentiated Responsibility
REACH	Registration, Evaluation, Authorisation and Restriction of Chemical Products
REDD	Reducing Emissions from Deforestation and Forest Degradation
RIOD	International NGO Desertification Network [Réseau international des organisations non gouvernementales sur la désertification]
SSC	South-South Cooperation
TEEB	The Economics of Ecosystems and Biodiversity
TREMs	Trade-Related Environmental Measures
TRIPS	Trade-related intellectual property rights
UNCCD	United Nations Convention to Combat Desertification
UNCSD	United Nations Conference on Sustainable Development

UNDP	United Nations Development Programme
UNEO	United Nations Environment Organization
UNEP	United Nations Environment Programme
UNESCO	United Nations Educational, Scientific, and Cultural Organization
UNFCCC	United Nations Framework Convention on Climate Change
USAID	United States Agency for International Development
WEO	World Environment Organization
WHC	World Heritage Convention
WTO	World Trade Organization
WWF	World Wildlife Fund

Redoutant plus l'isolement que l'erreur, ils se joignent à la foule.[1]
Tocqueville, *L'Ancien régime et la révolution*

Toute idée devient fausse au moment où l'on s'en contente.[2]
Alain, *Les Marchands de sommeil*

*C'est une mission de l'intellectuel que d'empêcher
la métamorphose d'un moyen politique en article de foi, en mythe.*[3]
Claude Aveline, *Les devoirs de l'esprit*

---

1   More afraid of being isolated than wrong, they join the crowd.
2   Any idea becomes false as soon as we settle for it.
3   One of the missions of the intellectual is to prevent political means from becoming articles of faith or myths.

ACKNOWLEDGMENTS

This book grew out of a series of lectures given as holder of the International Francqui Professor Chair at three Belgian universities (Université Saint-Louis, Université Libre de Bruxelles, Gent University) in 2015–16. I am deeply grateful to the foundation for the honor thus bestowed as well as to these three institutions (and particularly Amandine Orsini, Barbara Delcourt, and Thijs Van de Graaf) for having sponsored and welcomed me, thereby allowing me to enjoy the fruits of stimulating and lively intellectual environments. Through this chair, the Francqui Foundation granted me the invaluable and rare opportunity to go back to some of my earlier work in order to organize my thinking around some of its implications. The Université Saint-Louis provided the work space, the resources, and the intellectual environment in which I could toy with those ideas. I owe a special debt to Amandine Orsini for having suggested themes that proved to constitute sound departure points for a general inquiry about the nature of the ecopolitical doxa and complex governance.

INTRODUCTION

Challenging the doxa of global ecopolitics

The emergence and resolution of global environmental problems constitute one of the major challenges to humanity's quest for security and justice. Through its concern for the relationships between these issues and traditional political issues, for the various roles that international actors play in their dynamics, for the bases of international cooperation, and for the interactions among international and national arrangements, global ecopolitics opens a window onto the very nature and foundations of contemporary international relations.[1]

This book is about the need to go beyond the received wisdom of international environmental politics and reflect on how a complex systems approach might help define the contours of a new model of international environmental governance likely to help maintain the capacity of societies to choose their own future. The increasing complexity of environmental questions, the relentless degradation of ecosystems, the difficulty of changing the behavior of international and national actors, and the need to reconcile the traditional aspirations of societies and individuals with the transformations of their physical and social environment all make the definition of new forms of governance ever more urgent. The temptation then is great to turn to miraculous solutions. Under pressure from the twin logics of politics and bureaucracy, the assertions and generalizations they represent navigate back and forth from the local to the global, and because they are plausible they become necessary, thereby mutating into unquestioned principles of action. Slogans, half-truths, and common wisdom have diverse roots, be they political interests, belief systems, experience, or scientific knowledge. They constitute a doxa; that is, a set of ideas and propositions shared by members of a community that are taken for granted and guide thinking and action.

The quest for a new model of governance, however, requires shedding untested or unqualified articles of faith, disguised as knowledge, that help interpret the world and guide human actions. These beliefs operate as so many intellectual straightjackets that may hinder international, national, and local cooperation, and constrain learning capacities through an illusory quest for universal recipes. Many of them are held and disseminated by intergovernmental organizations (IGOs) and nongovernmental organizations (NGOs), as well as bilateral aid agencies. They shape the prevailing international discourse and, consequently, the definition and resolution of global environmental problems.

Global ecopolitics cannot avoid relying on such slogans and half-truths, since it is the realm of scientific and political uncertainties, of evolving values, and of formulaic incantations on which both activists and politicians rely for rapid decision making and support. The ideas they disseminate reflect the experience, knowledge, assumptions, and values of a small number of countries, mostly from North America and Northern Europe. Although this common wisdom has resulted in many positive outcomes, it has also excluded entire bodies of knowledge as well as cultural areas from the definition of environmental problems and solutions. These beliefs may also blind and prevent decision makers from asking questions more likely to help them apprehend better the existing problems and discern the contours of available options. They even become dangerous when they substitute for political thinking, as if environmental protection and politics were two separate universes. These articles of faith, whose empirical foundations are often shaky, have real political consequences on the distribution of authority, power, wealth, and values, as well as on the probability to realize collective aspirations. They often ignore the history and research findings from areas that lie beyond the horizon of those organizations that dominate the discourse on the environment. They prevent national experience from contributing to international debates and widen the gap between the expectations of the "international community" and the local understanding of problems. Consequently, they may hinder the hard task of organizational and social learning as well as the search for models that reconcile the evolution of the international system and the need to address environmental problems in a coordinated fashion.

It seems important, therefore, to reflect not only on the dimensions and foundations of these sets of received ideas but also on the processes that generate and disseminate them, on their transformation into dogma, and on their impact on the behavior of international, national, and local actors. The alternative is not to accept or reject them; the behavior of individuals and groups is always rooted in belief systems, and the values many of them embody are indeed laudable. These beliefs also have important sociopolitical and heuristic functions. Our purpose, then, is not so much to condemn their use than to ascertain their limits. Our task is to decipher the propositions regarding the origins of environmental problems and the solutions deemed most appropriate, and to identify their scientific and empirical foundations, as well as the mechanisms under which they operate, including the conditions under which they hold.

At least five drivers explain the prevalence of these articles of faith as well as the propensity of certain actors to appeal to them. First, they may represent plausible hypotheses. Too often, however, plausibility mutates into truth. Second, bureaucratic factors come into play. Common wisdom makes the job of task managers in aid agencies easier and protects the organization from criticisms in case things go wrong. One does not have to think about the best way to tackle a given problem in a specific set of circumstances, only apply recipes or follow a process. Third, from a political viewpoint, intellectual slogans are convenient rallying cries for NGOs and IGOs alike. Value-based NGOs find them to be powerful tools for mobilizing people and attacking those opposed to their preferred course of action. For IGOs, they may be convenient means with which to try and bypass states. Fourth, this common wisdom has a decidedly cultural origin. NGOs are particularly forceful generators and vehicles of such beliefs. Many precepts, for example, reflect a basic distrust of the state that lies at the heart of Anglo-Saxon political philosophy. The state is a potential tyrant, not a liberator against the power of local elites (as in France) or a protector in exchange for support (as in Asia). Finally, they may reflect an absence of memory.

Widely held beliefs embody successful issue framing, a single process by which problems are identified, causes diagnosed, moral judgments inferred, and solutions promoted (Entman 1993). Framing determines which issues get on the political agenda, reveals connections with more widely held values and helps build support with groups that may not be keen on taking action (Mitchell 2002; Young 1998). Issue framing is a political process, involving power relationships among various networks of interests and knowledge (scientists, IGOs, NGOs, governments, business, local communities, etc.); yet we still know little about the process through which a discourse becomes widely accepted and the propositions it carries common wisdom (Ibid.). In the case of climate change, the way the issue was cast alienated significant sections of society and failed to convince many of the necessity of taking concerted action. Fear of immediate, high mitigation costs trumped vague risk estimates for the distant future. A remarkable and partly successful strategy was to reframe the issue in economic terms, with the publication of the 2006 Stern Review, which emphasized the long-term economic costs of inaction. Similar considerations surrounded the drafting of the report on The Economics of Ecosystems and Biodiversity (TEEB) in 2010 which built, in part, on the Millennium Ecosystem Assessment (MA) that sought to reframe the biodiversity *problématique* in terms of ecosystem services.

Slogans and assorted myths then respond to the need for simplification in the face of complexity. Unravelling the connections among multiple factors, and identifying the uncertainties surrounding knowledge and the conditions under which such knowledge holds is difficult and may complicate political mobilization and education. Hence complex problems are reduced to simple challenges, and contextual solutions become universal remedies. When discourse is dominated by groups eager to promote a message of action, environmental information is portrayed in simple often value-laden terms; with the inherent risk of demobilization when confronted with failure. The semantics of this discourse are often vague: concepts such as participation (why? whose participation? how?), sanctions (what types?), effectiveness (what kind?) are ill defined when they are not outright false ("the encroaching desert," "the lungs of the earth," "indigenous populations in tune with their environment," "the need for agreements with teeth," etc.).

Received ideas abound; this book will only evoke a few of them. They have been selected because they are representative of the main assumptions driving the discourse about international environmental governance and tend to guide the thinking and actions of national and international actors, as well as local populations. Identifying them and examining them critically is the first step in the process of designing a new model of international environmental governance that takes into account the results and uncertainties of existing research, as well as the contextual complexity of environmental problems.

Indeed, the early 1990s saw the affirmation of a broad governance shift away from the centralization of authority and toward decentralized governance and polycentricism. Whereas decentralized governance (subsidiarity, polycentrism, scales and levels of governance, etc.) has been widely documented and discussed at the domestic level (Ostrom 1990; Smith and Wolfish 2002), the international governance discourse on the environment has long favored some sort of centralized authority as the only solution to the globalization of environmental problems, despite trends to the contrary and a growing number of scholars challenging those assumptions in the name of complexity (see chapters 2 and 6).

"Complexity," however, has become a buzzword. Though the reality it aims to describe has been well mapped out, its specific implications remain undeveloped. International relations theorists have been looking at complexity at least since the late 1990s. Research groups have developed, seminars have been held,[2] special issues of scholarly journals published.[3] But it has yet to be as institutionalized as in the mathematics, engineering, economic, natural and health sciences.[4] As the 2009 Lancaster seminar outlined,

> The Complexity approach… can provide both a new, more realistic, paradigm and a range of simple and common-sensical tools (both metaphorical and modelling based) that can help move academics and practitioners beyond the limits of the current debates [in IR theory].

Indeed, authors, since the late 1990s, have amply documented the potential usefulness of this approach and suggested ways in which it could alter our thinking and advance systemic approaches (e.g. Bousquet and Curtis 2011). Nevertheless, although it helps transcend the old agent-structure debate and provide a way of conceiving and modelling decentralized governance systems, it has yet to fulfill its promises and be widely used. Much of the literature remains hortatory.

The current search for new models of international governance away from a centralized perspective forces us to take a harder look at the common wisdom and reconceptualize traditional questions pertaining to the definition of the problem, the context and nature of governance, the role of knowledge in policy, the emergence of governance by units of the systems (such as regions), the role of developing countries in shaping a new environmental order, and the contours of a complex governance system of the environment.

Thinking about the doxa means reflecting about what goes without saying. The premise of any book about the environment is that the latter matters. Asking why it matters appears to be a useless and trivial question with an obvious scientific answer. But it is fruitful to reflect on the different reasons various actors active in international environmental governance would think of it as obvious. This allows us to point out again that environmental problems are politically and socially constructed, an idea that is as widely acknowledged as it is subsequently ignored. Accordingly, chapter 1 first outlines the convergence of concerns that have made global environmental problems a political, social, scientific, and moral issue. It then proceeds to identify some of the dimensions surrounding not the question "whether" but "how?" Ultimately, the answer to the question "why should we care?" is to call upon a social virtue, that of accountability.

Chapter 2 addresses the general quest for effective international environmental governance. It first recalls well-known developments in international relations that render indispensable a wholesale reconceptualization of governance. The latter also entails shedding some received ideas, a few of which are considered here, such as the record of environmental progress, the role of the state (and by extension of other units of the system), the value of simple solutions, and the tendency to model an international order based on domestic political arrangements. The limited progress of global environmental governance (GEG) reform suggests the need to reflect on the contours of a governance that takes advantage of the complex nature and of the evolution of the system instead of fighting them, one that reflects the intractable nature of the issues, and that acts as a counterpoint to existing models that are more straightjackets than means to put in place the conditions for the adoption of legitimate, meaningful, and effective actions.

The relation between science and policy, the role of regions, and the evolving role of the Souths are aspects of international environmental governance where the dynamics of complex governance are emerging. Chapter 3 examines the prevalence of a traditional linear model of the relationship between science and politics as well as a new conceptualization of that relationship, using the Intergovernmental Platform on Biodiversity and Ecosystems Services (IPBES) as a reference point. A crucial function of such organizations in a complex system is their ability to act as agents of learning, enabling other agents gradually to develop shared interpretations of a given problem, where these interpretations come to define identities, institutions, and the contours of cooperation.

There is a wide consensus that the European Union (EU) has played an important leadership role in agenda setting and in fostering multilateral agreements in a number of issue areas. Yet questions about its effectiveness arise. Indeed, its failures in some areas have been spectacular, as in the case of climate change. The aim of chapter 4 is to examine what is the most achieved version of regional integration through the concept of role as a tool that can help understand the interplay of various factors that affect EU actions and identify the conditions under which regions could play a leadership role in a complex international environmental governance system.

The fifth chapter examines the evolving contribution of the Souths to global environmental governance. The received wisdom is that developing countries have largely been "policy takers" rather than policy makers in international environmental negotiations and have struggled to avoid the imposition of an environmental agenda and policy commitments that, in their view, threatened their economic prospects as well as their national autonomy; all this in the name of solving problems they had not created or the importance of which they deemed secondary to their primary objective of improving human security. In fact, many of the initial fears of the developing countries have not come to pass. Rather, one could argue that they have successfully resisted obligations they rejected, and managed to use environmental issues to pursue their own political and economic priorities, even though their hopes have sometimes been dashed. It remains, however, that they have largely failed to develop definitions of the problem and offer solutions that are not reactive to developed countries' initiatives, a shortcoming that the emerging international environmental governance has the potential to overcome.

Complexity theory has been around in international relations for about 20 years. Although it has been applied to socioecological systems, how one should approach international environmental governance deserves more sustained attention. The final chapter builds on previous chapters, notably chapter 2, in an attempt to define better what embracing complexity would mean for global environmental governance, with particular reference to biodiversity and climate change. Complex governance is not a set of new recipes, but a different way to define and approach problems. After a brief overview of the etiology of complexity in the study of international relations, the chapter discusses the main features of complex systems in light of that concern, pointing out that the empirical building blocks of such a conceptual shift already exist, and then sketches some of the contours of a complex governance of global environmental issues.

Notes

1 With a nod to Pirages (1978), "global ecopolitics" here refers to the set of political dimensions governing the identification and resolution of global and worldwide environmental issues and, in particular, to attempts by a variety of international actors to impose their own definition of security with regard to nature and people's welfare, and to use emerging environmentally induced scarcities for their own ends (see Le Prestre 2005).
2 Fruitful meetings have been the workshop organized by David Earnest at ISA in 2008 and the seminar on "Complexity and the International Arena" held in November 2009 at Lancaster University.
3 See, for example, the *Cambridge Review of International Affairs* 2011 special issue.
4 Many universities around the world have created centers, institutes or research groups on complex systems; most are dominated by natural scientists, engineers, and mathematicians with a few scattered economists.

References

Bousquet, A. and S. Curtis. (2011). "Beyond Models and Metaphors: Complexity Theory, Systems Thinking and International Relations." *Cambridge Review of International Affairs* 24 (1): 43–62.

Complexity and the International Arena seminar, Lancaster University, November 6, 2009. Available online at www.lancaster.ac.uk/fass/centres/cemore/event/2877.

Entman, R. M. (1993). "Framing: Toward Clarification of a Fractured Paradigm." *Journal of Communication* 43 (4): 51–58.

Le Prestre, P. (2005). *Protection de l'environnement et relations internationales: les défis de l'écopolitique mondiale*. Paris: Armand Colin.

Mitchell, R. B. (2002). "International Environment." In *Handbook of International Relations*, edited by W. Carlsnaes, T. Risse, and B. A. Simmons. Thousand Oaks, CA: Sage.

Ostrom, E. (1990). *Governing the Commons: The Evolution of Institutions for Collective Action*. New York: Cambridge University Press.

Pirages, D. (1978). *Global Ecopolitics*. North Scituate, MA: Duxbury Press.

Smith, G. and D. Wolfish, eds. (2002). *Who's Afraid of the State?* Toronto: University of Toronto Press.

Young, O. R. (1998). *Creating Regimes: Arctic Accords and International Governance*. Ithaca, NY: Cornell University Press.

1

THE INJUNCTION OF THE ECOLOGICAL CRISES

A few days before global political leaders gathered at the United Nations in April 2016 to sign the 2015 Paris Agreement on climate change, a group of interfaith leaders presented a "Statement on Climate Change" to the president of the UN General Assembly, emphasizing that "Caring for the Earth is our shared responsibility. Each one of us has a moral responsibility to act" and "[t]he challenges ahead require honesty and courage and we all must take action to reduce emissions."[1]

Why should we all care about the global environment? Deceptively simple as they are, such questions are often the trickiest for the answer seems obvious. The operative words here are of course "all," "global," and "caring." So the first question is, why global more than local issues? And if global problems are important, why should we *all* be concerned (either as individuals or members of a group or of an international community)? Finally, "how" should we care?

Certainly, a pastoral farmer in Africa, a miner in South America, a slum-dweller in a megalopolis, a rice grower in Madagascar, or a landless farmer or factory worker in Asia might have other priorities. Everybody cannot afford to care. But even in advanced industrialized countries, why invest energy in trying to solve or understand global environmental issues or putting pressure on those who could, if these problems are beyond reach and disconnected from people's immediate welfare?

Secondly, why should we care about the environment rather than other problems that threaten the survival of humanity (such as nuclear war) or the well-being of humankind (access to health, physical security, food security, shelter, etc.)? To be sure, one can care about many things at the same time, but the more one does, the fewer the resources available to each and the greater the number of trade-offs faced.

We can also ask why, as a society, we should care about the environment at all. The answer may seem obvious today; it was not 50 years ago in industrialized countries, and it is not self-evident in many parts of the world. For example, in the

1970s, the European Left was deeply suspicious of the emergence of the environmental protection movement that it feared would distract people from more important political issues (such as the class struggle) or, worse, perpetuate inequalities. Or, if they acknowledged the extent of environmental degradation, it would be approached as one more instance of the existence of an unfair capitalistic and consumption-based economic system which had to be reformed if not overthrown. We hear echoes of this position today in Naomi Klein's 2014 best seller as well as in Pope Francis's own words to which we shall return.

Yet thinking has evolved not only among various political obediences but also throughout the world. We are indeed witnessing a strong convergence of concerns (I). Thus, if not whether, then how should we care? Which raises the issues of environmental justice and equity at the international level (II). Finally, we shall reflect on the challenge of action, for caring is one thing, and acting another (III).

A convergence of concerns

Environmental norms disseminate and appear on the political agenda as a result of concerns expressed by a variety of actors, notably the environmental scientist's, the political scientist's, the politician's, the concerned citizen's, and the ethicist's.

The environmental scientist's answer

"Environmental scientist" here refers to those researchers, primarily natural but also social scientists, who are studying issues related to global change and global environmental problems. They differ considerably regarding the importance they attach to various phenomena, their causes, and consequences; but they all express deep concerns regarding the trajectory of humanity's impact on its environment and all share a deep feeling of urgency.

Eloquent litanies and reports about current environmental trends abound and need not be repeated. More importantly, environmental problems are not given. Politics and international environmental politics in particular start with attempts to impose one's own definition of a problem. Is the issue climate change or biodiversity loss? Land degradation or chemical contamination? Urban health problems or access to water? Population growth or technology? Poverty or the nature of the economic system? Modes of consumption or inequalities? Which problems should we tackle first and why?

In November 1992, prestigious scientists signed a solemn declaration that once again warned humanity that it was on a collision course with the earth system likely to endanger life as we know it.[2] This declaration mentioned the ozone layer, air pollution and acid rain, overuse of fresh water, the state of the oceans (fisheries, pollution), soil productivity loss, the destruction of forests, and species extinction. But it is one thing to point out environmental trends that scientists, out of their own field of specialization, find worrisome; it is another to prescribe remedies. Yet they did not hesitate to call on states to limit their destructive activities, conserve resources, stabilize population growth, eliminate poverty, and grant women full equality. Finally, military operations were also condemned for their destructive impact on the environment. This was an extreme example—alas, all too common but fortunately all too obvious—of ideology masquerading as science, for the links between the solutions proposed and the nature of the problems were far from obvious. This oft-repeated tendency is easy to identify and condemn; less so is keeping in mind that politics indeed starts with issue framing—in this case with the definition of the environmental problem, of its dimension, and of its relative importance.

The model we use to represent the problem of the protection of natural resources determines the parameters of the political debate and the range of possible solutions. To speak of "global public goods,"[3] for example, means defining the issue as the underprovision of a given good. In contrast, defining it as a "common property resource" means emphasizing questions linked to the distribution of benefits derived from its overconsumption. Science and politics help redefine the nature of these goods.[4] A case in point is the atmosphere, which has moved from the status of a global public good to that of a common property resource, as scientists argued that humanity would face catastrophic consequences from too rapid and too high a concentration of greenhouse gases. In both cases, we cannot ignore those actors that refuse to cooperate and thus reduce the collective enjoyment of the good either by underproducing it or by overexploiting it. We will, therefore, eschew repeating the litany of environmental problems that nations face collectively and focus on three general dimensions that embody negative environmental trends.

The first dimension pertains to disequilibria, though the very notion of equilibrium may be thought of in a variety of ways. Concerns about the cycle of elements fundamental to sustaining life were already raised in a seminal article back in 1986. In that article, Peter Vitousek *et al.* estimated that, on land, "organic material equivalent to about 40% of the present net primary production in terrestrial ecosystems was being co-opted by human beings each year" (Vitousek *et al.* 1986). The co-option, diversion, and destruction of these terrestrial resources "could cause a greater reduction in organic diversity than occurred at the Cretaceous-Tertiary boundary 65 million years ago," thus foreclosing "numerous options for humanity because of the loss of potentially useful species and the genetic impoverishment of others that may survive." This is the root of the notion that we have entered a new geological age, that of the Anthropocene.

Ten years later, another much-cited article (Vitousek *et al.* 1997) stressed the extent and acceleration of human alteration of earth. Between one-third and one-half of the land surface has been transformed by human action. Atmospheric carbon dioxide concentrations have increased by nearly 30 percent since the beginning of the Industrial Revolution.[5] More atmospheric nitrogen is fixed by humanity than by all natural terrestrial sources combined; more than one-half of all accessible surface fresh water is put to use by humanity, and about one-quarter of the bird species on earth have been driven to extinction. We are changing our planet more rapidly than we are understanding its dynamics and discovering its richness.

An avatar of this line of thought is found in the recent popularization of the concept of planetary boundaries proposed by Johan Rockström and colleagues (Steffen et al. 2015; Rockström et al. 2009). In a way, it is an attempt to revisit the notion of limits popularized by Dennis and Donella Meadows (1972) in the early 1970s (which contributed to the rise of the environmental movement but was also heavily criticized from a methodological viewpoint) and define the problem in terms of thresholds that should not be transgressed lest our societies are forced to deal with dynamics with unpredictable and possibly dire consequences. The authors identify nine "boundaries" (of which three might have already been overstepped) whose simultaneous transgression may lead the earth system close to a tipping point (see chapter 6). This framing has been criticized, notably by Nordhaus et al. (2012), who question some of the authors' assumptions (notably regarding the link between ecosystemic services and human welfare) as well as the concept of boundary, and, more importantly perhaps, argue that the notion of threshold had only a local and regional meaning.

The second dimension worth stressing is the convergence of crises. Without climate change, there would still be a biodiversity crisis and overexploitation of resources. But not only are those crises simultaneous, they reinforce each other. And to make things even more complicated, we cannot always assume that solutions are synergistic. At least in the short term, reducing atmospheric aerosols in the northern hemisphere may significantly reduce Arctic sea ice.[6] Trade-offs among various ecosystem services abound. Political scientists like to say that one does not solve environmental problems; one merely displaces them (Dryzek 1987). Politics is about managing these trade-offs.

Finally, the third dimension does not deal with the evolution of the natural environment but with the impact of environmental trends on societies. The question no longer is whether trends are negative but which trends could be reversed and, above all, how can societies adapt to those that are inevitable. This entails both acting on the trends and addressing their impacts; and it constitutes much of the interdisciplinary work under way. The international "community" has recently given itself some means to undertake this challenge through the establishment of the Future Earth Program, a global research platform designed to provide the knowledge needed to support transformations toward sustainability.

Scientists who are active in the political realm have often used a utilitarian argument in order to overcome political or social inertia. This has notably been evident with respect to biodiversity issues: who knows, the argument goes, where the next cure for cancer will come from? Where would agriculture be without pollinators? It goes back to a time-tested strategy for mobilizing in favor of the environment. Given that governments and societies have a variety of concerns, starting with physical security and economic growth, and that environmental issues rank generally much lower, it is helpful to tie environmental concerns to more widely shared values in order to put them on the political agenda. Thus, action against climate change is justified in terms of its economic impacts, the greater probability of the spread of infectious diseases, or the threat posed by so-called environmental refugees. Indeed, it was by tying pollution to health concerns that environmental issues first became politically salient. That is the reason why *The Stern Review on the Economics of Climate Change* (Stern 2006) attempted to make the economic case for strong measures to reduce greenhouse gas (GHG) emissions, or why The Economics of Ecosystems and Biodiversity (TEEB) report did the same for biodiversity in 2010. Politics, then, is part and parcel of the environment. It is the concern of a great variety of actors, among which governments naturally stand out.

The political scientist's answer

Why should governments care about global environmental problems? First, because global environmental policy is not just about global environmental problems. For example, there are strong connections between climate on the one hand, and trade, energy, and development, not to mention a host of other environmental issues on the other. Global and local issues are linked through science, trade, and communications. National environmental policies are no longer made in isolation; they very much depend on what takes place outside national borders. The nature of global environmental change and the solutions that one adopts to face it have political consequences for the way societies govern themselves, the distribution of values and resources, the definition of the common good, the distribution of power among groups, and the relationship between the individual and the collective. Environmental issues reflect both scientific concerns as well as social values. Neither problems nor solutions are given. Conflicts and trade-offs are part and parcel of environmental politics. Further, in developing countries where the state often is weak, environmental problems and the solutions promoted to deal with them may question existing political arrangements.

The politician's answer

Indeed, to a politician, environmental problems are important through their political impacts insofar as they are linked to the access and retention of power. The politician's main answer to our initial question might then be simply because people (or some key groups) care. Studies after studies have shown that public awareness matters. In many developed countries (but not all, to be sure) environmental issues were put on the political agenda thanks to citizens' movements.[7] Although one could object that citizens from developing countries have other concerns, the rise of environmental demands that follows a growing middle class in emerging and middle-income countries, and specifically the case of China, show otherwise. Awareness of global environmental matters is not insignificant in the developing world where the politically influential groups and the incipient middle-class attitude differs from that of other socioeconomic groups that may be primarily concerned with local pollution problems. The challenge, then, is showing how local and global problems may be linked.

In the absence of strong public opinion, elected officials may have little to gain from spending scarce political capital on global environmental issues, especially when costs are concentrated and benefits both spread out and remote in the future. This is something that US presidents have long understood and respected except (i) when any constituency against environmental regulation no longer existed (as in whaling) or (ii) having been forced to adopt environmental protection policies through domestic pressures, it then had an interest in seeing them adopted by other countries (see chapter 4). For example, barring strong public or industry pressure, US presidents have little to gain from a fight with Congress over the ratification of the Convention on Biological Diversity (CBD) or Biodiversity Convention, a convention that entered into force in 1994, with the United States the only UN member state not a party. They have instead preferred hortatory lectures, as in the case of Jimmy Carter's farewell address. President Obama has sought to go further than his predecessors on climate change, primarily during his second and last term.

Dynamics differ among countries, of course. For middle or small powers such as Canada or the Netherlands, the active pursuit of common solutions to global problems also provides a means of exercising diplomatic leadership. For some developing countries, concern for global issues is strongly dependent on the additional resources they can gain from adopting and implementing policies designed to address them. In other cases, ambitious local politicians may use environmental issues to attract foreign resources that will enable them to become a political force with which to reckon domestically. Environmental protection can be instrumentalized and provide the argument needed to mobilize opposition to the central government or acquire foreign resources to challenge it. But this is truer for local environmental problems than for global issues.

The concerned citizen's answer

Global issues by definition are beyond the reach of any individual. How, as an individual, can I contribute significantly to protect the climate, the oceans, the ozone layer, or the biodiversity of distant countries, when success depends on the cooperation of numerous other individuals, countries, and international actors? It might be more fruitful to start with one's neighborhood or country.

Indeed, we could go back to the old slogan of the 1970s: Think globally but act locally. Local problems are often the manifestation of larger problems, that is, problems shared by all and that cannot be solved except through cooperation (the classic collective action problem). There is no excuse, therefore, for passivity: acting at an individual level (through changing modes of consumption, for example) helps address larger problems. This slogan sought to impress upon all others that we have a responsibility toward the earth as individual citizens and consumers; it is not only up to governments and corporations. Thinking about global issues means reflecting on what should or could change in order to meet the challenges they pose. Global issues are not abstract problems; they affect our capacity to lead our daily lives and fulfill our aspirations by restricting the range of our and society's future options.

An example of this type of argument based on enlightened self-interest is reflected in a report that the British government released in the fall of 2014, as a preparatory document for the 20th and 21st Conferences of the Parties (COPs) of the United Nations Framework Convention on Climate Change (UNFCCC) (DECC 2014). Not only will climate change have direct impacts on the United Kingdom, but its indirect risks and costs might even be more pronounced through rising food prices and potential shortages of certain foodstuffs, higher costs of materials and goods due to the impact of extreme weather on critical infrastructures and supply chains, loss of trade and earnings as climate change impacts on key trading partners, and growing regional instability, insecurity, and health risks, especially in the world's poorest areas expected to be hit hardest from coastal flooding, land loss, and heat waves. Climate change will affect the governance of societies, our habits, and our way of life. The issue here is not whether we shall have to change our behavior or modify our values but at what pace and in what direction.

Finally, the question of environmental justice, long neglected by traditional political parties, looms large, perhaps (and paradoxically) more so at the international than at the national level. Instead of embracing it, political parties of the Left first sought to deny the importance of environmental issues altogether. Although they have since changed enormously, as many Leftist militants sought in ecology a way of pursuing their questioning of the capitalist system, this dimension has remained neglected. Yet it is clear that the way problems are defined as well as the solutions adopted have a profound ethical dimension. And it affects both national and international environmental politics, regarding, for example, the principles that should govern burden sharing of greenhouse gas emission reductions or the distribution of the costs of adaptation to the impacts of climate change.[8]

The ethicist's answer

Two aspects of the question of environmental justice are worth mentioning: eco-citizenship and the change in Western religions' approach to the ecological crisis.

In line with several political ideologies, the prevailing discourse of environmental activists calls for the advent of a new human being, in this case the eco-citizen. In addition to presenting themselves as key intermediaries between governments, corporations, and citizens, environmental nongovernmental organizations (ENGOs) also question our relationship with nature and present themselves as the embodiment of a new "ecological ethics." This goes back to the very origins of the movement of which Henry David Thoreau's *Walden* and Aldo Leopold's *A Sand County Almanac* are oft-cited illustrations. The contents of this ethics are a matter of complex debates, of course. Suffice it to mention that it is customary to distinguish among three main strands: human-centered, bio-centered, and eco-centered (Aspe and Jacqué 2012).

Remarkable in this regard has been the evolution of Western churches. Perhaps surprisingly, more than biodiversity issues, it is climate change that has triggered a marked evolution in their approach to ecological issues, culminating in the 2015

Encyclical from His Holiness Pope Francis, the June 2015 Declaration of Religions of France, and the "Summit of Conscience for the Climate" in July of the same year.[9] The latter's "Call to Conscience" condemns man's sin of pride and calls upon each individual "to approach these complex challenges from our own individual personal consciences." It precisely answers the question "Why do I care?" particularly in the context of COP-21 where each delegate is urged to "come to the COP primarily as a conscious human being not just a representative of a Government or agency." Further, in July 2015, representatives from the six main religions of France (Catholic, Protestant, Orthodox, Muslim, Jewish, and Buddhist) released a common declaration calling for a binding agreement applicable to all at COP-21. Although rooted in long-standing inter-religious discussions, this echoed the strong call made by Pope Francis in the papal Encyclical, *Laudato Si* (Francis 2015).

Back in 2002, US evangelical churches had already expressed their concern and called upon US citizens to rethink their modes of transportation in light of the threat of climate change. And Pope Francis's predecessors spoke eloquently about the ecological crisis. Indeed, John-Paul II went as far as arguing that "Every effort to protect and improve our world entails profound changes in lifestyles, models of production and consumption, and the established structures of power which today govern societies," a sentiment that Pope Francis will strongly echo.[10] Several bishop conferences underlined important dimensions of the environmental crisis, and called for action. In 2001, for example, in the face of US inertia, US Catholic bishops called for a genuine dialogue on those issues.[11] But it is Pope Francis who made climate change and the protection of our planet, "our Sister Earth," a personal matter of our own beliefs and values. His Encyclical is not addressed solely to the Catholic faithful but to all persons of goodwill.

For Pope Francis, the environment is foremost a moral problem and thus demands renewed ethics. But the Encyclical also denounces "a system of commercial relations and ownership which is structurally perverse" (Francis 2015, 38), and calls for a "bold cultural revolution" (Ibid., 85).[12] It contains all the buzzwords of today's environmental discourse regarding the nature of problems, the solutions, and the key concepts to be used such as complex systems, bioaccumulation, problem displacement, circular model of production, climate as common property resource or public good, ecosystem services, vicious circles (negative feedbacks), biological corridors, sustainable use, the subsidiarity principle, and, of course, the importance of future generations. It endorses ecological economics, the principle of common but differentiated responsibility (PCDR), as well as the precautionary principle. It condemns individualism, obsessive consumerism, the dictatorship of the market, the myth of infinite economic growth and narrow economic interests pursued by states and corporations at the expense of the common good, as well as blind faith in technology. It deplores the poor implementation of existing legislation and the process of cultural homogenization, and thus the idea that there exist universal solutions to common problems (§144). In sum, it insists on the respect that Man must have in his common house and for all of God's creatures, and on environmental justice. In so doing, it refutes the long-standing accusation of absolute anthropocentrism levied against Judeo-Christian thought (see White 1967).

Pope Francis goes further than various eco-citizenship movements, and, in fact, rejects both anthropocentrism and biocentrism. Protecting the environment is a moral but also a structural problem. Institutions, governments, corporations, markets, inequalities, and nationalism restrict individual choices. Thus environmental problems inescapably are social problems. Not only a matter of conviction but also of responsibility, it calls also for an ethics of consequences.

Not whether but how? Justice and ethics in global ecopolitics

The issue remains, as Hugh Stretton (Stretton 1976) asked some 40 years ago, according to which values or concerns is the environment to be protected? According to what ends should we manage resources? How are solutions linked to other values we hold dear, such as reducing inequalities or promoting democracy?

I shall leave aside the large question of domestic environmental justice, well summarized in *Laudato Si* (Francis 2015, 31–34).

> In some places, rural and urban alike, the privatization of certain spaces has restricted people's access to places of particular beauty. In others, "ecological" neighbourhoods have been created which are closed to outsiders in order to ensure an artificial tranquillity. Frequently, we find beautiful and carefully manicured green spaces in so-called "safer" areas of cities, but not in the more hidden areas where the disposable of society live… Both everyday experience and scientific research show that the gravest effects of all attacks on the environment are suffered by the poorest.

International environmental justice has several aspects. First, how can we prevent some nations from inflicting harm on others, as well as other nations from becoming free riders, that is benefiting from the efforts of others without contributing to solving the problem? Second, given the ecological debt owed by richer countries to poorer ones (Francis 2015, 36–37), and in the context of climate change where it is most acute, how should the burden of mitigation be allocated? What is the fairest way of allocating national efforts in emission reductions? Further, how should the burden of adaptation be distributed in order to minimize the negative impacts of climate change on the poorer segments of national or international society? Least developed countries have stressed both the catastrophic impacts of climate change and their inability to face them without massive help. Their argument is basically moral: the main victims of climate change are not those who have or are contributing to it.

Mitigation and adaptation are twin questions that outstrip their technical or political dimensions. They are also a matter of ethics. As Shue (2014) argues: "to call for binding commitments to a joint plan to mitigate emissions reductions without binding commitment to a joint plan for everyone to adapt, is clearly unfair in demanding similar contributions from nations in radically different circumstances. According to the US, the burden of mitigation has to be shared by all, but not the burden of adaptation. In effect, climate now, justice maybe later."

In global ecopolitics, equity questions permeate the international discourse and profoundly affect the dynamics of negotiations. Yet one should not confuse justice and moralism. The discourse on climate change is full of moralism; but defining the problem in terms of moral responsibility makes compromises more difficult as climate change becomes the battlefield of competing ideologies. Moralism may be useful to mobilize citizens and decision makers. However, political solutions are empirical questions that must be addressed in the context of an ethics of consequences (Hoffmann 1988).

Equity and fairness issues lie at the heart of sustainable development that places human well-being, rather than the environment, at the core of our definition of our relation to nature and the quality of life that individuals should be able to lead. In particular, they are expressed in terms of solidarity (intergenerational equity, North-South solidarity) and the promotion of certain political rights (local democracy, participation, respect for the rights of minorities, protection of cultural identities, etc.). Specific conventions are devoted to their advancement, such as the Convention on Access to Information, Public Participation in Decision-Making and Access to Justice in Environmental Matters (Aarhus Convention 1998). In other cases, they are embedded in larger agreements. For example, the third objective of the CBD is "the fair and equitable sharing of the benefits arising out of the utilization of genetic resources." In yet other cases, they represent the basic rationale of other conventions, such as the Convention on the Control of the Transboundary Movements of Hazardous Wastes and Their Disposal (Basel Convention 1989).

A regime complex (see chapter 6) often is the place where different ethical and social justice principles compete; it does not necessarily embody the victory of one over the other. This competition often explains their dynamics, as can be seen in the case of the CBD (conservation vs. indigenous rights) or the UNFCCC (mitigation vs. adaptation; burden-sharing principles, etc.). The CBD embodies the confrontation of various and legitimate principles of equity and justice grounded in a particular place and time. Clashes, therefore, are inevitable. In this sense, the quest for global regimes based on principles deemed to be universal, a heritage of the enlightenment, may be both elusive and illusory, if not counterproductive. Indigenous groups have instrumentalized the CBD in order to advance their political claims, with the result that the notion of equity and justice developed by the CBD essentially refers, when applied to humans, to their own definition of the problem and to their interests. One should then ask, along with Zerner (2000), whether and how one should develop a notion of justice not limited to indigenous communities but that also encompasses the landless, marginal populations, local communities and the city poor. In short, to what extent is the quest for justice at the expense of others and under what conditions can it lead to inequitable outcomes?

Although the 1986 Universal Declaration on the Right to Development affirms that Development is both a collective and an individual right, a mere assertion of their complementary character does not obviate the real tensions that may exist between the respective rights of states, groups, and individuals. The CBD, again, creates new state rights, notably through the extension of the concept of sovereignty and the right to development, but it also enables indigenous groups to assert their own rights vis-à-vis the state. And then, what about individuals? In order to respond to this problem, in 2007 France proposed the adoption of a universal declaration of the rights of peoples in matters of the environment and sustainable development. Nothing was heard about it after President Chirac left power.

Questions of fairness and equity can be a fundamental driver of negotiating stands. Equity concerns, it has been argued, have been a major determinant of China's diplomacy on climate change (Zhang 2013). An agreement perceived as fair has a greater probability to be concluded and to be effective. Dominant models of cooperation tend to insist on the rationality of actors and on the difficulties affecting the provision of global public goods (see Barrett 2007). Moral and ethical considerations, however, can affect this rational calculus. At the UNFCCC, the concern for equity takes several forms, the most important of which is the principle of common but differentiated responsibility (PCDR). This principle is often pointed out as having enabled a wide and meaningful participation in the negotiations by developing countries, and largely explains the near universal ratification of the treaty. The definition of what is just is not static, however. With the rapid rise in greenhouse gas emissions from emergent powers and the greater knowledge about the sources and impacts of climate change, the determination of what is fair and equitable is changing, and the operationalization and legitimacy of the PCDR have been questioned.

The negotiation of the Kyoto Protocol initially saw Europe deeply opposed to the proposed Clean Development Mechanism (CDM), the scope of which it wished to limit in the name of the moral obligation that countries primarily responsible for the problem should strongly commit to reduce their own emissions rather than attempt to pay their way out. Accordingly, Article 6 (1d) of the Kyoto Protocol stipulates that "[t]he acquisition of emission reduction units shall be supplemental to domestic actions for the purposes of meeting commitments under Article 3." *The Economics of Climate Change* (Stern 2006) placed equity issues at the heart of its approach to the discount rate (which it set close to zero), which represents the importance one attaches to the well-being of future generations. In this case, the report sacrifices the present generation for the sake of future ones: to what extent should we redistribute current wealth in favor of a more opulent future? This fundamentally is an ethical issue (Nordhaus 2008).

The ethics of consequences also pervades various manifestations of what has been called "green imperialism," that is the imposition of richer countries' environmental values and options on poorer societies. The preference and procedures of the United States Agency for International Development (USAID) regarding the exportation and use of pesticides (notably DDT) have virtually prevented the direct provision of pesticides to developing countries where they are potentially valuable weapons in the quest to manage pests (Tobin 1996).

This leads to another dilemma. It may not be fair, because of the ethics of consequences, to apply similar environmental criteria to all countries; yet is it just to apply different criteria? Are all lives not equally valuable? Should we oppose a treaty on climate change because it fails the test of justice, or should we support it because it will finally reduce greenhouse gas emissions and protect the options of future generations?

Faced with the relative paucity of ethical guidelines to adaptation (according to which principles define and support adaptation policies?), as well as with competing ethical criteria that threatened further to complicate negotiations rather than provide a reliable ethical compass, an international meeting was convened in 2004 to discuss the ethics of climate change. Though it did not settle the debate, it helped clarify the scope of discussions and identified the major relevant ethical issues. These included responsibility for damages, the determination of atmospheric targets and emission rights, as well as procedural justice.[13] One of the two main principles mentioned in the UNFCCC COP-21 Agreement on climate change (2015) that should guide its implementation is, along with the PCDR, that of equity whose scope is in line with this understanding although its contents remain largely unspecified.

The choice of a particular theory of justice that should govern international agreements reflects both ethical and political concerns. Though politics often masquerades as ethics, the reverse is also true. Opposing conceptions of justice provoke conflicts and dilemmas. A classic dilemma pits the environment against sustainable development, although they often are presented as mutually reinforcing. Is whaling, for example, an environmental or a sustainable development problem? Should we emphasize the intrinsic value of whales or the needs of coastal whaling communities when it can be shown that whales can be hunted sustainably? Indeed, to what extent is sustainable development an unconditional good? More generally, does an international community exist in whose name one could legitimize action in favor of managing or solving global environmental problems?

Caring is not acting: Of political will and courage

We may be convinced that we must care for our environment and that global environmental issues deserve strong sustained action from citizens and politicians alike, based on shared conceptions of fairness; still how do we get from awareness to political action and positive outcomes? This is, of course, the stuff of international environmental politics.

Even though the environment has been successfully implanted into local, national, and international political agendas, lasting solutions seem elusive. So-called political will and capacity often seem to be in short supply. Much could be said about such an impression, starting with questioning its premise that progress has been limited and diplomacy has failed (a question taken up in chapter 2). Answers to criticisms regarding the lack of lasting solutions to global environmental issues range from institutionalized forms of unsustainability, domestic politics, and collective actions problems to the nature of the international political and economic system. But this does not always explain why progress has been more forthcoming in certain areas than others and why some countries are leaders and other laggards on different issues and at various times. In this case, the following factors seem to be at work: availability of financing, linkages among sectors and concerns, socialization efforts of epistemic communities, interministerial dynamics, domestic interests, and capacity. With respect to climate change, mitigation and adaptation present political, technical, and institutional challenges stemming from cyclical attention to climate change since 2009, the social and economic dimensions of the problem and solutions proposed, differences in countries' interests and motivations, and the absence of easy and cheap technological fixes.

Despite the progress that has occurred in some areas, a popular answer to the question "what now?" is to talk of political will. Fighting climate change, we are told, requires political will. If only that were so simple. What is political will? How do we generate it? And is it so easy to find a way when there is a will?

Economists and political scientists have long shown that even when rational people agree on the nature of the problem and on the direction required to solve it, cooperation may remain elusive. This is the essence of the Tragedy of the Commons (Hardin 1968). One solution may lie in the exercise of power that enables the use of a stick or the provision of carrots. Another is building the right kind of institutions that will change the calculus of interests and reduce uncertainty regarding the actions of other actors as well as the consequences of one's own. Yet another is changing minds. These directions are not incompatible. A vast literature in international relations in the last 25 years looks at the conditions for the emergence of cooperation, the evolution of institutions, the conditions for their effectiveness, and their interrelationships. Although we now know a lot more, debates endure.

The notion of "political will" is one of those concepts (like political culture or the national interest) whose discursive function is far superior to its analytical usefulness. If it means anything, it is that there must be a recognition that a problem exists and that one must create the right incentives to act. The urgency is to change behavior first, not minds, even though norms are ultimately the pillars of sustainable change. What incentives that are both fair and politically feasible may work? Under what conditions? On whom? What aspects of the problem call for specific incentives? Which principles should govern their identification and use?

Lack of political will explains nothing. We know from the prisoner's dilemma (the model of the Tragedy of the Commons) that it may be rational to defect from the course of cooperation even though our preferences may lie elsewhere, and even when we know the long-term negative consequences of doing so for the common good as well as ours. Actors do not always face a choice. In many cases, decision makers feel they have very few options. Invoking a lack of political will does little to understand those situations.

It may simply denote a lack of courage, however; another vague notion that again is repeatedly invoked in the face of policy inertia. In one episode of the

1980s British series *Yes Minister*, Sir Humphrey Appleby, Minister Jim Hacker's Permanent Secretary of the Department of Administrative Affairs, wishing to thwart another "brilliant" idea of his minister, tells him that to go ahead would be very commendable for it would show "courage"; whereupon, of course, his minister, preoccupied with electoral survival and his good standing in cabinet, promptly backs off. Governments, we are told, lack it. Back in 1978, Solzhenitsyn already bemoaned its short supply in the West (with echoes of Spengler, of authoritarian regimes' typical view of democracies, and of contemporary declinists): "A decline in courage may be the most striking feature that an outside observer notices in the West today... Such a decline in courage is particularly noticeable among the ruling and intellectual elites, causing an impression of a loss of courage by the entire society" (Solzhenitsyn 1978). And on the last day of the 2009 Copenhagen Summit on Climate Change (COP-15), the Secretary-General of the UN, Ban Ki-moon, urged delegates to boldly go where no one had gone before: "Now is the time again for common sense, compromise and courage... Political courage, political wisdom and political leadership should prevail. And this afternoon, let me add, conscience. It will be your legacy for all time. It will be the legacy. Let us today seal a deal for the common good" (Ban 2009). A similar appeal is heard on the eve of many major international meetings.

Many observers refer to a lack of political courage in order to explain the apparent inability of the international community to take the bold steps required to solve national and global problems or to promote the very values upon which it bases its legitimacy. Appeals to courage underline the difficulties that individual leaders have in balancing national and international priorities while they attempt to cooperate in solving global problems that threaten the very survival of their societies such as ecological degradation, climate change, poverty, cultural homogenization, civil war, or terrorism.

In this context, three sets of questions arise that deserve further thought. A first set pertains to the nature of political courage. Along with prudence, justice, and temperance, courage (or fortitude) is one of the four cardinal virtues if not the foundation of all the others. The courageous act makes sense only if it is the product of deliberation. It is the product of rational thinking: as Nicias in Plato's *Laches* submitted, it assumes knowledge of what should be feared and of what one should trust and hence of what one should dare.

Though definitions of personal courage abound, those pertaining to political courage are fewer. Courage is widely defined as the willingness to incur severe personal costs (in terms of physical well-being, emotional balance, social status, reputation, financial well-being, political future, career goals, etc.) in order to uphold some idea of the collective good (such as security, economic well-being, environmental protection), the integrity of one's own person (such as dignity before death) or social cohesion. In global ecopolitics, it usually means putting the common good ahead of narrow national interests, and it is as much the attribute of a group as that of a given individual. Political courage, then, is the science of what one should dare for the sake of the common good. Time and purpose are intrinsic to its nature and manifestation: "the intention waiting for the moment" said Vladimir Jankelevitch (2011).

In *Profiles in Courage*, John Kennedy features eight senators who have defied their constituents or party line to uphold their convictions, suggesting that he too was prepared to display this virtue. Can we assume that individual acts of courage should translate into acts of political courage? This has certainly been the assumption in various cases involving US presidents and presidential candidates. From Roosevelt's illness to John McCain's wartime record, Americans have tended to associate personal and public virtues. Other questions that might be asked pertain to the evolution of this notion over time and across societies and political systems and the conditions under which it can be considered a virtue.

A second set of questions pertains to the individual, social, or structural variables with which it is associated. Here the focus is on identifying factors that are closely associated with the perceptions that an individual act has been courageous and with the characteristics of the individual, group, society or situation that may have been conducive to the emergence of such acts. One nagging question concerns the legitimacy of acts of political courage when the potential costs of such actions fall on individuals and groups that do not take part in the decisions involved.

Finally, a third set of questions pertains to the impacts of acts of courage. Under what conditions do they lead to the expected outcome? Is political courage considered as such only when the consequences of its exercise are deemed good in the long term? When can a courageous act be considered legitimate? Indeed, when do acts of political courage clash with democratic values and with what consequences? Would a political system peopled only with "courageous" politicians be desirable?

In light of all these questions and many others, political analysts tend to dismiss the concept as meaningless. Lack of courage would only reflect the absence of strong political incentives to go in a certain direction. Guzman (2013), echoed by Pope Francis, for example, identifies the lack of popular awareness and understanding of the seriousness of the climate change threat as one of the main reasons for politicians' lack of motivation to address the issue. Others, as mentioned previously, attempt to tie climate change to other issues such as security and economic or public health. Courage implies a choice; as mentioned previously, decision makers often feel that they have very little. It also implies costs; there is no courage without risks.

This brings us back to the importance of education, which entails reframing problems, as well as redefining and reordering values so that they converge. In this sense, education aims to make sure we are playing the same game; that is, that there exists a symmetrical preference order, such as sharing the same loss aversions. In this regard, the courageous politician, among other things, must be an opinion leader rather than an opinion follower. Not necessarily convincing the public that the problem is scientifically sound, but showing the soundness of the political solutions that should be adopted.[14] It is precisely what is often meant by lack of political courage: disincentives to lead public opinion on a certain issue even at the expense of political survival.

Naturally, in democratic polities, courage is a virtue as long as it is not divorced both from prudence and accountability. Courage without prudence is temerity; courage without accountability is irresponsibility. Accountability means being answerable for one's acts and decisions and for their consequences before those who came before us, as well as those that are or will be affected by these actions; and it is in that sense that accountability is also a foundation of political courage.

Ultimately, the answer to our initial question "why should we care?" is to call upon virtue. We should care because it is the right thing to do. From there we can either rely on individual virtue, favor external inducements, or combine both. The first pathway emphasizes education, and it has deep religious foundations. The second pathway entails entrusting the state (or some supranational authority) with promoting virtue, following what Ophuls (2011) calls the "classical conception of the polity." Instead of acting as a referee, "the state has a duty to make men and women virtuous in accordance with some communal ideal" (Ibid., 16). We should care because we are responsible toward our fellow human beings, if not all living things.

Why should we care for the global environment, then? Simply because all of us, from individuals to governments, are *now* accountable for our actions or inertia. This was the lesson of the Holocaust, it is the message of Pope Francis, and it is the injunction of the ecological crisis.

Notes

1 Statement by Religious and Spiritual Leaders on the Occasion of the UN Secretary-General's High Level Signature Ceremony for the Paris Climate Change Agreement, April 18, 2016. See www.interfaithstatement2016.org#Faiths4ParisAgreement.
2 Union of Concerned Scientists, "World Scientists' Warning to Humanity (1992)," Cambridge, MA, November 18, 1992.
3 Defined as the range of goods available to all states that, however, do not necessarily share an individual interest in producing them. This is due to their twin nature of nonexclusion (no state can be prevented from enjoying it) and nonrivalry (consumption of the good does not reduce the amount available to others). See Kindleberger 1986 and Kaul et al. 1999. Defining a good as a global public good, however, is the result of a political process.
4 Hulme (2009) has nicely shown how important framing is in the context of climate change politics.
5 Methane increased by 145 percent. The rate of CO_2 increase which steadily accelerated since then has stabilized, though.
6 "Cleaner air in the high north could reduce Arctic sea ice by an area of about one million square kilometers this century. Air pollution has a net cooling effect on the climate, and has partially offset the decline of Arctic sea ice since the mid-1970s. In a model with high greenhouse-gas emissions and large projected reductions in air pollution, the Arctic Ocean became seasonally ice-free in 2045—12 years earlier than when aerosol emissions were held at 2000 levels." Source: *Nature* 526 (8).
7 Whereas in the United States, Japan, or Britain, political activism in favor of the environment was essentially the outgrowth of social movements, in France, for example, the initial policy stimulus came largely from the bureaucracy and the press.
8 On domestic environmental justice, see Bullard (2005). On climate justice, see Roberts and Parks (2006); Ciplet et al. (2015).
9 The Summit of Conscience for the Climate is a joint initiative by Nicolas Hulot (special correspondent for the French president), the Alliance of Religions and Conservation

(ARC), Bayard Presse (a media publisher for young readers, seniors, and Christians), the R20 (a network of local authorities and businesses founded by Arnold Schwarzenegger), and the Economic, Social, and Environmental Council (ESEC). See www.whydoicare.org/fr.
10 Encyclical letter, *Centesimus Annus* (May 1, 1991), n. 38: *Acta Apostolicae Sedis* 83 (1991), n. 58: p. 863. Quoted in *Laudato Si*, p. 5.
11 "Global Climate Change: A Plea for Dialogue, Prudence, and the Common Good." Statement, United States Conference of Catholic Bishops, June 15, 2001, Washington, DC.
12 Even the latest IPCC Assessment Report (AR5) of Working Group III notes that an "effective response to climate change may require a fundamental restructuring of the global economic and social systems, which in turn would involve overcoming multiple vested interests and the inertia associated with behavioural patterns and crafting new institutions that promote sustainability" (IPCC 2014, 297). This idea, however, was not taken up in the synthesis report.
13 "The Buenos Aires Draft Declaration on the Ethical Dimensions of Climate Change," Buenos Aires, Argentina, December 9, 2004. See http://manitobawildlands.org/pdfs/BA_draftDECLonCC_dec04.pdf.
14 In this context, see Sarewitz 2011.

References

Aspe, C. and M. Jacqué. (2012). *Environnement et société. une analyse sociologique de la question environnementale*. Paris: Éditions de la Maison des Sciences de l'Homme/Quae.
Ban, K. (2009). "Remarks to Informal High-Level Event." Address, Copenhagen, December 18.
Barrett, S. (2007). *Why Cooperate? The Incentive to Supply Global Public Goods*. Oxford: Oxford University Press.
Bullard, R. D. (2005). *The Quest for Environmental Justice: Human Rights, and the Politics of Pollution*. San Francisco: Sierra Club Books.
Ciplet, D., et al. (2015). *Power in a Warming World: The New Global Politics of Climate Change and the Remaking of Environmental Inequality*. Cambridge: MIT Press.
"Climate Change: Clean Air Puts Arctic Ice in Peril." (2015). *Nature* 526 (7571): 8–8. DOI: 10.1038/526008d.
"Convention on Access to Information, Public Participation in Decision-Making and Access to Justice in Environmental Matters." United Nations Economic Commission for Europe, Aarhus, Denmark, June 25, 1998. Available online at www.unece.org/fileadmin/DAM/env/pp/documents/cep43e.pdf.
DECC (Department of Energy and Climate Change). (2014). *Paris 2015. Securing Our Prosperity through a Global Climate Change Agreement*. London: DECC.
Dryzek, J. S. (1987). *Rational Ecology: Environment and Political Economy*. Oxford: Blackwell.
Francis. (2015). "Encyclical Letter Laudato Si of the Holy Father Francis on Care for Our Common Home." Vatican City, Italy: Holy See.
Guzman, A. (2013). *Overheated: The Human Cost of Climate Change*. New York: Oxford University Press.
Hardin, G. (1968). "The Tragedy of the Commons." *Science* 162: 1243–1248.
Hoffmann, S. (1988). *The Political Ethics of International Relations. Seventh Morgenthau Memorial Lecture on Ethics & Foreign Policy*. New York: Carnegie Council on Ethics and International Affairs.
Hulme, M. (2009). *Why We Disagree about Climate Change: Understanding Controversy, Inaction and Opportunity*. Cambridge: Cambridge University Press.

IPCC (Intergovernmental Panel on Climate Change). (2014). *Climate Change 2014: Mitigation of Climate Change. Contribution of Working Group III to the Fifth Assessment Report of the Intergovernmental Panel on Climate Change*. Cambridge and New York: Cambridge University Press.
Jankelevitch, V. (2011). *Traité des vertus II: Les vertus et l'amour*. Paris: Flammarion.
Kaul, I., et al. (1999). *Global Public Goods: International Cooperation in the 21st Century*. New York: Oxford University Press.
Kennedy, J. F. (2006) [1956]. *Profiles in Courage*. New York: Harper Perennial Modern Classics.
Kindleberger, C. (1986). "International Public Goods without International Government." *American Economic Review* 76 (1): 1–13.
Klein, N. (2014). *This Changes Everything: Capitalism vs. the Climate*. New York: Simon & Schuster.
Meadows, D., D. Meadows, J. Randers, and W. W. Behrens III. (1972). *The Limits to Growth: A Report for the Club of Rome's Project on the Predicament of Mankind*. New York: Universe Books.
Nordhaus, W. (2008). *A Question of Balance: Weighing the Options on Global Warming Policies*. New Haven: Yale University Press.
Nordhaus, T., et al. (2012). *The Planetary Boundaries Hypothesis: A Review of the Evidence*. Oakland, CA: Breakthrough Institute.
Ophuls, W. (2011). *Plato's Revenge: Politics in the Age of Ecology*. Cambridge: MIT Press.
Roberts, J. T. and B. C. Parks. (2006). *A Climate of Injustice*. Cambridge: MIT Press.
Rockström, J., et al. (2009). "A Safe Operating Space for Humanity." *Nature* 461: 472–475.
Sarewitz, D. (2011). "Does Climate Change Knowledge Really Matter?" *WIREs Climate Change* 2: 475–481.
Shue, H. (2014). *Climate Justice: Vulnerability and Protection*. Oxford: Oxford University Press.
Solzhenitsyn, A. (1978). "The Decline of Courage." Address, 327th Commencement of Harvard University, Harvard University, 1978.
Steffen, W., et al. (2015). "Planetary Boundaries: Guiding Human Development on a Changing Planet." *Science* 347 (6223): 736–746.
Stern, S. N. (2006). *The Stern Review on the Economics of Climate Change*. Cambridge: Cambridge University Press.
Stretton, H. (1976). *Capitalism, Socialism and the Environment*. Cambridge: Cambridge University Press.
TEEB (The Economics of Ecosystems and Biodiversity). (2010). "The Economics of Ecosystems and Biodiversity: Mainstreaming the Economics of Nature: A Synthesis of the Approach, Conclusions and Recommendations of TEEB." Available online at www.teebweb.org/our-publications/teeb-study-reports/synthesis-report.
Tobin, R. J. (1996). "Pesticides, the Environment, and U.S. Foreign Assistance." *International Environmental Affairs* 8 (3): 244–266.
UNEP (United Nations Environment Programme). (1989). "Convention on the Control of the Transboundary Movements of Hazardous Wastes and Their Disposal." Basel Convention, 1989. Available online at www.basel.int/portals/4/basel%20convention/docs/text/baselconventiontext-e.pdf.
UNFCCC (United Nations Framework Convention on Climate Change). (2015). "Adoption of the Paris Agreement." FCCC/CP/2015/L.9/Rev.1 (December 12, 2015). Available online at https://unfccc.int/resource/docs/2015/cop21/eng/l09r01.pdf.
United States Conference of Catholic Bishops. (2001). Statement, "Global Climate Change: A Plea for Dialogue, Prudence and the Common Good." June 15, 2001.
Vitousek, P. M., et al. (1986). "Human Appropriation of the Products of Photosynthesis." *Bioscience* 36 (6): 368–373.

Vitousek, P. M., et al. (1997). "Human Domination of Earth's Ecosystems." *Science* 277: 494–499.

White, L., Jr. (1967). "The Historical Roots of Our Ecological Crisis." *Science* 155 (3767): 1203–1207.

Zerner, C. (2000). *People, Plants, and Justice: The Politics of Nature Conservation*. New York: Columbia University Press.

Zhang, H. (2013). "China and International Climate Change Negotiations." WeltTrends. Available online at www.welttrends.de/res/uploads/Zhang_China-and-International-climate-change-negotiations.pdf.

2
INTERNATIONAL ENVIRONMENTAL GOVERNANCE
Beyond cosmopolitanism

Introduction

Along with nuclear war and development, the transformation of the biosphere represents one of the three major political challenges of our time. Environmental governance, however, has long been at the margins of the discipline of international relations. This is ironic, for international environmental politics have contributed much to the evolution of the field and its study should be one of its major endeavors.

To be sure, the days since a preeminent international relations (IR) scholar could argue that the environment would largely remain "at the periphery of international relations" seem long gone (Smith 1993). For the foreseeable future, the clear and present danger that climate change and other issues present have triggered the attention of an increasing number of preeminent scholars, and more scholars of international environmental politics now enjoy professional recognition. Calls for an active involvement of the profession in those issues have multiplied (Keohane 2015; Javeline 2014). Political science departments, at least in North America and Northern Europe, look to hire specialists in that field rather than merely considering that subject a marginal bonus likely to attract students. This evolution is to be welcomed for it is indeed where the next grand theories of IR will originate.

Before addressing the issue of global environmental governance which has become the Holy Grail of global ecopolitics since the late 1990s, it is fitting to address two other topics that help put the problem in context: (i) the relationship between the environment and the study of IR, and (ii) several received ideas regarding international environmental governance. Indeed, many of the premises underlying efforts to develop new models of governance are based on assumptions and "half-truths" that at best need be placed in context, and at worst do not rest on solid empirical foundations.

The environment and the new international relations

Diplomats and realist observers of international relations traditionally distinguish between high and low politics, with the former being concerned essentially with territorial integrity, the independence of national institutions, and the security of populations, and the latter with more sectoral concerns, ranging from economic growth to environmental protection and human rights. This distinction has less and less relevance. Indeed, through the study of global ecopolitics, one catches a glimpse of the dynamics that characterize contemporary international relations. It reveals features that governments have difficulties understanding, and that increase the number and complicate the nature of the political dilemmas they face. Although international political economy has also contributed much to this new vision, the field of global environmental governance has been at the center of the articulation of new concepts and theories and of the emergence of a new vision of international relations. To illustrate, the next section identifies four trends that the domain of the environment embodies particularly. These trends will be very familiar to any student of IR.

Interdependence, globalization, and the interpenetration of domestic and international politics

For a long time, it was traditional, as Senator Vandenberg used to say back in 1948 in reference to the United States, to assert that "politics stops at the water's edge." This attitude and the capacity to draw a clear line between the two realms of politics, domestic and international, have long since vanished. In the case of environmental policy, environment officials long ago recognized that national policy depends on what takes place abroad. In some instances, such as in Canada, this has led to end-run strategies whereby domestic bureaucracies formed coalitions with external actors (their counterparts in other countries, for example, or NGOs) in order to create an international context that would enable them to overcome domestic obstacles to their objectives (such as reducing stratospheric ozone or controlling air pollutants). But this "intermestic" situation (to use James Rosenau's (1990) term) has dimensions that go beyond the reciprocal influence between domestic and international issues.

Interdependence, globalization, and free trade have accelerated that trend. We know that many environmental problems are either transborder or global. Many are transposed to the national level by transnational actors (be they corporations, NGOs, or networks). Fewer and fewer domestic environmental issues can be addressed on the basis of domestic concerns, values, and priorities only. Conversely, before they can be successfully tackled, most global problems and their solutions must rest on a consensus among all stakeholders, both international and domestic, including civil society (as in the case of the control of pesticides). This phenomenon, of course, has increased the importance of two-level games (Putnam 1988) in international negotiations, making the latter ever more complex. In sum, the number of relevant stakeholders increases, and so does uncertainty regarding the nature of the problem and of the appropriate solutions.

In their 1977 classic study, Keohane and Nye laid the grounds for a theory of interdependence and later of regimes. Interdependence is usually thought of as having two dimensions: sensitivity to developments abroad, and vulnerability, that is the degree to which one can avoid the consequences of negative developments. Sensitivity does not automatically entail vulnerability. Indeed, Waltz (1979) has defined great powers precisely as being better able than other powers to resist external pressure. Globalization as a property of the international system is an extension of this concept and adds to the unpredictability of the system, for it entails the multiplication of actors claiming a legitimate role in governance. It also means the densification of their relations, the existence of more or less competing norms embedded in various regimes, and a multiplicity of forums (public, private, public-private) where norms and regulations are negotiated. Interdependence and globalization increase the uncertainty attached not only to the actions of others, but also to the consequences of one's own actions, which contributes to the nonlinear behavior of the system. In sum, it creates a system where things "ramify" (Jervis 1997). Actions have unintended consequences in distant places. And in such a system, raw power is not a good predictor of the outcome of environmental negotiations. Further, power is not fungible; rather, it is relative to the nature of the issue area. And matters become much more complex when the boundaries of the issue area expand through linkages.

Issue linkages

These linkages first affect environmental issues themselves. For example, efforts to reduce atmospheric pollution may, at first, increase global warming or its negative impact. Some substitutes for chlorofluorocarbons (CFCs) proved much more potent greenhouse gases than carbon dioxide or methane. The development of carbon sinks (such as forest plantations) can be at the expense of biodiversity. At another level, linkages take place between environmental issues and a variety of other issues such as economic growth, trade, human and political rights, or security. Synergies among them are possible, but trade-offs are more common.

Related to this dimension is indeed the illusion that all good things go together. Not unique to ecopolitics, it refers to the tendency to think that everything one highly values is positively related, such as conservation and democracy, human rights and environmental protection, or biodiversity conservation and poverty reduction. Likewise, we tend to assume the existence of a positive relationship among our fears, for example between demographic growth, poverty, and environmental degradation, when in fact they may not always be so related.[1] Eckersley (2004), for example, contends that democracy creates more ecologically conscious states. Yet, quantitative research does not show a positive correlation overall between democracy and environmental protection; it even may be negative, although the relationship varies by issue area (Midlarsky 1998). Nazi Germany implemented forceful environmental protection policies, after all (Ferry 1992).

Ecopolitics, like all politics, is the realm of trade-offs and dilemmas that come in at least two forms: (i) between values we want to achieve (environmental quality and human security; conservation and access to parks; protection and development; etc.); and (ii) between solutions to environmental problems. These solutions all have a downside; many will have unintended consequences (one of the properties of a complex system). For example, Quebec's legislation on the overuse of fertilizers has led to an increase in deforestation as many hog farmers cleared land in order to increase their leach field, even though the higher the deforestation, the greater the resulting pollution of waterways. As will be further argued in chapter 6, effective governance is not simply about eliminating trade-offs (the result of seeing the system as complicated) but recognizing that these trade-offs are inevitable, and integrating this inevitability into models of governance (the result of seeing the system as complex).

Multiple actors

Environmental problems are caused by the actions of numerous agents that are, in turn, affected by them. Global ecopolitics, as is true of many other areas of international politics, is no longer the sole province of states. Other actors come into play who claim a legitimate role in shaping the definition of the common good and the search for the most acceptable and effective policies to pursue it. Alongside states, intergovernmental organizations (IGOs), nongovernmental organizations (NGOs), business and subnational authorities (federated states and provinces, regions, local authorities) shape the dynamics of the system. Between 2000 and 2010, for example, local authorities have established themselves as a strong voice on biodiversity and climate change. Cities have organized into a network of networks on environmental issues. These networks of actors, in turn, form so-called "complexes" that govern a specific issue area. In 2008, at COP-14 (held in Poznan), Yvo de Boer, then executive secretary of the United Nations Framework Convention on Climate Change (UNFCCC), recognized that 50 percent to 80 percent of effective mitigation actions, and almost 100 percent of adaptation measures were conducted at the substate level. Until 2015, local authorities were the only international level of governance that had concluded agreements committing themselves to long-term action against climate change.[2]

Emblematic of the readiness of some states and provinces to compensate for perceived federal inaction, is the Western Climate Initiative, which combines seven US states and four Canadian provinces. It has been working since 2007 to develop policies to address climate change, including a regional, economy-wide cap-and-trade program and forest offset mechanisms. Only some of the initiative's members— California, Quebec, and British Columbia—have taken concrete steps toward implementing this program, however.

Naturally, these actors are not monolithic. Some businesses have mobilized against climate change while others are promoting clear and sustained policies of emission reductions. Environmental NGOs can be at odds with development

NGOs and both with scientists. Ministries can ally with IGOs and NGOs to promote certain courses of action and pressure other parts of governments more reluctant to move forward.

Emerging forms of governance

Finally, international environmental politics is also a laboratory where new forms of governance are invented and tested. These include:

- governance at various levels of authority, from the global to the regional, the national, the subnational, and the local; this leads to issues regarding (i) where to locate various instruments of governance (see the European Union's [EU's] subsidiarity principle), (ii) the conditions under which one can upscale, downscale or disseminate findings and solutions internationally, and (iii) the management of interscalar relations (the impact of global-local links on the national level of policy making, for example);
- the use of a variety of instruments, be they legal, political, administrative, economic, or social, notably command-and-control as well as market instruments;
- the challenge of reconciling various and sometimes contradictory objectives, and thus of devising political arrangements that set norms and goals, define commitments, allocate resources, manage conflicts; and find ways to implement effectively such arrangements, including through the formalized involvement of a variety of actors (civil society);
- which leads to the emergence of new forms of governance, notably regarding the relationship between science and policy (see chapter 3) but also between various sources of authority.

Private governance is indeed a remarkable development of the last 20 years. This includes not only the adoption by business of new forms of self-regulation (environmental certification—ISO 14000 and ISO 21000, codes of conduct, voluntary labeling) as well as public-private partnerships, but also agreements between private actors (business and NGOs) to define, implement, and enforce new norms governing business conduct and production. Well-known examples are the various forest certification schemes and the Marine Stewardship Council, as well as agreements between NGOs and fast food chains.

In the context of a more turbulent international system, global ecopolitics has contributed handsomely to the development of theoretical approaches to account for the evolving nature of international relations such as institutionalism and regime theory, negotiation theory, governance, transnational networks, and how to address the agent-structure problem. Regarding methods, the field's main contribution lies probably in the development of new thinking about interdisciplinarity and the promotion of a holistic posture, as opposed to a reductionist analytical approach. In this regard, the notion of adaptive complex systems seems particularly well suited to the field, either in its environmental or political dimensions (see chapter 6).

Yet although no one disputes the transformation of international politics, there remains a strange disconnect between this recognition and the solutions that have been pursued in order to improve international environmental governance. These solutions, largely based on hierarchy and centralization, correspond to a dominant discourse about global environmental governance that needs to be put in perspective before we can hope to entertain new models of governance that recognize and even take advantage of these new features of international politics.

Questioning the doxa

As mentioned in the introduction, the field of international environmental politics harbors an extensive doxa that needs questioning. Among them, a cosmopolitan approach to the definition and resolution of environmental problems looms large. Five commonplace assertions will illustrate the prevalence of this approach.

Has diplomacy failed the earth?

As in 1992 and 2002, Rio+20, in June 2012, again provided an opportunity to take stock of progress accomplished or lack thereof. This exercise, each time, is meant to revive the dynamics of international cooperation; again, it remained limited, and again, the usual criticisms regarding inaction in the face of ecological catastrophe flourished.

Indeed, confronted with the multiplication of international meetings and often dramatic assessments of their results, with growing interdependence among environmental, with development, security, trade, foreign and domestic policy, and with the expansion of knowledge that seems to increase rather than reduce uncertainties, many find it difficult to understand the usefulness of multilateral talks, and appreciate the progress made in terms of cooperation in the resolution of environmental problems. Climate change negotiations are often portrayed as embodying what is wrong with international environmental diplomacy, notably the prevalence of narrowly defined national interests over the collective interest, the perceived influence of key lobbying groups, the politicization of science, and rules of procedure that reward blockers over leaders.

Pessimists will emphasize the worsening of the state of the environment such as global warming, reduced sea ice cover, the frequency of extreme events, disruptions of agricultural production, development impairment, the emergence of new threats to security; biodiversity loss (from big mammals to pollinators and ocean life, Butchart et al. 2010), land degradation, or the diminishing primary tropical forest cover.

In addition, although one may hope that more knowledge will lead to an increased capacity to solve problems, it also brings out their complexity: the more we know, the more complex an issue, such as climate change, becomes; and perverse effects abound. The multiplication of problems and growing interdependence exhaust diplomatic resources and, along with a general lack of significant and obvious progress, threaten to demobilize both leaders and citizens. The "great international masses" of Rio in 1992, Johannesburg in 2002, or Rio again in 2012, are increasingly perceived as decoys and generate frustrations in the face of unrealized hopes. Ambitious commitments are painfully negotiated then seemingly abandoned. Subsequent meetings try to revive these earlier efforts, rather than go forward by renewing the thinking about environmental problems or take on new commitments to resolve them.

Progress, if any, seems indeed limited in the face of the urgency to act, and discouragement appears logical when one remembers the words of Sweden's Prime Minister Olof Palme, who, at the opening of the 1972 Stockholm conference exclaimed, "People are no longer satisfied only with declarations. They demand firm action and concrete results. They expect that the nations of the world, having identified a problem, will have the vitality to act."[3]

Many observers, confronted with the magnitude of environmental problems and the perceived failure of international cooperation, therefore, will develop a dangerous cynicism used to justify inaction and the abandonment of efforts under way or stifle research on new avenues for action. Others, such as many NGOs and experts, will highlight problems that remain or worsen in order to mobilize support for their preferred course of action. Governments will ascribe to their opponents or on other countries the responsibility for a lack of action, or hide behind the public's ambivalence to whom environmental measures are presented as so many opportunity costs. The political instrumentalization of environmental issues adds to this problem for it subordinates the definition and attention given problems to external political goals. This pessimistic attitude, when it is not a mere political tactic, needs to be put in perspective. Indeed, the criteria used to assess success or failure need be questioned, the indirect impact of international meetings recognized, real progress acknowledged, and the political context of environmental cooperation taken into account.

Judgments about success or failure first are rooted in the criteria adopted. For example, Amartya Sen, winner of the 1998 Nobel prize in economics, denounced the overwhelmingly negative opinions regarding the notorious 2009 Copenhagen meeting on climate change, arguing that the widespread perception of failure stemmed from unrealistic expectation by the EU,[4] which led observers to overlook that the reality of the problem and the need to act were now widely acknowledged, even by emergent economies, and that new financial resources in favor of adaptation measures of the most vulnerable countries were adopted.[5] The 2002 Johannesburg Summit was also heavily criticized by environmentalists worried about the pre-eminence of the Millennium Development Goals, but it also stimulated thinking about sustainable development and its environmental dimensions, such as land degradation or water use. Johannesburg, through its preparatory process, initiated a deep examination of the UN institutional architecture regarding the environment and sustainable development. New questions were put on the agenda, such as corporate responsibility, transparency of decision-making procedures, the notion of global public goods (as promoted by the United Nations Development Programme [UNDP]), or the relationship between human rights, on the one hand, and health and religious practices on the other.

One could also question the concepts used to assess progress. A classic case is that of regime effectiveness. Asking the question "are international agreements effective?" may have various meanings: have they been implemented, that is translated into national and local legislation and policies? Have they helped solve the initial problem they were intended to address? Have parties complied with its provisions? Have they led to changes in the behavior of key stakeholders? Have they helped disseminate new norms? Etc.

Further, often difficult to notice, the indirect impacts of global meetings vary from location to location, or organization to organization and are heavily dependent on states' engagement during the preparatory phase. Indeed, a summit can strengthen the conditions associated with the adoption and implementation of sound policies in favor of the environment such as improving coordination among administrations and creating new ones, strengthening key ministries, facilitating transparency and the participation of citizens in the decision-making process, supporting public education, stimulating research, mobilizing NGOs, or increasing external political and financial support. They are also an opportunity for civil society to forge new transnational alliances, for IGOs to showcase their work and build new links, and for the general public to become more aware of these issues. In many cases, parallel summits are taking place among various stakeholders, alongside the negotiation of the main intergovernmental text.

Progress, albeit limited, has occurred. First, recent decades have seen a steady institutionalization of environmental concerns, both at the national and international levels. States have created dedicated political and legislative structures. New principles such as the right to a healthy environment, and norms, such as the precautionary principle, have been inserted into national constitutions. The obligation to take sustainable development considerations into account when making decisions is increasingly found in national legislations. Internationally, the number of institutions has increased exponentially. New organizations have been established; existing ones have created new departments or made environmental protection or sustainable development firmly a part of their mission. The strengthening of international law has been significant. It now takes less the form of the adoption of new agreements than that of progress in the legal architecture, notably through the improvement of compliance systems or through monitoring implementation.[6]

More importantly, the last 20 years have seen a strengthening of the trends expressed at the 1992 Rio Summit, regarding, for example, the overall objectives to be pursued (contained in the Millennium Declaration, the Cartagena Protocol, the World Trade Organization [WTO] Doha Declaration, or the Monterrey Consensus), the principles to be followed (common but differentiated responsibility, precaution), the approaches to be adopted (such as the ecosystem approach of the Convention on Biological Diversity [CBD]), the decision-making process (transparency, good governance, participation) or the impacts of globalization and trade liberalization.

Finally, most of these agreements lift national and regional policies and play a driving role in fostering collective action at the international level. Regarding water resources, for example, the work of the International Law Commission and the 1997 Convention on the *Law of Non-Navigational Uses of International Watercourses* have influenced the adoption of other instruments at the level of the region or the watershed (Boisson de Chazournes and Tignino 2011).

In terms of financing, the picture is indeed far from rosy, both at the national and international level. National environmental structures are starved of resources. National plans (such as national desertification plans or national biodiversity strategies) elicit little interest from investors. Current funding is inadequate and unreliable. In general, many special funds created to support the activities of multilateral environmental agreements (MEAs) remain empty or devoid of significant resources. At the CBD COP-10, for example, developing countries explicitly linked the adoption of a new strategic plan and the adoption of a protocol on access and benefit sharing to the mobilization of new sources of financing. Indeed, developing countries have long fought the tendency to pile up new obligations without the provision of new financial resources to carry them out. Efforts to overcome this situation have led to the adoption of innovative instruments, such as tri-partnerships, debt for nature swaps, the Clean Development Mechanism and Reducing Emissions from Deforestation and Forest Degradation (REDD) under the Kyoto Protocol, or payments for ecosystem services. Moreover, the Global Environmental Facility (GEF) has become an important source of financing for projects with global dimensions as well as the financial instrument of an increasing number of MEAs.

Thus, although conventions are great producers of norms, more decentralized discussions, such as on water or forests, have also progressively legitimized norms of exploitation that could form the basis of future international agreements or strengthened norms that remain fragile (such as the precautionary principle and public participation). The inspection panels of development banks also act as a source of harmonization and dissemination of norms. Even the governance of tropical forests has made significant progress. States have agreed on a basic driving principle (sustainable forest governance) that brings together the main concepts included in various governance tools adopted over the last two decades.

Apart from the multiplication of actors, agreements, and numerous declarations of good intentions, what is to be retained from the international efforts in favor of the environment in the last quarter century? Although numerous scientific evaluations have indeed shown the growing negative impact of humans on ecosystems, one should not overlook progress that has occurred, although too often it remains geographically limited and fragile. Climate change and the biodiversity crisis (in the South) have tainted our overall appreciation of the evolution of cooperation. But states have taken significant steps to prevent a further deterioration of the stratospheric ozone layer and enable its recovery. Pollution has decreased in northern cities and northern inland waters; persistent organic pollutants are subject to stricter (although insufficient) control; the forest cover in northern latitudes is increasing along with biodiversity; developing countries are much more aware of the importance of environmental protection, even though their priorities may differ from that of the North (UNEP 2011; see also chapter 5); protected areas have multiplied. Damages are reversible: the Aral Sea and the Mesopotamian marshlands are slowly recovering, and the number of tanker oil spills recorded and the quantity of oil involved have declined. Examples of improvements abound. This is not to minimize the scope of the current ecological crisis (see chapter 1), but one should also acknowledge significant progress in certain areas. The overall picture remains bleak because new problems have emerged that seem more intractable, because questions are raised concerning the ecological limits of the earth (see chapter 1), and because the international community started with the easiest measures.

Indeed, the first measures to remedy environmental problems are the most economical and politically feasible to implement for results that are often easily noticeable. The first 30 percent in pollution reduction is easier than the last 20 percent (given a compromise over an acceptable level of pollution). To establish national parks where few people live or where no resources of significant economic value are thought to exist is easier than displacing populations or shutting them off from the area, excluding industries, or developing and implementing access rules.

When negotiating international agreements, states, often under pressure from public opinion or for political reasons, are reluctant to acknowledge failure. Often, they put off the difficult questions until after the signature of the agreement, in the hope that the new political dynamics thus created will help remove obstacles to more extensive commitments. It is in fact what underlies the Framework Convention-Protocol technique where a framework agreement is signed outlining a general direction and the norms adopted, to be later complemented by protocols detailing more specific commitments (the UNFCCC and the CBD embody this approach). So it is little surprising that subsequent discussions often seem to be trapped in quicksand, although this has proven to give much needed flexibility in negotiations.

Negotiations also increasingly touch upon issues set aside originally as too complex or in areas where scientific uncertainty is significant, whereas the costs of remediation seem considerable. Cooperation also leads to the adoption of norms and solutions likely to affect the distribution of power or interests, which may exacerbate equity considerations as well as political rivalries. Solutions are never politically neutral: they affect the resources (diplomatic, political, financial, human, scientific) available to key actors. Some individuals, groups, and states win; others lose (or win less). For example, the reconciliation of different norms, obligations, and organizational cultures that structure various environmental and nonenvironmental (e.g. trade) regimes is now at the heart of global ecopolitics and presents an acute challenge to environmental diplomacy.

Finally, initial success may bring later failures, depending on who has learned what from previous negotiations. For example, if Japan was opposed to listing red tuna in the Convention on International Trade in Endangered Species (CITES) appendix II, which would limit the catch and trade of that species, it was because of the poor flexibility of the instrument, in particular, the difficulty to change the level of protection. In the case of elephant populations, those southern African cone countries that managed their populations well were prevented from benefiting from their own efforts.[7] Similarly, though the principle of common but differentiated responsibility continues to be a pillar of North-South cooperation, it has also created categories of countries subject to different obligations. Countries with little obligations then have no interest in changing category.[8] By freezing inequalities in terms of responsibility (commitments), this principle enabled minimal agreements on the paths to be taken, at the price of a lack of flexibility in future negotiations (as the dynamics of the UNFCCC illustrates). Although an utter pessimistic vision may not be warranted, there are indeed challenges to international cooperation that need to be overcome if those presented by humans' impacts on the earth system are to be met.

These challenges emphasize building relationships among actors more than overcoming existing obstacles to the resolution of environmental problems. The obvious priority, for example, lies in implementing existing agreements and in creating the conditions that will enable necessary changes in behavior to take place. Among the challenges to be met, the most preeminent are leadership, devising new forms of governance, and reconciling sustainable development and environmental conservation.

According to one of the main negotiators of the Montreal Protocol, the achievement of an international consensus rests on leadership by great powers and major international institutions. US leadership, in that case, helped identify a general strategy for ozone protection, and its economic weight allowed it to overcome traditional North-South divisions (Benedick 1998). Yet power redistribution after the Cold War and the transformation of traditional coalitions did not lead to renewed leadership in environmental matters. Even though North-South bargaining gave way to more flexible coalitions (such as over climate change or genetically modified organisms), internal divisions within each group have increased. The South has fragmented into Souths, without emerging powers playing a leadership role yet, be it diplomatic, intellectual, or financial. EU enlargement made it more difficult to arrive at a common position, which weakened diplomatic flexibility. Moreover, its leadership remained elusive (see chapter 4). Past leaders became blockers. The US distanced itself from multilateral cooperation by expressing formal reservations to past agreements or refusing to join new ones, while Canada, a traditional leader on many environmental issues, became a blocker as more environmental issues touched upon trade interests, intellectual property rights, or could have an impact on domestic constitutional arrangements.

Emerging powers failed to take up the responsibility to lead, although China's participation in international discussions has increased significantly. In this regard, COP-21 of the UNFCCC may have heralded the gradual advent of a new model of governance away from the traditional North-South opposition (see chapter 5), a model not limited to the politics of climate change.

This question has several aspects that touch on the quest for a decentralized model of governance, on regime interplay, and on the growing lack of legitimacy of rules of negotiations. Faced with the dead end of the past 20 year's efforts to revamp the international environmental architecture, it has become urgent to develop a new model of governance. Rather than a centralized model predicated on edicting norms, rules, and procedures at the global level, one should be articulated that rests on the new dynamics of international politics, that is on the development, control, and harmonization of various governance networks, on regional differentiation, and on the integration of various levels of governance (see chapter 6).

A second aspect is reconciling the norms and commitments of different environmental regimes as well as other regimes, such as trade, that interact with the former. To be sure, international financial mechanisms (development banks, the Development Assistance Committee of the Organisation for Economic Co-operation and Development [OECD], the GEF) are playing a welcome role in meeting the challenge of reconciling differing norms; yet this challenge remains daunting. In the case of water, for example, instruments relative to environmental protection, human rights, trade and investments all partake in the management of inland waters.

Finally, a third aspect lies in the risk that current rules of negotiations be perceived as less and less legitimate. As UNFCCC COP-15 has shown forcefully, this risk stems from controversies over the roles of civil society, the nonrespect of the rule of consensus, and from a concert diplomacy where a few states get together on an issue then submit their agreement to the larger body of states who have but very little possibility to amend it. As global ecopolitics affects more closely the core interests of states (security, economics, health, control over territory and resources), procedural questions assume more importance. This is not to say that concert diplomacy is not appropriate. Rather, it means recognizing the tension between legitimacy and effectiveness in international environmental governance.

The third challenge, namely reconciling sustainable development and environmental conservation, may seem paradoxical since environmental conservation is one of the pillars of sustainable development, so much so that the two are often thought to be synonymous. But these two values may clash. Indeed, the fracture between sustainable development and the environment is widening, as symbolized by the Millennium Development Goals that granted only limited attention to traditional environmental questions, as well as by the evolution of the names of the so-called "Earth Summits" (from the 1972 Stockholm "Conference on the Human Environment," to the 1992 Rio "Conference on Environment and Development," the 2002 "World Summit on Sustainable Development," and the 2012 "United Nations Conference on Sustainable Development" or Rio+20). The central importance of sustainable development leads one to emphasize local development concerns (at the expense of transnational environmental issues or the management of the global commons), redistributive considerations, and poverty reduction. This is one of the great tensions of global ecopolitics. It reflects less a lack of concern for the environment than an agenda dominated by the priorities of developing countries, centered on the provision of goods and services (access to water, sustainable agriculture, water- and sewerage-treatment facilities; see chapter 5).

Diplomacy has not failed the earth. Because of the evolution of knowledge and norms, environmental protection is a moving target. New problems arise, old problems become more complex. The international community has made significant progress and has largely put together the basis of future and more forceful actions, provided incentives be there. Naturally, a lot remains to be done, and one can only deplore the existing inertia regarding the most pressing issues. It is also clear that societies will transform their relationship to the natural world away from a mythical harmony with it. The challenge is to survive as functional societies, but also to redefine our relationship to the natural world. Rather than attempting to build ideal societies and international institutions, it would be more reasonable to tackle the most important underlying problems rather than pursue false emergencies. Significant steps have been made to that end. We should not despair of politics. Far from being an impediment, it is there to help change come about.

Must effective governance transcend the state?

In the 1970s, the state was seen as the solution to environmental problems. In his influential parable of the Tragedy of the Commons, Hardin (1968) concluded that the solution was "mutual coercion, mutually agreed upon." What was good at the national level, it was assumed, also applied to the international level. Yet the state has also been seen as an obstacle at that level. Environmentalists have bemoaned either its weaknesses (lacking autonomy in the North; autonomy, authority, and capacities in the South), or national selfishness when the national interest is placed above the environmentalists' conception of the collective interest. States, it is said, should not be allowed to endanger humanity in the name of sovereignty, which has led to the doctrine of the right to intervene to prevent an ecocide (and to countervailing criticisms of green imperialism).

Today, the state is challenged from below (with the rise of new actors from civil society and multilevel governance) and from above (IGOs and transnational business). The current environmental "wisdom" points out states' inability to solve economic and environmental problems by themselves. The advent of global environmental issues, the transborder character of many environmental threats, the evolution of interstate relations, global flows and networks, and interdependence not only make interstate cooperation necessary but are also deemed to make the move toward supranationalism inevitable. Specific institutions and processes are required, it is argued, in order to manage the global system and enforce supranational norms and regulations, and in so doing, help redefine agency, authority, leadership, and even citizenship (Martello and Janasoff 2004). Yet at least four reasons point to the continuing importance of the state as a source of environmental progress (understood as greater cooperation around the protection of the environment).

First, environmental politics has historically been a politics of the local. It derives emotional force from people's attachment to particular places, landscapes, and livelihoods, and to an ethic of communal living that can sustain stable, long-term regimes for the protection of shared resources (Ostrom 1990). The state has a strong role to play, even when dealing with the management of common-pool resources, which relies on the state to enforce certain rules (idem).

Second, international progress often starts at the national level. This has taken two forms: (i) what Vogel and others have termed "regulatory politics" (see chapter 4) and (ii) unilateral acts. The first instance refers to efforts by a particular state (or group of states) to impose its own model or extend its own environmental norms abroad, as in the case of the United States and the protection of the ozone layer. It has been one of the major determinants of the few environmental successes of recent decades.

The literature on international regimes, in its realist variant, has also stressed the role that a hegemon can play in the emergence and maintenance of international regimes, either through the threat of sanctions (as in the case of the US and International Convention for the Prevention of Pollution from Ships [MARPOL]) or by shouldering a larger share of the maintenance cost of that regime. Boycotts, sanctions, or outright assumption of control have been potent drivers of cooperation. Unilateralism may apply to norms asserted through declarations and promises of support that contain new rights and obligations, or more often to implementation and enforcement, as when a state claims the capacity and even the right to enforce rules either in its own interest or in the name of the international community.[9] In this regard, it is important to distinguish between acts that fit or do not fit in a larger legal context, such as an international treaty. Examples abound, from the bombing of the Torrey Canyon in 1967 to Canada's 1970 Arctic Water Pollution Prevention Act, which asserted jurisdiction over shipping up to 100 miles, or the US boycott of shrimp imports from Mexico. These actions may lead to the adoption of new instruments, to a refinement of existing ones, or to the development of legal doctrine.

Third, states have insisted on being at the center of international environmental developments and regime evolution from the creation of the Intergovernmental Panel on Climate Change (IPCC) and Intergovernmental Platform on Biodiversity and Ecosystems Services (IPBES), to the drafting of scientific evaluations, the negotiation of international agreements, and the elaboration of the compliance systems of treaties.

Finally, the state retains an autonomy of decision far superior to that of other actors, unique capacities, as well as the legitimacy to define and pursue the collective good. It is the only player that has general knowledge of the problems and interests of all stakeholders and that is capable of identifying, negotiating, and enforcing a solution acceptable to all, and thus of staking out a domain in which it is free to act. In other words, the diffusion of power increases the state's need to play referee and mediator among actors within and outside national boundaries.

Far from undermining the role of the state, global ecopolitics offers striking examples of efforts to use environmental issues in order to reinforce national sovereignty, from the right to develop natural resources to the extension of sovereignty into new areas. This trend took on four aspects: (i) the reaffirmation of the sacrosanct character of national sovereignty and of the right to develop natural resources on the sole basis of national priorities; (ii) the willingness of certain states to make this sovereignty effective by controlling the entirety of their territory, usually by settling it (e.g. Brazil); (iii) the extension of the geographic boundaries of territorial sovereignty to the oceans and space (such as the Exclusive Economic Zone [EEZ]); and (iv) a broadening of the scope of sovereignty, to genetic materials for example, as through the CBD.

The last two, which illustrate the emergence of a new dynamics of enclosure since Rio 1992 (Lipietz 1992), are not necessarily associated with better protection of resources. In the case of fisheries, for example, weak states may have difficulty policing their own waters. Likewise, the ability to control access does not guarantee a sound exploitation of the resource, as the dramatic fall of the Canadian cod fisheries has shown.

Research supports the central role of state power. Regimes influenced by learning and norm diffusion tend to be weaker, in terms of implementation, than regimes based on structural power (Andersen 2008). Moreover, global governance does not mean the weakening of states, which may form power concerts. Drezner (2007), for example, has reintroduced a great powers-based theoretical perspective which he tested with four cases: the internet, genetically modified organisms, intellectual property rights (IPR) and public health. Through these cases, he shows why a great power concert is a necessary and sufficient condition for effective global governance. His argument is not strictly realist and limited to states' actions since it takes into account the role of IGOs and NGOs and argues that domestic actors shape states' preferences.

Although it is no longer the only important actor, the state remains the indispensable actor. With regard to climate change, only it has the necessary regulatory authority.[10] And without some states taking on a leadership role either at home or abroad, or within supranational arrangements, international cooperation on many environmental issues would be far more limited. Far from disappearing, the state is demonstrating immense capacity to adapt to the new realities of international relations and even to direct them (Bauer and Le Prestre 2001). Environmental governance then takes the form of collaborative problem-solving arrangements where the state relies on the support of other actors to fulfill its functions (Karkkainen 2004).

Do global problems require global solutions?

The quest for global solutions to environmental problems has been the leitmotiv of international efforts of the past 50 years. Starting in the 1970s, nations rallied around such issues as acid rain, ozone depletion, hazardous wastes, marine pollution, biodiversity loss, desertification, and climate change (Martello and Jasanoff 2004). There are few truly global problems, however. There are worldwide manifestations of a given environmental danger, but their status as a "problem" depends on their local impact and on the values and priorities of local societies. Defining a problem as "global" may help raise awareness, but it also obscures their differential impacts and thus the various priorities that countries place upon them, as well as the unequal responsibilities of countries in addressing them.

At one level, one may argue that it is not the scale of problems but their nature that drives solutions. There is a difference between global problems, such as ozone depletion or climate change, where nobody can escape being impacted, and worldwide problems, such as biodiversity loss, that may affect all states but whose solutions are essentially local and national. Global problems, though they may be collective action problems, do not imply, by their very characteristic, that their solutions must include all actors and all related issues. It is not because everything is related to everything else that everything must be part of the analysis and solution. Thus as Hulme argued (2009, 333, quoted in Keohane 2015), framing climate change as a "mega-problem" may have "led us down the wrong road, creating a political log-jam of gigantic proportions."

This does not mean that there is no need to search for solutions at the international level and for coordinating solutions devised at other levels, which explains why international agreements are necessary. But neither does it mean that all actors have to be included in the solution. Indeed, defining global problems as requiring global solutions leads to an all-or-nothing approach and to a higher risk of failure (either through blackmail or through the refusal to act alone). The key issues are what happens at the national level in key states, the prospects for the diffusion of these policies and norms both horizontally and vertically, and whether potential free riders can significantly jeopardize the effectiveness of the regime in the long term. Globalizing problems does not hide national differences and may even exacerbate them. The call to transcend the state tends to assume that there are universal solutions to global problems, thus negating the importance of the local. Over the past 30 years, some of the most interesting balancing acts between the global and the local have come from the domain of environmental governance. Indeed, a strong research agenda now focuses on the articulation of the global with the local and among all intermediary levels of governance.[11]

Do stronger treaties lead to better international environmental policies?

We commonly hear that to be effective, international environmental protection must rest on strong treaties, i.e. treaties that are said "to have teeth." This is a particularly popular idea with NGOs and legal scholars who are wont to attribute what they deem the poor effectiveness of international agreements to the lack of specific obligations and the absence of enforcement provisions. On the eve of UNFCCC COP-21, calls for a strong legally binding agreement abounded, from EU environment ministers (September 18, 2015) to the Pope (although later what was deemed legally binding became the object of much casuistry). This belief calls for a few caveats.

First, compliance (that is, the extent to which parties fulfill their obligations) is not effectiveness (the extent to which the agreement helps change the behavior of relevant actors). In part, because states negotiate the obligations they believe they can fulfill; in part also, because states can be in compliance even though they have done nothing to implement the provisions of an agreement (Victor et al. 1998). So treaties that focus on compliance may miss the mark.

Second, this approach may also assume the problem to be solved: If states are ready to accept strong measures that demand specific actions (with little room left for interpreting the obligations in light of their own circumstances) under threat of sanctions, then those measures are probably not needed since all will be convinced of their value and none would have an incentive to cheat. The problem then moves from achieving cooperation among states to managing the coordination of national efforts.

Third, the search for stronger treaties may also make their conclusion less probable and reduce the possibility of future cooperation. States will not ratify an agreement without knowing the details of the sanctions for noncompliance (as the negotiations on the implementation of the Kyoto Protocol illustrated) and without being convinced that the process will be fair both in its spirit and outcomes. The definition of a fair and equitable process is itself unclear and likely to be questioned.

Sanctions also have to induce compliance and a gradual strengthening of commitments, rather than make the latter more difficult to achieve. In the case of the Kyoto Protocol, these sanctions, although notionally legally binding, were not credible and failed to guarantee domestic implementation of commitments (particularly in federal systems) and also made it less probable that noncompliant states would later agree on a follow-up treaty. Treaties need to be flexible in order to adapt to specific implementation contexts that differ widely. For example, transboundary water issues require legal norms that can fit the characteristics of each case (Sohnle 1998).

Finally, far from weakening international law, even a weak treaty may induce positive political dynamics within governments and civil societies that help disseminate norms and principles. It defines yardsticks for evaluating behavior, identifies a direction, and helps mobilize actors.

This is not an argument against sanctions in principle. Rather, it is that lack of explicit sanctions does not mean that an agreement is worthless; and, under some conditions, sanctions may have no meaning or may even be counterproductive. The call to include tough sanctions into MEA attempts to transpose a domestic model of enforcement to the international level. The role of coercion at the international level is very different, however. This position also ignores studies of compliance that emphasize the importance of utilitarian calculations or of processes leading to a redefinition of interests and identities.

Are powerful international institutions required for concerted and effective international environmental policy?

Historically, environmental scholars have largely favored central regulatory mechanisms resting on coercive powers, as a condition for effectively addressing environmental issues. This domestic model has been largely transferred to the international arena, thanks to lawyers fond of binding agreements and NGOs eager to reshape value systems authoritatively. Yet this has led to a dead end as the environment continues to deteriorate (despite the progress mentioned above), issues to expand, actors to multiply, and values and interests to clash. Complexity science, on the other hand, suggests that the environment is too complex to be treated by a centralized monolithic organization, and calls for complex and adaptive management.

The belief in greater centralization at the international level is widespread and remains the default position of most nonacademics and of a majority of academics themselves. When it proposed the creation of "an IPCC for biodiversity" in 2005, which later became the IPBES, the French government envisaged "a single steering center that issues specific directives."[12] This belief in the virtues of centralization modelled after domestic arrangements often takes the form of a call for a World Environment Organization (WEO), an idea variously raised by German and French leaders in the 1990s as well as by the former executive director of the WTO, Ernest Ruggiero. Various Popes have recently called for a world authority from Pope John XXIII to Pope Francis, who echoed the words of Pope Benedict XVI:

> To manage the global economy; to revive economies hit by the crisis; to avoid any deterioration of the present crisis and the greater imbalances that would result; to bring about integral and timely disarmament, food security and peace; to guarantee the protection of the environment and to regulate migration: for all this, there is urgent need of a true world political authority, as my predecessor Blessed John XXIII indicated some years ago (quoted in Francis 2015, 175).

At first sight, arguments in favor of this solution appear convincing for more and more MEAs contain commercial provisions (such as the 1987 Montreal Protocol on stratospheric ozone, the Basel Convention on hazardous waste, and the Cartagena Protocol on biosafety) that may clash with the free trade provisions of the WTO and be successfully challenged in that forum, thus reducing their effectiveness. A WEO, it is argued, would have the weight required to force the WTO to integrate environmental concerns into its activities. Furthermore, it would have greater authority and thus improve the enforcement of treaties. It would overcome current institutional fragmentation (a source of weakness), integrate the goals and procedures of existing sectoral conventions, ease the diplomatic burden of states, speak with one voice, and protect environmental values as well as the WTO protects the principles of free trade.

Here again, however, is a solution in search of a problem. Leaving aside the current travails of the WTO, are there really that many conflicts between the rules of the WTO and those aimed at protecting the environment? No economic provision designed to facilitate the enforcement of an environmental treaty has yet been denounced in the WTO. The WTO itself is not opposed to using environmental concerns in decisions about trade, but it is concerned with the results of such decisions and with using trade-related environmental measures (TREMs) in a discriminatory fashion.

More fundamentally, as Victor (1999) has pointed out, there is no dominant environmental paradigm comparable to that of free trade. This has a triple meaning: (i) current institutional diversity reflects the diversity of perspectives and interests at play; (ii) states hesitate to grant extensive powers to a single institution they do not control; and (iii) a WEO will, in effect, have difficulties speaking with one voice. This difficulty is enhanced by a lack of coordination at the national level. Fragmentation at the international level also reflects domestic tensions and rivalries among ministries and levels of government, tensions that are enhanced by participatory and decentralization policies. Such tensions could quickly paralyze a WEO. If the latter manages to possess the authority and resources that its supporters would like, states will then be all the more eager to control its outputs: competition among different priorities could then quickly lead to stalemate or incoherence. States will first want to negotiate the mandate and authority of such a WEO before committing to it, which will be the surest way of defeating it.

Indeed, why would states agree to give a WEO such extensive powers? Either it will be too powerful or useless. If the latter, there is no need for it. And if the former, then as Calestous Juma (2000) has pointed out, "Drawing on their experiences with the World Bank and the International Monetary Fund, many developing countries are concerned that a new environmental agency would only become another source of conditions and sanctions."

The influence of most states might also be far more modest in a WEO than in individual regimes. Issue linkage may encourage successful bargaining over some issues but impede progress on others. It is unclear why such an agency would be better able to facilitate implementation of national legislation and international agreements, and the scope of its potential responsibilities might create new fears of green imperialism (at the expense of sustainable development) among developing countries. Finally, nothing suggests that a WEO could demonstrate the ability to adapt and escape the ills of other large organizations, namely uncertain legitimacy, waste of resources, internal paralysis, incoherence of activities, and competition with other institutions. Better coordination does not automatically follow geographical or administrative centralization, especially in the absence of an overarching consensus on the norms and principles that should be promoted. Faced with these obstacles, this solution has had little traction, and international environmental governance reform seems to be trapped in quicksand.

The nature of the current dead end

Sustained efforts at reforming international environmental governance (IEG) have been under way since the mid-1990s.[13] They accelerated in the build-up to the 2002 Johannesburg Summit and subsequently with the French initiative to transform the status of the United Nations Environment Programme (UNEP). They are now stalled, having only led to a bit of tinkering with the current structure rather than to an overhaul of the governance system. Several questions then arise: (i) what is the problem? (ii) what has been attempted and achieved? (iii) why so little progress? and (iv) where are we headed? I shall briefly address the first three in this section and leave the fourth question for a final conclusive section.

What is the problem supposed to be?

Between the middle of the 1990s until 2012, the debate about how to reform international environmental governance has been dominated by efforts from the UN system to rationalize its activities in that field. But the question of IEG dates back to 1972, with the creation of UNEP whose mandate, resources, and scope were deliberately kept limited. This question emerged again in the mid-1990s with various calls for the establishment of a WEO. It then dominated the preparatory meetings of the Johannesburg (2002) and Rio+20 (2012) Summits.

Reaching a consensus on the nature of the problem has not been easy. Extensive consultations with states after Johannesburg pointed to six basic concerns:

i the lack of coherent and authoritative scientific assessment capabilities, overlaps in the scope and actions of subsidiary bodies, and the absence of early-warning systems;
ii institutional fragmentation deemed to foster inconsistencies, waste, as well as impose a heavy administrative and diplomatic burden.[14] For example, both the CBD and the agreement on Trade-Related Intellectual Property Rights (TRIPS) are key institutions in the regulation of the provisions dealing with Access and Benefit-Sharing of biodiversity resources. Institutions and instruments pertaining to environmental protection, human rights, or trade all contribute to the governance of water. Their reconciliation presents a challenge that is found in many other areas;
iii poor national implementation of international commitments;
iv complex and scattered financial instruments;
v weak authority and limited resources of UNEP;
vi insufficient partnerships with civil society (broadly conceived).

The functions of international environmental governance that should be strengthened, according to this consensus, include the assessment of the state of the environment, the production of norms and policies, implementation at all levels, policy support, and policy evaluation. How one is to translate these concerns into effective and politically acceptable solutions remains elusive, however.

What has been attempted and achieved?

Though the diagnosis rests more on impressions and anecdotes than on rigorous empirical analyses, the debate regarding international environmental governance has mostly revolved not around problems but around solutions, including the transformation of UNEP into a specialized agency of the UN, the relationship between environmental and sustainable development governance, the status and coordination of MEAs, or the potential contradiction between a governance model designed to rationalize the distribution of competencies, and one centered on the national implementation of international agreements. These dynamics where solutions drive the definition of the problem (or the attitude toward the science that supports it) can be found in a variety of areas, including climate change.

At the UN, the measures have remained modest. In the case of UNEP, though the adopted changes have somewhat strengthened its political weight and improved the predictability of its financial resources, they have not widened its scope of action, increased its resources significantly, or changed its status. Its structure and operations were modified with the creation of the Environment Management Group in 1998 and of the Global Ministerial Environment Forum (GMEF) in 1999; the adoption of a voluntary scale of contributions in 2002; and the universal membership of its governing council in 2012. The proposition, strongly promoted by France and the EU, of changing its status into that of a specialized agency did not succeed.

The idea of gathering all MEAs under a UNEP umbrella, of transforming the trusteeship council into a sustainable development council, or of creating a dispute settlement mechanism on the model of WTO's were never seriously considered. The Rio+20 Summit only approved the transformation of the Commission on Sustainable Development, created in 1992 to oversee the implementation of the Rio Summit Action Plan (Agenda 21), into a high-level political forum. The usefulness of this reform remains to be seen. In addition, some efforts have been made to improve coordination among MEAs and an experimental attempt at clustering chemical conventions appears to be holding.

This does not mean an absence of points of convergence around a few principles, including the need to maintain the autonomy of MEAs (that is, oppose the establishment of a WEO); the rejection of any new and significant financial commitments; the desire to adopt an incremental rather than a revolutionary approach by strengthening the existing structure; the value of encouraging clustering; and the necessity to improve the links between various governance levels.

In general, three questions have structured recent discussions:

1. Should we create a new institutional framework? Faced with political opposition to a deep reform of the system and disagreements over the definition of the problem and of the appropriate solutions, there is only room for limited institutional reform.
2. Should we adopt a centralized or a more decentralized and bottom-up approach? This dimension has largely opposed the EU to the US, with developing countries siding with the latter. The debate remains open, although, in practice, at least in the case of climate change, it is moving toward a more decentralized model.
3. Finally, should the objective of global environmental governance be to strengthen national capacities or cooperation on questions that have an impact on the effectiveness of national policies? In other words, is international centralization of authority necessary for the successful implementation of policies negotiated at the international level?

Beyond cosmopolitanism: The need for a new approach

Faced with this dead end, either we deem the existing situation better than any alternative or we look for ways to define the problem differently—that is, not on the basis of a solution deemed a priori desirable. I shall use the term "cosmopolitanism" in its political aspects, to refer to the desirability of centralizing authority at the global level so as to fulfill the universal aspirations of humankind either sectorally (the environment) or comprehensively (world government).

Fueled by the desire to bring order, cosmopolitan theses have a long tradition in international relations, and recur periodically. Nonstate actors are fond of it: It remains largely behind the approach to international relations of transnational corporations and is strongly endorsed by other transnational actors, such as the Catholic Church. This translates into specific propositions that correspond to two distinct visions: world government and global governance (Campbell 2008).

There is a certain revival of the first approach with prominent theorists advocating the inevitability as well as necessity of the advent of a world government if humanity is to hope ever to manage the problems it faces (Deudney 2006; Wendt 2003). The various theses largely amount to an update of Kant. For some, the fear of a common danger (such as climate change) must lead to exceptional unity in the face of it, and to concerted actions and associations among former rival states. For others, following the Kantian tradition, the destructive power of modern military technology will make cooperative arrangements inevitable. Others, such as Wendt, see it as an inevitable process, albeit deep in the future, thanks to the twin logics of globalization and recognition.[15]

In the second approach, that of global governance, the various problems triggered by globalization and environmental degradation can be managed through the gradual strengthening of existing institutions (McGrew and Held 2002). While the former utopian vision still holds sway, even though it remains highly unlikely, for the impact of perceived danger on group unity is not linear but more like a normal function, it is the global governance vision that dominates, with sometimes the idea that it could prove a first step toward the former.

With respect to international environmental governance, a few discordant voices emerged almost from the beginning, but they were largely ignored, in part because they did not offer the same clearly understood though misleadingly simple solution as did the proponents of a WEO (Hoffmann 2011; Victor 2011; Haas 2004; Najam 2003; Le Prestre 2001). Overall, the prevailing discourse (be it from scholars, activists, or politicians) hardly changed. It was dominated by solutions based on some sort of centralization of authority and, with few exceptions, neglected scholarly studies about international relations that identified the new emergent dynamics. Among the features of current IR that centralizing solutions do not fully integrate into the models proposed or with which they are at odds are multilevel governance (the importance of the region as a locus of political action (see chapter 4), the decentralization of authority, and the need to coordinate actions across various levels of authority), the democratic imperative (that is, the push in favor of participation in decision making, but see chapter 3), institutional diversity, network governance, and the properties of complex systems (such as the different evaluation of institutional fragmentation; see chapter 6).

Conditions are not ripe for the adoption of a centralized model of governance, even were it advisable. The establishment of a UN Environmental Organization lacked the support of key states, triggered suspicions from emerging and developing countries, and faced resistance from established UN agencies (Le Prestre 2006). The Group of 77 (G77) continues to claim the need to speak of sustainable development governance rather than environmental governance, that is, to place more emphasis on social and economic issues (see chapter 5).

If international environmental governance reform remains elusive, perhaps it is because it is illusory to want to centralize authority and the production of norms, knowledge, and policies in this area. Even though more and more studies emphasize the multiscalar dimension of problems and acknowledge that current MEAs do not exclude that dimension or even rely on regional mechanisms to fulfill their objectives (such as the United Nations Convention to Combat Desertification [UNCCD]), the rule of multilateralism emphasizes strategies that all states commit to pursue, leaving only the development of specific measures to additional efforts by states. This "globalist" approach discourages the development of regional levels of governance (outside of the EU) even though most problems and solutions are regional.

The limited progress and current dead end suggest the need to think anew about the nature of international environmental governance, a governance that takes advantage of the evolution of the system instead of fighting it; one that reflects the complexity of the issues and that acts as a counterpoint to existing models. The contours of such an approach are sketched out in chapter 6.

Notes

1 For an argument against the existence of such a relationship, see Mathieu (1998).
2 Soon after Rio, cities started organizing themselves as a global network on environmental issues, notably on climate change. Eight declarations and pledges have been concluded since 1994: the Aalborg Charter (1994), the Montreal Declaration (2005), the Mayors' Convention (2008), The Saint-Malo Declaration (2008), the Dunkirk Declaration (2010), the Mexico Global Cities Pact (2010), the Carbon Cities Climate Registry (2010), and the Nantes Declaration (2013). In some countries, labels were created to recognize local authorities' actions against climate change and to protect the environment.
3 UNEP. (2005). GEO: Global Environmental Outlook 3. London: Earthscan, 6.
4 Raising the bar high can also be a political tactic designed to put pressure on laggards and blockers.
5 Interview of Amartya Sen, January 14, 2010 by RTL-Belgium. See www.rtl.be/info/magazine/science-nature/pour-le-prix-nobel-amartya-sen-copenhague-a-ete-un-succes-147334.aspx.
6 Examples of strengthened compliance systems are found in the Kyoto Protocol (perhaps the most elaborate and innovative), and in the Montreal protocol. The CBD, for its part, has considerably developed its monitoring system, both internally and through its links with the biodiversity governance system as a whole.
7 Source: *The Economist*, March 27, 2010, 90.

8 Regarding climate change, the outcome of the UNFCCC COP-21 has changed this situation somewhat since each party is now asked to "prepare, communicate and maintain successive nationally determined contributions that it intends to achieve" (Art.4 [2]), and "Developing country Parties should continue enhancing their mitigation efforts, and are encouraged to move over time towards economy-wide emission reduction or limitation targets…" (Art.4 [4]). Source: United Nations (FCCC/CP/2015/L.9).
9 Such as successful US moves in the 1970s to impose regulations designed to reduce intentional oil spills, or to raise the level of protection of cetaceans; or, in the 1990s, US attempts to impose fishing practices less destructive of ancillary species (as illustrated by the Tuna/Dolphin and Shrimp/Turtles WTO cases).
10 On the role of states and power politics in climate change, see Vogler 2015.
11 This is usually presented by MEAs as well as scholars of international regimes, as ensuring that decisions made at the international level are implemented at the local level, making it an issue of translating the global into the local. But such a top-down approach surely is insufficient if not the wrong way to think about those links. Rather than attempting to mould the local into the global, a recursive model that defines principles at the global level informed by lower levels, and lets the regional and local levels devise implementing norms and procedures would fit better with the complex nature of the governance problem (see chapter 6).
12 Renaud Dutreil, France's minister of civil service, Address to the International Conference on "Biodiversity, Science and Governance," Paris, January 24–28, 2005.
13 Uncertainties surrounding the meaning of "governance" do not simply stem from the confusion between governance and government (the latter being subsumed in the former) but also from the use of the term in both an analytical and normative way. In the first instance, it simply refers to nonhierarchic modes of regulation involving many actors (agents) operating on different levels. In the second instance, it corresponds to a political program with the aim to manage the challenges of globalization or simply to ensure sound management of public or private affairs. Generally, governance can be approached as the various arrangements (authoritative or not) that societies have developed in order to pursue the common good, that is, legitimize a certain conception of what constitutes a problem, identify appropriate principles, norms, rules, and solutions to be applied, and mobilize the means needed to modify the behavior of relevant actors in accordance with stated goals.
14 Keeping in mind that a distinction can be made between cooperative fragmentation, where different institutions and decision-making procedures embodying different norms are loosely integrated, and conflictive fragmentation where institutions are hardly connected, operate differently, and represent conflicting sets of norms (see Biermann et al. 2009, 22).
15 Unlike their predecessors, modern cosmopolitans argue that the trend is inevitable, whether or not states want it. Wendt (2003) assumes a tendency of systems to develop toward stable end-states, which is a systemic approach rooted in physics. Ecology, however, although it did embrace that view early on with the notion of climax, now reasons in terms of multiple equilibria and regulatory catastrophes.

References

Andersen, R. (2008). *Governing Agrobiodiversity: Plant Genetics and Developing Countries*. Aldershot, UK: Ashgate.

Bauer, J. and P. Le Prestre. (2001). "Ménage à Trois: The State between the Domestic and International Systems." In *Who's Afraid of the State?* edited by G. Smith and D. Wolfish. Toronto: University of Toronto Press, 29–88.

Benedick, R. E. (1998). *Ozone Diplomacy: New Directions in Safeguarding the Planet*. Cambridge: Harvard University Press.

Biermann, F., et al. (2009). "The Fragmentation of Global Governance Architectures: A Framework for Analysis." *Global Environmental Politics* 9 (4): 14–40.

Boisson de Chazournes, L. and M. Tignino. (2011). "Gestion Internationale de l'eau et développements du droit international." In *Vingt ans après: Rio et l'avant-goût de l'avenir*, edited by P. Le Prestre. Québec: Presses de L'université Laval, 245–262.

Butchart, S., et al. (2010). "Global Biodiversity: Indicators of Recent Declines." *Science* 328 (5982): 1164–1168.

Campbell, C. (2008). "The Resurgent Idea of World Government." *Ethics & International Affairs* 22 (2).

Deudney, D. H. (2006). *Bounding Power: Republican Security Theory from the Polis to the Global Village*. Princeton: Princeton University Press.

Drezner, D. W. (2007). *All Politics Is Global: Explaining International Regulatory Regimes*. Princeton: Princeton University Press.

Dutreil, R. (2005). "Articulation Local-Global dans la Gouvernance de la Biodiversité." Address, International Conference on Biodiversity, Science and Governance, Paris, January 24–28, 2005.

Eckersley, R. (2004). *The Green State: Rethinking Democracy and Sovereignty*. Cambridge: MIT Press.

The Economist. (2010). "How the Elephants' Success Hurt the Bluefin Tuna." *The Economist*, (March 27): 90.

Ferry, L. (1992). *Le Nouvel Ordre Écologique. L'arbre, L'animal et L'homme*. Paris: Grasset.

Francis. (2015). "Encyclical Letter Laudato Si of the Holy Father Francis on Care for Our Common Home." Vatican City, Italy: Holy See.

Haas, P. M. (2004). "Addressing the Global Governance Deficit." *Global Environmental Politics* 4 (4): 1–16.

Hardin, G. (1968). "The Tragedy of the Commons." *Science* 162: 1243–1248.

Hoffmann, M. J. (2011). *Climate Governance at the Crossroads: Experimenting with a Global Response after Kyoto*. New York: Oxford University Press.

Hulme, M. (2009). *Why We Disagree About Climate Change: Understanding Controversy, Inaction and Opportunity*. Cambridge: Cambridge University Press.

Javeline, D. (2014). "The Most Important Topic Political Scientists Are Not Studying: Adapting to Climate Change." *Perspective on Politics* 12 (2): 420–434.

Jervis, R. (1997). *System Effects: Complexity in Political and Social Life*. Princeton: Princeton University Press.

Juma, C. (2000). "The Perils of Centralizing Global Environmental Governance." *Environment Matters* 6 (12): 13–15.

Karkkainen, B. C. (2004). "Post-Sovereign Environmental Governance." *Global Environmental Politics* 4 (1): 72–96.

Keohane, R. O. (2015). "The Global Politics of Climate Change: Challenge for Political Science. The 2014 James Madison Lecture." *PS: Political Science and Society* (January): 19–26.

Keohane, R. O. and J. S. Nye. (1988) [1977]. *Power and Interdependence*. Boston: Little, Brown.

Le Prestre, P. (2001). "Releasing the Potential of Emerging Trends: For a Canadian Initiative on Strengthening Convention Governance Systems." Workshop on International Environmental Governance (Environment Canada). Vancouver, BC.

Le Prestre, P. (2006). "Gouvernance internationale de l'environnement: une initiative française." In *Annuaire français des relations internationales*, edited by S. Sur. Bruxelles: Bruylant.

Lipietz, A. (1992). *Towards a New Economic Order: Postfordism, Ecology and Democracy*. Cambridge: Polity Press.

Martello, M. L. and S. Jasanoff. (2004). "Introduction: Globalization and Environmental Governance. " In *Earthly Politics: Local and Global in Environmental Governance*, edited by S. Jasanoff and M. L. Martello. Cambridge: MIT Press, 1–29.

Mathieu, P. (1998). "Population, pauvreté et dégradation de l'environnement en Afrique: fatale attraction ou liaisons hasardeuses?" *Natures-Sciences-Sociétés* 6 (3): 27–34.

McGrew, A. and D. Held, eds. (2002). *Governing Globalization: Power, Authority and Global Governance*. Cambridge: Polity Press.

Midlarsky, M. (1998). "Democracy and the Environment: An Empirical Assessment." *Journal of Peace Research* 35: 341–361.

Najam, A. (2003). "The Case Against a New International Environmental Organization." *Global Governance* 9: 367–384.

Ostrom, E. (1990). *Governing the Commons: The Evolution of Institutions for Collective Action*. Cambridge: Cambridge University Press.

Putnam, R. D. (1988). "Diplomacy and Domestic Politics: The Logic of Two-Level Games." *International Organization* 42 (3): 427–460.

Rosenau, J. N. (1990). Turbulence in World Politics. Princeton: Princeton University Press.

Smith, S. (1993). "Environment on the Periphery of International Relations: An Explanation." *Environmental Politics* 2 (4): 28–45.

Sohnle, J. (1998). "Irruption du droit de l'environnement dans la jurisprudence de la C.I.J: L'affaire Gabcikovo-Nagymaros." *Revue Générale de Droit International Public* 102 (1): 85–121.

UNEP (United Nations Environment Programme). (2005). GEO: Global Environmental Outlook 3. London: Earthscan.

UNEP (United Nations Environment Programme). (2011). Progress Towards Meeting Internationally Agreed Goals (Findings from GEO-5 Draft 2 as at 26 September 2011). Nairobi: UNEP.

UNFCCC (United Nations Framework Convention on Climate Change). "Adoption of the Paris Agreement." FCCC/CP/2015/L.9/Rev.1 (December 12, 2015). Available online at https://unfccc.int/resource/docs/2015/cop21/eng/l09r01.pdf.

Victor, D. G. (1999). *The Market for International Environmental Protection Services and the Perils of Coordination*. Tokyo: UNU.

Victor, D. G. (2011). *Global Warming Gridlock: Creating More Effective Strategies for Protecting the Planet*. Cambridge: Cambridge University Press.

Vogler, J. (2015). *Climate Change in World Politics*. Basingstoke, UK: Palgrave Macmillan.

Victor, D. G., et al. (1998). *The Implementation and Effectiveness of International Environmental Commitments: Theory and Practice*. Cambridge: MIT Press.

Waltz, K. (1979). *Theory of International Politics*. Chicago: Addison-Wesley.

Wendt, A. (2003). "Why a World State Is Inevitable." *European Journal of International Relations* 9 (4): 491–542.

3
BRIDGING THE SCIENCE-POLICY DIVIDE

Introduction

Around midnight on December 12, 2015, as delegates were about to vote to adopt the COP-21 agreement, UN Secretary-General Ban Ki-moon exclaimed that "we have to do as science dictates." This was a remarkable statement for two reasons: (i) it showed the prevalence of a traditional linear model of the relationship between science and politics at the time when this model was being questioned and an alternate one promoted in new international entities, and (ii) it assumed not only that scientific knowledge was clear but also that from it sprung inescapable courses of action. Yet already back in 1988, a British Parliamentarian could observe during the debates over the Montreal Protocol in the House of Lords that "politics is the art of taking good decisions on insufficient evidence" (Lord Kennet, quoted in Benedick 1998, 2). Indeed, we have gradually come to accept that policy initiatives and "progress" in solving environmental problems do not depend on the mere accumulation of knowledge. We often seem to face a paradox exemplified by the case of climate change: the better the problem is known scientifically, the less the global and political community appears capable of addressing it.

This issue has two dimensions. First is the question of the relevance of science to policy. Natural scientists rarely ask themselves that question since they assume their science is relevant, but it pervades the social sciences (or at least those sciences that develop research topics that are not directly responding to the needs of policy makers), such as international relations theory. Second is the matter of how to improve the science–policy interface.

Thinking about these issues, we could adopt a broad or a narrow vision of science. The broad vision encompasses all science, if not all knowledge (whether or not of rational Western origins), whether natural, social, or humanistic. For example, in the case of the social sciences, we may be concerned not only with research results of particular significance but also with the dialogue (or lack thereof) between theory and policy. This chapter is mostly concerned with the relationship between the natural sciences and policy, which is the main topic of the literature. But as the importance of the social sciences increases, as it is bound to do in the Intergovernmental Panel on Climate Change (IPCC) and other international assessments programs, we will need to see whether similar dynamics obtain. We shall first contrast how scientists, politicians and political scientists see the problem, then illustrate the science-policy relationship using international assessments and the Intergovernmental Platform on Biodiversity and Ecosystems Services (IPBES) as examples before closing with a few concluding observations.

Contrasting perspectives

The scientist's view

Despite decades of close relationships between scientists and politicians as exemplified by the appointment of chief scientists or scientific advisors in cabinets, despite governments themselves employing large numbers of scientists and holding advanced expertise in many fields, despite the use of government scientists to represent and negotiate on their country's behalf, and despite the calls for and endorsement of interdisciplinary research, the prevalence of fairly caricatural attitudes among natural scientists regarding the relationship between science and policy remains striking.

The traditional viewpoint sees scientists as belonging to the lab. Scientists should leave policy and politics to others for fear of being contaminated by it and losing credibility. That attitude changed first thanks to nuclear physicists, who became concerned with the consequences of their discoveries and injected themselves actively into the policy process, and then through the environmental movement where scientists became opinion makers alongside journalists and civil servants.

Subsequently, natural scientists came to think the problem was twofold. First was the belief that lack of scientific training (by which they meant training in the "hard" sciences) prevented policy makers from understanding their scientific message. *A contrario*, Margaret Thatcher's openness to the arguments regarding the need to do something to protect the ozone layer might have been facilitated by her training in chemistry. This is reminiscent of Socrates' famous admonition in Plato's Republic:

> Until philosophers rule as kings in cities or those who are now called kings and leading men genuinely and adequately philosophize, that is, until political power and philosophy entirely coincide, while the many natures who at present pursue either one exclusively are forcibly prevented from doing so, cities will have no rest from evils, Glaucon, nor, I think, will the human race. And, until this happens, the constitution we've been describing in theory will never be born to the fullest extent possible or see the light of the sun.[1]

But it could also make decision makers more impervious to the arguments presented if they thought of themselves as experts. Claude Allègre, a distinguished French geochemist and former minister of education, was a leading climate skeptic and used the prestige gained in his field to disseminate his doubts.

The second assumption is lack of access. Indeed, it was one of the main arguments behind the creation of the future IPBES. Scientists are wont to reduce the problem to one of access. If only policy makers had the right information on their desk, then surely they would make the right decision (that is, the decision that meets the preferences of the scientists). But scientists must run labs, write grants, give papers and publish; they seldom have the time to be active in the policy process. Yet who better than the scientists themselves to identify the implications of their research and the nature of their concerns to policy makers and the public alike? Preeminent scientists in many different countries took on the mantle of attempting to convince their colleagues that science indeed should be brought to policy by scientists themselves rather than by political brokers or through the development of institutions that would define consensual knowledge and make it available to policy makers.

It is indeed striking to see how much scientists have a tendency to minimize their influence. In the United States (and that is true of many countries), the mechanisms and procedures put in place by the government for selection and support of scientific research, for accountability of funds, and for rights of publication were established according to the principles and criteria used in the scientific community itself. In what has been called a quasi *coup d'état* (Skolnikoff 1968, 535), the mechanisms for allocating resources were staffed largely by scientists. Studies abound that have shown the extent to which scientists have shaped the political agenda and the range of options that have been considered in response to problems they identified, their needs, and their concerns.

With respect to international environmental governance, science has played an important role in at least three ways (Miller 2011):

- through the concepts it developed (such as the biosphere and ecosystems) as well as the empirical data it provided, which helped shape the political agenda;
- by globalizing science, science conceived as a universal language and intellectual endeavor that transcends borders and sovereignty (of which the IPCC and Future Earth are examples);[2]
- and by legitimizing policies; i.e. it has shaped what is considered legitimate political discourse.

The idea that science provides knowledge and politics implements its implications (as determined by scientists) corresponds to the linear model of the science-policy interface (see Figure 3.1).

This model ascribes a special role to science, deemed to possess the moral authority of speaking truth to power (Koetz *et al.* 2011). Science helps define problems and solutions. It is consensual, neutral, and universal, whereas politics is

FIGURE 3.1. The linear model of the science-policy interface
Source: Philippe Le Prestre

conflictual, partial, and contextual. Scientists provide the knowledge that decision makers should use. In such a model, if the decision makers or the public are resistant to the scientific message, the fault lies either in politics or in their lack of scientific knowledge, combined with poor performance on the part of science communicators (Hulme 2009).

Now, one could also submit that when scientists minimize their influence, they actually mean the influence of their own discipline rather than that of science in general. The science-policy interface is also the arena of power struggles among epistemic communities (see below).

The politician's view

Decision makers and politicians like to present science as the ultimate justification of environmental policies. According to the 2000 Malmö Declaration, for example,[3]

> [S]cience provides the basis for environmental decision-making. There is a need for intensified research, fuller engagement of the scientific community and increased scientific cooperation on emerging environmental issues, as well as improved avenues for communication between the scientific community, decision makers and other stakeholders.

This belief in the centrality and power of science also reflects a liberal faith in the virtue of knowledge. More knowledge and better access to knowledge are necessary and sufficient conditions for changes in behavior. Faced with evidence of the negative impacts of their behavior, individuals and groups will modify it. It is assumed that knowledge facilitates decisions: the more one knows about the factors that lead to the degradation of the environment, the easier the identification and selection of enlightened policies. This argument is presented both as a plea (for more science) and as an observation (that it matters).

But for politicians, to be useful, science first has to be intelligible and clear. There is, therefore, a well-known tension between the politician asking for clear indicators and absolute assertions in order to justify policy and mobilize support, and scientists' prudence. The adoption of the 2-degree climate change target illustrates these dynamics as it serves as a means to prod and evaluate commitments, even though it may be contested from a purely scientific viewpoint.[4]

Politicians also tend to hold unrealistic expectations of what science can do, namely give them high probabilities. They yearn for assessments and predictions over explanations. Policy making involves dilemmas and trade-offs. Some politicians may hope (and most scientists believe) that more knowledge will help solve those dilemmas. Yet knowledge often complicates matters. The more we know about climate change, the more intractable the situation appears. The better the distributional aspects of a problem are known, the more difficult the politics surrounding the quest for a solution. Why should victims share in the burden of alleviating the problem (see chapters 1 and 5)?

Science is also instrumentalized. Scientists are cautious, deal with probabilities, and stress the uncertainties attached to their conclusions. Even when they largely agree as to the nature of the problem, uncertainties can arise in the minds of legislators when scientists attempt to convey their message. These uncertainties, or varying descriptions of the phenomena involved, may be enough to support opposite stands in the very name of science. Paradoxically, then, a turn toward scientific expertise often polarizes or prolongs debate rather than leading to closure. As Zehr (1994) points out, in this context, science is of limited value for resolving controversies that are fundamentally political.

Calls for science can serve to improve decisions or block action. For example, the World Trade Organization (WTO) rejects the precautionary principle and argues that only absolute scientific certainty should be used to justify any environmental decision likely to have negative trade impacts.[5] This led to the conclusion that scientists' message should not be policy prescriptive (i.e. specify the solutions to be adopted), which would also be considered illegitimate since we do not live in Plato's Republic, but policy relevant (that is, help improve decision making). This principle underlies the procedures of the IPCC, for example (IPCC 2010).

The story of the "Bali Box" in the IPCC fifth report (IPCC-AR5) also shows that choices and values always lie behind numbers, that science is method and interpretation, and that, in a political context, it is always instrumental and accepted in the context of a political deal (Lahn and Sundqvist 2015; see also Sundqvist and Lahn 2015). The Bali Box purports to give a scientific estimate of the range of the difference between emissions in 1990 and emission allowances in 2020/2050 for various greenhouse gas (GHG) concentration levels for the groups of Annex I and non-Annex I countries in order to meet the 2-degree target. In the version published in AR4, its authors gave only a range of reductions needed from developed countries; in a proposed avatar for AR5, they also sought to quantify their estimates to include developing countries. A controversy then arose, in the form of a political challenge by developing countries, which led to the removal of the box from the final draft of AR5. In essence, the two scholars behind the Bali Box had challenged the established political agreements around the climate.

Opening up the Bali Box helps understand climate change as a social and political phenomenon and gives a glimpse of the tensions created by the inescapable political nature of the work of the IPCC and the need to maintain scientific credibility. To be accepted, the political choices behind the numbers have to be clear (what to measure, how to measure, etc.) and agreed upon. "Arguments from scientists are perceived as more scientific when they follow and adapt to established political and institutional principles, while they are perceived as more political when they diverge from the existing institutional framework" (Sundqvist and Lahn 2015, 13). The problem, according to these authors, stems not from the impossibility of maintaining clear boundaries between science and politics (as exemplified by the removal of the box), but from attempts to maintain rather than manage the boundary, that is from "building climate policy on a view of pure science located outside of the political realm." In that case, "[t]he slightest contact between science and politics will overturn the ambition to establish a policy based on science into just politics…" (Ibid., 15).

Incidentally, it also helps to question the current emphasis on targets as a means of prodding action, assessing national efforts, and mobilizing funds (as in the national commitments under the UNFCCC or the Convention on Biological Diversity [CBD] strategic plan). Although supported by many government officials, intergovernmental organizations (IGOs) and nongovernmental organizations (NGOs), many countries are suspicious of such attempts and will then insist on clarifying the political understanding of these targets.

The political scientist's view

Scientists are no longer confined to their laboratories; they are embedded in national and international institutions and interact extensively with public officials, legislatures, and bureaucracies. This has taken the form of numerous and novel institutional arrangements, from "chief scientific advisors" to top executives and presidents, to the creation of so-called boundary organizations which bridge science and politics (see Miller 2001).[6]

In the case of biodiversity (see also chapter 6), these institutions include (i) learned societies (academies), national research agencies (natural history museums, agricultural science research organizations), advisors (national science advisors), and international professional associations; (ii) NGOs (International Union for Conservation of Nature [IUCN], Conservation International [CI], World Wildlife Fund [WWF]); (iii) networks (Diversitas, GEOBON), notably the International Council of Scientific Unions (ICSU), a network of national academies and international scientific unions pursuing the promotion of science for society. Two organizations similar to ICSU are the InterAcademy Panel (IAP) and the InterAcademy Council (IAC), which are both multinational networks of academies. The following two categories are truly boundary organizations (or hybrid organizations, to use Miller's term) that mix scientific and political elements (a managerial committee appointed by government officials combined with working groups or *ad hoc* expert groups selected from both the scientific community and government representatives): (iv) IGOs' technical bodies and Multilateral Environmental Agreement (MEA) subsidiary scientific bodies; and (v) global assessment panels (IPCC; International Panel on Chemical Pollution; IPBES, International Assessment of Agricultural Knowledge Science and Technology for Development [IAASTD], etc.).

The current international landscape of scientific advisory systems is therefore extremely dense. Each nation embraces its own system. Efforts in favor of an international dialogue on scientific advice have only recently begun. Meanwhile, the number of international bodies providing scientific advice has been growing, which raises the issue of how to make all those national and international systems work more effectively (Sato et al. 2014). Clearly, there is no dearth of arenas where science meets politics. So what is the problem?

The usual answer is to submit that it is a problem because one holds the wrong idea about the relationship between science and policy. Science is made by scientists, but which scientific facts are produced and transmitted into the policy arena depends on extrascientific factors. The conditions affecting the influence of scientists is subject to much debate. Political opportunities (Zito 2001), alliances with environmental NGOs (Meijerink 2005; Gough and Shackely 2001), support from key bureaucrats (Haas 1992b), types of scientific knowledge mobilized (Dimitrov 2006), and stages of policy making have all been put forward as key determinants. It remains that science needs knowledge brokers. The theory of epistemic communities sees scientists and fellow travelers as political actors, moved by convictions and political objectives that pertain both to their notion of the common good and to the influence of their own discipline. Their impact, in turn, depends on their capacity to create winning coalitions.

The monopoly of Western science over legitimate knowledge is also being questioned. This is particularly evident in issues dealing with the international environment. Several conventions, notably the CBD, accept indigenous knowledge as a form of knowledge equally appropriate on which to develop policy. The IPBES is tasked with operationalizing this trend. This corresponds to an evolving conception of the relationship between science and policy, where the linear model is being replaced by a collaborative or co-production model (Koetz et al. 2011; Pielke 2007; Cash et al. 2001). According to this model, political agreement often precedes science (as in the case of the Montreal Protocol on ozone depletion) and science co-evolves with politics. In particular, it insists on process and on the importance of involving a variety of disciplines and stakeholders in the production of knowledge relevant for policy. This approach is at the heart of the IPBES. The participation and the type of knowledge that these actors bring (be they states, NGOs, local communities, science communities, or business) are judged to be legitimate.

This shift to an apparent nonlinear model is likely to remain elusive if the problem is defined as one of integrating a variety of knowledge bases into a coherent whole. From a complex system perspective, however, though procedural aspects are important, the issue is not so much chimerical integration than relating different knowledge to different worldviews and thus to different values, politics, problem definition, and solutions. It means devising ways where these views can surface, be confronted, and coexist in compatible paths of action. In addition, here again the process is less linear than one thinks. In many ways, politics has driven science, not in the sense of subordinating the interpretation of scientific "facts" to political expediency, but in that politics has not only identified which facts were relevant but also developed concepts for political purposes that scientists were then called upon to flesh out and apply. Worthy of investigation here is the passage from a policy instrument or one designed to mobilize citizens and policy makers to an analytical tool used to understand or explain. Examples are ecosystem services, nature-based solutions, ecological footprint, planetary boundaries, environmental impact assessments, etc. In other words, how do politically relevant concepts become scientifically relevant as well? How have scientific assessments impacted fundamental research, changed how scientific problems are defined, led to the articulation of new questions, triggered the collection of new data, and changed disciplines or contributed to the emergence of new ones (such as sustainability science or complexity science)?

IPBES: A new kind of boundary organization?

IPBES illustrates the evolution of current conception of the science-policy interface and of efforts to bring order in the international provision of scientific advice. As such, it could become a useful element of a decentralized governance system. In particular, it represents the latest incarnation of a new governance of international scientific advice, that of institutionalized international assessments.

The advent and lessons of international assessments (IA)

One of the more remarkable trends in the production of knowledge at the international level is surely the emergence of international assessments conceived as "the entire social process by which expert knowledge related to a policy problem is organized, evaluated, integrated, and presented in documents and otherwise to inform decision-making" (Farrell et al. 2001). Scientists from various disciplines engage in building a consensus on what is and should be known and on the associated policy challenges. These assessments have become part of the fabric of international scientific governance of environmental issues.

They cover many fields and vary in scope and legitimacy. The largest may involve hundreds of scientists and address global issues, such as the IPCC reports, the Ozone Trends reports (World Meteorological Organization 1988), or the Millennium Ecosystem Assessment. Others are of more limited scope, such as the Arctic Monitoring and Assessment Programme. International scientific assessments have a dual scientific and political function. From a scientific viewpoint, they serve to define the various dimensions of a problem, reach agreement on the significance of findings, and identify the knowledge gaps that need be filled. The political function has two aspects. One pertains to scientists themselves, the other to the polity.

Assessments provide scientists with a means to promote their research and their discipline. Not only scientists as individuals (and their labs) but disciplines themselves are in competition for what will always be regarded as scarce funds. Some evaluations reflect the concern of specific research communities with strengthening their influence in a given area, not only vis-à-vis decision makers but also vis-à-vis their scientific competitors from other disciplines or subdisciplines. Preeminence in an assessment may translate into more resources later (financial, human, prestige, etc.).

The main political functions of assessments are to place an issue on the international political agenda and drive forward the process of international cooperation in a given area. Assessments, however, cannot solve political problems and may even exacerbate them. Consensus is hard to build. It may be a necessary, but it surely is not a sufficient condition for cooperation. Assessments also enable governments to regain control of the scientific discourse around a particular issue. That is what lay behind the creation of the IPCC, for example. And that is utterly legitimate. It means that the relationship between research communities and decision makers is ambivalent. The parameters of international assessments are determined politically; otherwise, their results will be ignored. The main message to be drawn from an assessment is also negotiated among political representatives (and not scientists).

A major and pioneering study of assessments by David Cash, William Clark, and colleagues has identified three major necessary conditions that international assessments must fulfill if they are to be used by policy makers: salience, credibility, and legitimacy. Together, they define what is "usable" knowledge. These conditions have become a mantra in any discussions of assessments processes, notably in the context of the IPBES.

International assessments walk a fine line between science and politics, the price of failure being lack of legitimacy and credibility. For an assessment to be most directly relevant to a particular decision maker, it should be highly focused on the specific issue under consideration, and it should use mechanisms that would be seen by that individual to give it the greatest legitimacy and credibility. Yet narrowly focused sectoral assessments will inevitably underemphasize important trade-offs with other sectoral concerns, as well as concerns and perspectives relevant at other levels (Reid 2004). Further, from a complex governance perspective, beyond adopting a collaborative model, successful regional assessments would (i) integrate research, assessment, and decision making across multiple levels; (ii) be structured to assess and address global change in the context of local consequences; and (iii) identify, assess, and respond to the interactions between society and environment that cross levels (Cash et al. 2001).

International assessments exemplify the globalization of science. Reflection on what that means remains in its infancy. Little attention has been devoted to the ways in which assessments shape the topics that are chosen (the production of policy-relevant research has become a central mandate in the climate change scientific domain), the way research is conducted (large international teams), and the evolution of scientific disciplines. For example, how do increasing calls and pressure for research to be relevant (that is, problem solving and applied) affect inquiries and methods? In this regard, the IPBES provides an interesting experiment in the institutionalization of an effective science-policy interface.

The institutionalization of a scientific discourse

Politics starts with issue framing. Institutions created to pursue policies embody a particular conception of the relationship between human societies and the natural world. The IPBES aims to become the arena where the dominant discourse about biodiversity and biodiversity science is being constructed and legitimized. This discourse defines central concepts, identifies core questions, and offers a set of assumptions regarding the key relationships among them (Diaz et al. 2015).

The goal of the IPBES is to "strengthen the science-policy interface for biodiversity and ecosystem services for the conservation and sustainable use of biodiversity, long-term human well-being and sustainable development" (IPBES 2016).[7] Articulated in its conceptual framework, this discourse basically rests on a socioecological system perspective that sees both the social and natural worlds as co-constructed and where the core concerns are the complexity, resilience, robustness, sustainability, vulnerability, and adaptability of the system. The main concept that articulates the relationship between these two dimensions (social and natural) is that of ecosystem services. Finally, although nature still tends to be conceptualized as separate, social variables such as poverty alleviation and equity figure as prominent concerns.

The establishment of the IPBES rests upon a number of assumptions that reflect the dominant conception of the relationship between science and policy that still prevails among scientists, although it also embodies an evolution toward a new co-constructed model not devoid of challenges. Three of these assumptions give an opportunity to put the existing doxa regarding the science-policy interface in perspective.

Assumption #1: More knowledge is better

Behind the IPBES are biologists who not only felt neglected compared to climatologists and geophysicists but who were also convinced that they were far from knowing their object of study (such as the sheer number of species), let alone understand how it behaves. There was also a need for greater integration of biodiversity knowledge, which typically has been generated along national lines. Countries may know less about their own biological resources than their former colonial overlord; data banks are heterogeneous, preventing the development of an overall picture of the state and evolution of those resources; basic data are still lacking. Although the IPBES is not intended to generate new knowledge, it will nevertheless do so by synthesizing studies, assessing the relative importance of explanatory factors, drawing conclusions about trends, and evaluating the relative merits of alternate courses of policy.

Knowledge is not enough, however. If the aim is to facilitate international cooperation and inform national and international policy so that it will better take into account their dependence and impact on other species and life forms, knowledge will not suffice. First, in the case of the IPBES, many countries opposed to its establishment pointed out that biodiversity was not a matter of science but of values. More science will not help resolve conflicts over the latter.

Second, although scientific knowledge has provided significant arguments to justify policies and played a significant role in the identification of problems and in agenda setting, it has been less of a driving force when it comes to the decisions made or the probability of international environmental cooperation. This may sound surprising until one distinguishes among agenda setting, policy formulation, the scientific definition of problems, and the political solutions adopted. The adoption of a scientific discourse does not mean that scientific knowledge has determined the definition of the problem, the interpretation of the scientific findings, and the choice of solutions.

Third, more knowledge does not mean easier policy making; it often complicates it. The more we know about the climate, the more numerous the questions, so making the political decision dependent on greater knowledge may delay the moment of decision. Further, precise knowledge may hinder agreement on joint action: the more we know about the origin, movement, and impacts of pollutants, the clearer the winners and losers (P. Haas 1990). Indeed, a "veil of ignorance" about the distributional aspects of an issue can work in favour of cooperation. Only following rigorous and systematic studies did we find that the Mediterranean was not as polluted as once thought. But by that time, the negotiations of the Barcelona Convention were well under way (P. Haas 1990). In fact, such negotiations triggered data collection: science followed politics. Likewise, the Montreal Protocol showed that an agreement was possible even in the absence of empirical evidence, only based on mathematical models (Litfin 1994).

Fourth, states and societies may distrust "scientific" studies since data can be used to pinpoint good and bad pupils, allocate burdens, or redistribute aid. Indeed, the IPBES is not to perform local assessments. The same reluctance towards local data collection is present in the CBD and the IPCC, where governments oppose geographically specific assessments (Edenhofer and Minx 2014). In this context, calls for a greater scientific basis to decision making are bound to elicit suspicion.

Fifth, whose knowledge matters? In international relations, the origin of knowledge matters as much as its nature, since science is often suspected of masking interests. Governments still largely rely on the advice of their own scientists, at least in advanced and emerging economies. Hence the need to develop national expertise in order to challenge the monopoly of interpretations of scientific findings that may lead to inequities. UNEP and now the IPBES have capacity-building programs in order to promote the development of national expertise that, they believe, will relay their concerns.

Agarwal and Narain (1991), with their contention that contrary to the assumption of Western scientists and NGOs, not all molecules of CO_2 are alike since some derived from so-called "survival" behavior while other stem from consumerist preferences, have clearly shown that a globalizing discourse can engender policy prescriptions that may be unjust, even if the premises are not in dispute and scientists behind the globalizing argument cannot be suspected of manipulation. They simply do not share the same lens.

Sociologists have long asserted that the personal convictions and policy preferences of scientists influence their interpretation of the results of their research, as in the case of ocean dumping policy (see Spiller and Rieser 1986). Science is a social endeavor; knowledge processes are based in social contexts that may shift over time and place and are always influenced by the value systems of surrounding institutions, professions, and individuals (see Ascher et al. 2010).

Tocqueville used to contrast historians of aristocratic and democratic times, in order to show how the political systems to which historians belonged could affect their choice of causal explanations. Scientists hold givens which explicitly or implicitly color their work and conclusions from the definition of the problem to the type of conclusions they draw from the data. As comparative analyses of regulatory systems in different countries have suggested,

> the framing of risk, the norms and practices of expert advisory committees, and even the kinds of scientific evidence that predominate in policy deliberations differ from country to country in ways that reflect broader patterns of difference in political culture. Moreover, these differences also reflect back into the scientific institutions of the countries, shaping their organization and the kinds of knowledge produced.
>
> (Miller 2001, 487)

Finally, the question of what kind of knowledge is important needs to be raised. In so doing, we can make sense of apparently contradictory research findings. On the one hand, the intuitive expectations that information is a requirement of policy action are regularly contradicted by research findings that states create policy regimes in spite of large information gaps and scientific uncertainties. On the other hand, over the long term, international policy clearly corresponds with scientific research (Dimitrov 2006).

There are two ways of reconciling these findings. One is to argue that once in place, a regime will foster data collection and provide a means of integrating it into international regulatory measures, as well as constitute a matrix that fosters policy convergence through gradual socialization. Another way is to distinguish between the causes, the extent, and the structure of a given problem. For example, clear knowledge regarding the transboundary consequences of environmental degradation is linked to the dynamics of regime processes (such as acid rain). But conclusive information about the extent of a problem (i.e. reliable data) is not a critical requirement for more global international policy coordination (Ibid.).

In this context, negotiators will ask themselves three questions: i) who carries knowledge? (the messenger is as important as the message); ii) what interests does this scientific knowledge embody? and (iii) to what ends will this knowledge be used? A given problem does not have only one solution. There is a danger when one automatically derives solutions from the identification of a problem, since few solutions have win-win outcomes.

International governance often seeks to transform what are essentially political debates into scientific ones and calls upon international advisory or assessment bodies essentially to circumvent political debates and provide a scientifically legitimate rationale to political choices (Miller 2011). But one cannot ask of science to resolve political dilemmas when knowledge is uncertain and decisions also imply a choice among values. The scientific discourse articulates and rationalizes existing conflicts and interests (Litfin 1994, 197). The issue of genetically modified organisms has shown how controversial the notion of credible science can be. It is particularly difficult to separate science and politics in fields characterized by high uncertainty and value conflicts such as climate change and biodiversity. Sociologists would even argue that the scientific discourse tends to articulate and rationalize existing conflicts and interests.

Assumption #2: The problem is distance from policy

The impression that science is too removed from policy leads to two observations: (i) governments need to be involved and own assessments, and (ii) scientists themselves are too far removed from the locus of decisions. As the latter has already been addressed, I shall concentrate on the former.

The IPBES has been created with one basic lesson in mind: governments must play a role in assessments if the latter are to have any impact on policy. The Global Biodiversity Assessment (GBA) was faulted precisely for this failure. It was intended to serve as an IPCC-like assessment for the CBD, but the parties to the Convention rejected the report before the work even began and in the end refused to receive or use its findings. They did so in part because the report was prepared without any dialogue with its intended users (the governments), and focused more heavily on scientific debates than on debates with policy implications. It was a report by natural scientists for natural scientists (Borie and Pesche 2016).

This, of course, raises the issue of the independence of scientific assessment bodies. And this very question indicates that the three basic conditions for their impact (salience, credibility, and legitimacy) may not be positively related; trade-offs exist, an aspect that Cash et al. (2001) well acknowledge. The issue then, is to uncover the conditions that will favor synergies or trade-offs.[8] Further, actors on different sides of a boundary may perceive and value salience, credibility, and legitimacy differently (Cash et al. 2002).

Whether independence is a prerequisite of influence is open to debate. Research in comparative politics, international relations, public policy and theories of democracy suggests that the influence of scientists depends on their independence from politicians (close to policy but remote from politics). However, case studies point the other way. It probably depends on the nature of the issue, the amount of scientific uncertainty, and whether scientific debates hide conflicts over values (on the issue of autonomy from the political process, see also Lidskog and Sundqvist 2015). Moreover, this very debate assumes that science is neutral.

Indeed, in international relations, independence is suspect in the eyes of those states that believe that the membership of these scientific bodies is biased in favor of a particular definition of the problem and range of solutions as has been the case of the IPCC. The legitimacy of the assessment is then questioned. Independence enhances the credibility of the information transmitted, but this is less important when one wants this very information to be used in policy making.

Epistemic communities, as "expert networks in a given issue-area able to claim authority over knowledge relevant to public policy" (Haas 1992a), specifically bridge the gap between science and policy. Members share a common paradigm and values and seek to influence public policy and create regimes that reflect their perspective and values (Ibid.). These communities include scientists as well as the sociopolitical networks that share their convictions about the nature of problems and their solutions. Although this model is not exempt of difficulties, the concept can be useful to describe the pressure that decision makers are under from particular communities and their allies, whose main source of influence lies in their capacity to translate scientific knowledge into policy options.

Assumption #3: The virtues (and pitfalls) of multistakeholder participation

The third assumption, one that stems from the lessons learned from previous assessments, insists on the importance of stakeholders' participation in the definition of problems and on the degree of relevance of the knowledge to be used to address them. This has several dimensions, ranging from the call for greater interdisciplinary research and inclusion of more experts from developing countries, to taking into consideration different knowledge systems (such as that of indigenous communities), and the inclusion of groups affected by policies designed to protect biodiversity or groups that claim a role in its maintenance (such as farmers).

One of the problems that global assessments have faced is the underrepresentation of scientists from developing countries (such as the Ozone Trends panel or the early IPCC). This reflects in part the global distribution of expertise but also the belief in a universal character of science that transcends national boundaries. As mentioned previously, developing countries have been eager to demonstrate that the definition of a scientific problem and the interpretation of research results may also be different depending on where the scientists live and were trained.

Many developing countries, for example, do not trust evaluations in which their own scientists and decision makers have not participated. Naturally, this affects the legitimacy if not the credibility of their conclusions. As the new head of the IPCC recognized in 2015, as the organization moves more and more into adaptation, it will need to engage more scientists from developing countries with expertise in development, poverty reduction, and social mobilization.[9] In the case of the GBA, the relatively weaker participation of Southern scientists limited its relevance in the eyes of Indian researchers, notably concerning the socioeconomic dimensions of some issues, such as biotechnologies (Biermann 2002).

Along with its multiscale structure, one of the most experimental features of the Millennium Ecosystems Assessment (MA) and one with the greatest potential value to contribute to future global (and subglobal) assessments was an attempt to facilitate the incorporation of multiple sources of knowledge in the process. The MA included a mechanism for taking indigenous knowledge systems into consideration in order to foster a shared understanding of the nature and operation of complex systems (Koetz *et al.* 2011).[10] International biodiversity governance involves a variety of actors, each seeking to impose their own definition of the problem and preferred solutions. Their participation and the knowledge they bring to the issues are now considered legitimate. One of the challenges that the legitimacy of science faces is indeed public suspicion (see Haas 2004). Anthropologists and sociologists have opened the black box of scientific discovery, and the process of consensus building within scientific communities. The reliance on high-ranking science panels eliminates public participation, so it is imperative that a way be found to channel that input. The collaborative (or nonlinear) model of science-policy interface seeks to address this concern by emphasizing the necessity of a process-oriented approach regarding the development of useful knowledge thanks to the incorporation of a variety of disciplines and stakeholders.

IPBES did learn from the MA and the IPCC: NGOs as well as local and indigenous populations are included in the process through working groups whose conclusions then inform the discussions of the Multidisciplinary Expert Panel (MEP) of the IPBES. This does not eliminate the risk of clashes between academics (with their focus on knowledge building), local and indigenous populations (who bring a different kind of knowledge into play but also pursue political objectives) and NGOs (that promote values). It remains unclear how this juxtaposition will allow the development of a shared understanding of the nature and operation of complex biodiversity systems, leading to a true co-construction of all knowledge (Gupta *et al.* 2012). And indeed, as argued previously, this may be a fruitless endeavor.

Beyond the illusory construction of integrated legitimate knowledge, participation may exacerbate political conflicts by empowering new individuals and groups at the expense of established hierarchies. Provisions for public participation may make issues more intractable. It is indeed unclear whether opening up the process will encourage gridlock (see Victor 2011) or, rather, help build a shared understanding of issues that will be syncretic rather than a mere juxtaposition of antagonistic viewpoints.

Although the doxa largely trumpets the inherent virtues of participation, many studies have identified negative aspects too often ignored. Both the process and the effects of participation have been questioned. The problems go beyond mere bad practice and touch upon its assumptions. Proponents tend to overlook how calls for participation reflect and affect power relationships, favor external participatory schemes over internal ones, and neglect the influence of external constraints on the exercise and outcomes of participation (Giller *et al.* 2008).

In its weak avatar as concertation though, participation may help uncover potential political problems. It can also be used to control the nature of the discussions rather than promote an exchange of ideas. Participation may be used to impose a particular viewpoint (through the selection of participants) and thus steer policy dynamics in a preferred direction. When policy makers want to change decisions, they include more stakeholders (Howlett 1999). In the words of Isabelle Stengers (1997), "You who have the power to convene experts, show me which experts you have gathered and I will tell you how you intend to define the problem and the type of answers you hope to get." Public participation requirements alone are not sufficient to foster the development of a shared understanding of issues. Arguably it is not participation that will shape syncretic knowledge but the other way around.

Redefining the science-policy interface

Although several models of science-policy interface are likely to coexist (Dahan and Guillemot 2015), the relationship between science and policy has changed markedly over the last decades. Scientists are no longer confined to their laboratories but act as interest groups. Boundary organizations have been established where not only scientists and public officials but also other knowledge holders meet to discuss the definition of the problems and the range of options that should be considered to address them. This in turn shapes where science is going. Western science and scientists no longer have a monopoly on identifying politically usable knowledge. Whereas a dialectical model would emphasize its co-construction by scientists, policy makers, and representatives of other forms of knowledge that mix facts and values (see Miller 2001, 495), a complex system perspective would look into how different knowledge and relationships toward nature can be made to coexist and enhance the properties of the system (see chapter 6).

Ironically, by legitimizing other forms of knowledge and participations in the policy-making process, efforts by biologists to build an institution such as the IPBES that they hoped would give more visibility to their disciplines and concerns, may end up reducing their influence and complicating the message. The price of obtaining the IPBES is being actively engaged in an ongoing process of negotiating the boundaries between different kinds of knowledge and between science and policy (Jasanoff 1990). These boundaries are agreements about which issues matter and about for which of them each group holds authority. The issue is not whether there are boundaries, for both science and policy need to be salient, credible, and legitimate, but where they are located, how they shift, and with what consequences both for the process and the outcome (such as being able to resist being discredited).

Indeed, boundary organizations are organizations first. As such, their features and operations are the product of power and interests. They promote or maintain unequal power relationships (between groups, types of knowledge, disciplines, stakeholders, parties, etc.) and advance specific interests through a dominant discourse that itself defines what is considered relevant knowledge. In the case of biodiversity, conflicts over the configuration of the science-policy interface mask conflicts over the distribution of power and resources.

Ultimately, the key issue is learning, which can be approached at three levels of increasing depth: (i) simply as institutionalized error correction (learning by experience); (ii) as the capacity to integrate new knowledge into behavior, or to respond more quickly to new demands and new information (Hedberg 1981), which is crucial as the policy environment becomes more uncertain; and (iii) according to E. Haas (1990), as a fundamental change in the nature of the consensual knowledge of actors, i.e. a change in the norms built into theory-in-use accompanied by a change in the organization's model of the world. A crucial function of boundary organizations, then, should be their ability to act as agents of complex learning, enabling other agents gradually to develop shared interpretations of a given problem, where these interpretations come to define identities, institutions, and the contours of cooperation (see chapter 6).

Notes

1 Plato, *The Republic*, Book V, 473d-e, trans. G. M. A. Grube (2nd ed.), rev. C. D. C. Reeve, (Indianapolis: Hackett, 1992), 148.
2 Established and sponsored jointly by the International Council of Scientific Unions (ICSU), the International Social Science Council, the Belmont Forum (a consortium of national funding agencies), the United Nations Educational, Scientific, and Cultural Organization (UNESCO), the United Nations Environment Programme (UNEP), and the United Nations University in 2015, Future Earth is an international research platform on global sustainability. See www.futureearth.org.
3 Adopted at the first meeting of UNEP's Global Forum of Ministers of the Environment (UNEP/GCSS.VI/L.3).
4 The European Union (EU) adopted the 2°C temperature target in 1996 and argued that it was scientifically justified. It was subsequently formally adopted in 2010 by the United Nations Framework Convention on Climate Change (UNFCCC) COP-16 in Cancun (Geden and Beck 2014, 747, quoted in Sundqvist and Lahn 2015).
5 This is not to deny the legitimacy of this position in the context of the principles that the WTO is charged with upholding.
6 Boundary organizations are institutions that bridge two social worlds—in this case, science and politics (see Guston 2001).
7 See www.ipbes.net/about-us (accessed July 19, 2016).
8 As Cash *et al.* (2002, 6) suggest, "Engaging decision makers can increase salience by increasing the probability that the right questions will be asked and answered by experts, but it can also decrease the credibility of the information if it appears that science has been biased by the political process. In similar ways, efforts to increase salience can also have negative effects on legitimacy. Including more actors to increase salience may decrease legitimacy by including participants deemed not legitimate to certain other actors. Efforts to increase credibility, by increasing the isolation of science (maintaining strong boundaries) often have the cost of decreasing salience by removing the decision maker from the scoping or agenda-setting process." The reverse is also true: "Efforts to increase salience, for example, by engaging a broader range of decision makers may also increase credibility by better integrating local knowledge into the efforts of outside research or assessment."
9 Opening statement by Dr. Hoesung Lee, newly elected chair of the IPCC, in Dubrovnik, Croatia, October 7, 2015.
10 For a caveat, see above.

References

Agarwal, A. and S. Narain. (1991). "Global Warming in an Unequal World: A Case of Environmental Colonialism." *Earth Island Journal* spring: 39–40.

Ascher, W., et al. (2010). *Knowledge and Environmental Policy: Re-Imagining the Boundaries of Science and Politics*. Cambridge: MIT Press.

Benedick, R. E. (1998). *Ozone Diplomacy: New Directions in Safeguarding the Planet*. Cambridge: Harvard University Press.

Biermann, F. (2002). "Institutions for Scientific Advice: Global Environmental Assessments and Their Influence in Developing Countries." *Global Governance* 8 (2): 195–219.

Borie, M. and D. Pesche. (2017). "Making the IPBES Conceptual Framework: A Rosetta Stone?" In *The Intergovernmental Platform on Biodiversity and Ecosystem Services (IPBES): Meeting the Challenges of Biodiversity Conservation and Governance*, edited by M. Hrabanski and D. Pesche. London:Earthscan, 135–153.

Cash, D., et al. (2001). *From Science to Policy: Assessing the Assessment Process*. Cambridge: Harvard University-John F. Kennedy School of Government.

Cash, D., et al. (2002). *Salience, Credibility, Legitimacy and Boundaries: Linking Research, Assessment and Decision Making*. Cambridge: Harvard University-John F. Kennedy School of Government.

Dahan, A. and H. Guillemot. (2015). "Les Relations entre science et politique dans le régime Climatique: à la recherche d'un nouveau modèle d'expertise?" *Natures Sciences Sociétés* 23 (supplément): S6–S18.

Diaz, S., et al. (2015). "The IPBES Conceptual Framework—Connecting Nature and People." *Current Opinion in Environmental Sustainability* 14: 1–16.

Dimitrov, R. (2006). *Science and International Environmental Policy: Regimes and Nonregimes in Global Governance*. Lanham, MD: Rowman & Littlefield.

Edenhofer, O. and J. Minx. (2014). "Mapmakers and Navigators, Facts and Values." *Science* 345 (6192): 37–38.

Farrell, A., et al. (2001). "Environmental Assessments: Four Under-Appreciated Elements of Design." *Global Environmental Change* 11 (4): 311–333.

Geden, O. and S. Beck. (2014). "Renegotiating the Global Climate Stabilization Target." *Nature Climate Change* 4: 747–748.

Giller, K. E. et al. (2008). "Competing Claims on Natural Resources: What Role for Science?" *Ecology and Society* 13 (2): 34 [online].

Gough, C. and S. Shackely. (2001). "The Respectable Politics of Climate Change: The Epistemic Communities and NGOs." *International Affairs* 77 (2): 329–346.

Gupta, A., et al. (2012). "Science Networks." In *Global Environmental Governance Reconsidered*, edited by F. Biermann and P. Patberg. Cambridge: MIT Press, 69–93.

Guston, D. H. (2001). "Boundary Organizations in Environmental Policy and Science: An Introduction." *Science, Technology, & Human Values* 26 (4): 399–408.

Haas, E. B. (1990). *When Knowledge Is Power*. Berkeley: University of California Press.

Haas, P. M. (1990). *Saving the Mediterranean: The Politics of International Environmental Cooperation*. New York: Columbia University Press.

Haas, P. M. (1992a). "Introduction: Epistemic Communities and International Policy Coordination." *International Organization* 46 (1): 1–35.

Haas, P. M. (1992b). "Banning Chlorofluorocarbons; Epistemic Community Efforts to Protect Stratospheric Ozone." *International Organization* 46 (1): 187–224.

Haas, P. M. (2004). "Scientific Expertise: a Question of Legitimacy." In *Towards Collective Action*, edited by P. Le Prestre and L. Tubiana. Proceedings of the Conference on International Environmental Governance. Paris: Institute for Sustainable Development and International Relations, 193–195.

Hedberg, B. (1981). "*How Organizations Learn and Unlearn*." In *Handbook of Organizational Design*, edited by P. C. Nystrom and W. H. Starbuck. Oxford: Oxford University Press: 3–27.

Howlett, M. (1999). "Complex Network Management and the Governance of the Environment: Prospects for Policy Change and Policy Stability Over the Long Term." In *Governing the Environment: Persistent Challenges, Uncertain Innovations*, edited by E. Parson. Toronto: University of Toronto Press, 303–344.

Hulme, M. (2009). *Why We Disagree About Climate Change: Understanding Controversy, Inaction and Opportunity*. Cambridge: Cambridge University Press.

IPBES (Intergovernmental Panel on Biodiversity and Ecosystems Services). Available online at www.ipbes.net (accessed July 19, 2016).

IPCC (Intergovernmental Panel on Climate Change). (2010). "Statement on IPCC Principles and Procedures." Available online at www.ipcc.ch/pdf/press/ipcc-statement-principles-procedures-02-2010.pdf (accessed July 19, 2016).

Jasanoff, S. (1990). *The Fifth Branch: Science Advisers as Policy-Makers*. Cambridge: Harvard University Press.

Koetz, T., et al. (2011). "Building Better Science-Policy Interfaces for International Environmental Governance: Assessing Potential within the Intergovernmental Platform for Biodiversity and Ecosystem Services." International Environmental Agreements. DOI 10.1007/s10784-10011-9152-z.

Lahn, B. and G. Sundqvist. (2015). "Et Fast Punkt for Klimaet? Vitenskap og Politikk i den Svarte âBali-Boksenâ." *Sosiologi i Dag* 45 (1).

Lidskog, R. and G. Sundqvist. (2015). "When Does Science Matter? International Relations Meets Science and Technology Studies." *Global Environmental Politics* 15 (1): 1–20.

Litfin, K. T. (1994). *Ozone Discourses: Science and Politics in Global Environmental Cooperation*. New York: Columbia University Press.

Meijerink, S. (2005). "Understanding Policy Stability and Change. The Interplay of Advocacy Coalitions and Epistemic Communities, Windows of Opportunity, and Dutch Coastal Flooding Policy 1945–2003." *Journal of European Public Policy* 12 (6): 1060–1077.

Miller, C. (2001). "Hybrid Management: Boundary Organizations, Science Policy, and Environmental Governance in the Climate Regime." *Science, Technology, & Human Values* 26 (4): 478–500.

Miller, C. (2011). "Gérer la planète: gouvernance et sciences de l'environnement planétaire." In *Vingt ans après: Rio et l'avant-goût de l'avenir*, edited by P. Le Prestre. Québec: Presses de l'Université Laval, 45–52.

Pielke, R. A. (2007). *The Honest Broker. Making Sense of Science in Policy and Politics*. Cambridge: Cambridge University Press.

Plato. (1992). *The Republic*, Book V, 473d-e. Translated by G. M. A. Grube (2nd ed.), revised by C. D. C. Reeve. Indianapolis: Hackett, 48.

Reid, W. V. (2004). "Bridging Scales and Epistemologies in the Millennium Ecosystem Assessment." Paper, Conference on "Bridging Scales and Epistemologies—Linking Local Knowledge and Global Science in Multi-Scale Assessments." Alexandria, Egypt (March 24).

Sato, Y., et al. (2014). "Building the Foundations for Scientific Advice in the International Context." *Science & Diplomacy* 3 (3).

Skolnikoff, E. (1968). "The Difficult Political Choices of Science (Review Article)." *World Politics* 20 (3): 535–558.

Spiller, J. and A. Rieser. (1986). "Scientific Fact and Value in U.S. Ocean Dumping Policy." *Review of Policy Research* 6 (2): 389–398.

Stengers, I. (1997). *Sciences et pouvoirs: la démocratie face à la technoscience*. Paris: La Découverte.

Sundqvist, G. and B. Lahn. (2015). "What 'Fixed Point' for the Climate? Science-Policy Interactions in the Proposed Black Bali-Box." Paper, Eighth WIRE (Workshop on

International Relations) on "Boundary Organizations in International Affairs," Université Saint-Louis, Brussels, August 28.

UNEP (United Nations Environment Programme). (2000). "Malmö Ministerial Declaration." Declaration, adopted by the Global Ministerial Environment Forum, Sixth Special Session of the Governing Council of the United Nations Environment Programme, Fifth Plenary Meeting, May 31, 2000 (UNEP/GCSS.VI/L.3).

Victor, D. G. (2011). *Global Warming Gridlock: Creating More Effective Strategies for Protecting the Planet*. Cambridge: Cambridge University Press.

WMO (World Meteorological Organization). (1988). *Report of the International Ozone Trends Panel 1988, Global Ozone Research and Monitoring Project Report No. 18*. Geneva: WMO.

Zehr, S. (1994). "Flexible Interpretation of 'Acid Rain' and the Construction of Scientific Uncertainty in Political Settings." *Politics and the Life Sciences* 13 (2): 205–216.

Zito, A. R. (2001). "Epistemic Communities, Collective Entrepreneurship and European Integration." *Journal of European Public Policy* 8 (4): 585–603.

4

THE EUROPEAN UNION AND GLOBAL ENVIRONMENTAL DIPLOMACY

Introduction

The European Union (EU) undoubtedly has been very active in the international environmental arena. There is a wide consensus that it has played an important leadership role in agenda setting and in fostering multilateral agreements in a number of issue areas (such as hazardous wastes, biodiversity, trade in genetically modified organisms [GMOs], persistent organic pollutants, or public participation). Regarding climate change, Vogler (2011) credits it with providing the impetus in favor of an agreement based on targets and timetables under the 1995 Berlin mandate, implementing the world's first international emission trading system, and performing the complex diplomacy that led to eventual entry into force of the Kyoto Protocol. The EU has also participated actively in global summits and, together with the Group of 77 (G77), successfully opposed fundamental attempts to unravel existing principles. Perhaps more significant has been its impact on strengthening existing regimes such as the International Maritime Organization (IMO), the development of environmental guidelines (such as Registration, Evaluation, Authorisation and Restriction of Chemical Products [REACH]),[1] or its use of economic instruments (trade and aid) to change production norms or promote sustainable development principles.

Questions about its effectiveness, however, arise. Indeed, its failures in some areas have been spectacular, as in the case of climate change. This may sound surprising, but a quick examination of the record in climate change negotiations will illustrate this argument:

- The EU was unsuccessful in opposing the Clean Development Mechanism (CDM), and then, having accepted it, in using this turnaround to convince the US to remain in the Kyoto Protocol.
- Its intransigence at COP-6 (The Hague, 2000) is widely credited for having caused its failure.

- The EU was marginalized at COP-15 in Copenhagen (2009) which was deemed a failure precisely because the EU had raised expectations so high; it then failed to extend Kyoto beyond 2012.
- COP-16 in Cancun changed the model completely away from EU preferences. Both in 1997 and 2009–10, the EU had to accept a new model that it then tried to lead.
- At COP-17 (Durban), the EU failed to make the future 2015 agreement "legally binding" (regardless of the actual soundness of such an objective).
- The EU was unable to create conditions that would lead to a significant turnaround from the US (see below on pyrrhic victories).
- Progress at COP-21 hinged primarily on a bilateral deal between the US and China, although EU diplomacy (in support of France, the UK, and Germany) was instrumental in bringing developing countries aboard.

In other areas as well, the EU often seems to fall short of expectations. In particular, one could point to its failure to reform international environmental governance. Apart from marginal reforms of the United Nations Environment Programme (UNEP) and the UN Commission on Sustainable Development (CSD), and perhaps pilot clustering projects, the EU and its member states unsuccessfully pushed for a World Environment Organization (WEO), and for Multilateral Environmental Agreements (MEAs) and the World Trade Organization (WTO) to be considered on an equal footing. Then it failed to impose its fall-back position (a change in the status of UNEP into a UN specialized agency), despite an intense campaign. Likewise, the green economy approach it advocated, although taken up as one of the two main environmental themes of the Rio+20 conference, was largely rejected. The EU, however, was able to engineer the creation of the Intergovernmental Platform on Biodiversity and Ecosystems Services (IPBES) despite early reluctance from key states, and several EU member states (namely France, Germany, and the UK) played a key role in ensuring the successful outcome of COP-21 (2015).

Clearly, like UNEP (of which it has been a strong backer), the EU may have aspired to be the environmental conscience of the world, but it has failed to be its prime mover. This uneven record, however, does not seem to have initiated a change in role conceptions or in the means used to pursue them. What explains this gap between expectations and results and the difficulties in forging winning diplomatic coalitions? The idea of a gap between aspirations and realizations has been raised in the larger context of EU foreign policy. Schunz (2012, 208–9) asks how we can explain the discrepancy between, on the one hand, the EU's growing institutionalized foreign policy capacities, its activism and its relative success in promoting the multilateral framework of climate negotiations and in keeping the issue high on the diplomatic agenda, and, on the other hand, the meager results in terms of specifically reaching its foreign policy goals in this area?

Three main hypotheses have been proposed to account for the uneven performance of the EU (or the state of its leadership) in international environmental forums. One pertains to the relationship between the commission and the union (presidency).

Another points to conflicts among member states. And a third one emphasizes the degree of unity associated with the availability and successful use of power resources. For example, according to van Leeuwen and Kern (2013, 80), "[By] acting as a coalition represented by the EU presidency and by using the threat of unilateral action, the EU has been quite successful in changing decision-making processes within the IMO." In this case, power lies in its ability to adopt truly binding regional standards and to enforce them on all ships entering EU ports. Another example is the use of its economic position to promote guidelines (such as REACH) or of economic instruments in order to change production norms or promote sustainable development. The health of Indian workers and local populations has benefited from the requirement that Indian tanners modify their production process in order to comply with European norms prohibiting the use of certain fungicides and dyes (Repetto 1994).

Foreign policy roles, however, modify power in that they affect the nature of usable power vs. available power. The concept of role provides a framework that can help understand the interplay of these factors. Accordingly, this chapter explores (i) the evolution of role studies and the applicability of the concept of role to a collective actor, (ii) the nature of the EU's role in international environmental affairs, with a particular emphasis on climate change, and (iii) one notion in line with a general query on the impact of role conceptions on behavior, namely role entrapment.

Role theory and foreign policy

"Role theory in International Relations (IR) concentrates on the roles that individuals, states, and other international actors enact on the international scene" (Wehner and Thies 2014, 411). It posits that individuals often act more as role players than utility maximizers (Young 1989: 209–13). Although it could apply to a variety of actors, in practice this concept is primarily used in foreign policy analysis and applied to states or to the conceptions that their principal decision makers have of the role that their country should play on the international scene.

Roles correspond to social positions in an organized group and the concept is applied to any socially recognized category of actors, whether individual or collective (Stryker and Statham 1985, 323). This may be surprising as one would expect to encounter the fallacy of composition when the concept is applied to the state, to IGOs, or to the EU.[2] In fact, although

> [r]ole theory might be viewed as solely appropriate for the study of individuals, such as the leaders of states, [t]his view would be mistaken, since role theory developed in the interdisciplinary field of social psychology and can be appropriately applied to both individuals and corporate entities. Indeed, one of the purported advantages of role theory is precisely its ability to cross levels of analysis.[3]

In everyday parlance and in official speeches, role is a term used with multiple meanings. It can denote a function or contribution as in "the role of the US in the conclusion of a peace settlement"; an influence or impact as in "Our actions will, of course, play an important role in shaping the future of US-Soviet relations" (Baker 1989); expected behavior based on certain rules, written or unwritten, prescribed or achieved; a part in a larger script, a course of action as in "CSCE must also play a more effective role in addressing the actual and potential ethnic conflicts in the former Soviet Union by monitoring respect for human rights and minority rights throughout the CIS" (Eagleburger 1992); policy decisions as in "The nature of the problem, the interests and values at stake, the capacity of our friends to act, and the relevance of available multilateral mechanisms will shape our role" (Baker 1992); or rank, as in Henry Kissinger's (1994, 373) reference to one provision of the 1922 Washington Treaty, which reaffirmed "America's role as the dominant power in the Pacific alongside Japan" (see Le Prestre 1997).

In his seminal study, Kal Holsti (1970) adopted a definition closer to the one found in the sociology literature which emphasizes the normative aspects of the concept. According to Holsti (1970, 245–6), roles refer to

> the policymakers' own definitions of the general kinds of decisions, commitments, rules and actions suitable to their state, and of the functions, if any, their state should perform on a continuing basis in the international system, or in subordinate regional systems. It is their "image" of the appropriate orientations or functions of their state toward, or in, the external environment.

They define obligations and expectations that can be prescribed by external actors (role *prescription*) or self-generated by the policy maker's own definitions (role *conceptions*).[4]

One problem with the classic conception of a role is that it is conceived as the result of internal and external variables. But as Holsti's definition implies, in order to have an impact, role prescriptions must be translated and appropriated by policy makers. Thus it is more appropriate to view role conceptions as both rooted in internal variables and perceived external demands; these two sets of variables can be usefully combined into two distinct variables called identity (who we are) and status (*noblesse oblige*), which in turn encompass a variety of factors such as history, individuals and groups, institutions, domestic politics, or expectations from other international actors.

A second issue is the relationship between role conceptions and the means used to implement them. Given that various means may be used to fulfill a particular role, it is not helpful to make means endogenous to the definition of roles. Indeed, foreign policy debates are both about the proper role one should play and the legitimate means that should be used to pursue them. Roles may exclude some means, but they do not always prescribe particular means.[5] One should then leave open questions pertaining to the relationships between roles and means, which this endogeneity does not allow.

Simply then, a foreign policy role refers to the intersubjective understanding of appropriate behavior orientations in the international arena. The articulation of a national role betrays preferences, operationalizes an image of the world, triggers expectations, and influences the definition of the situation and of the available options. A role reflects a claim on the international system, a recognition by international actors, and a conception of national identity. It gives meaning and purpose to a foreign policy. This does not imply that a single role exists nor the existence of a consensus over them. Yet roles are remarkably stable. One of the issues is indeed how they change in response to domestic (political, economic, and social) and external (the distribution of power or the nature of the system) change.

The analytical attractiveness of the concept of role lies in three main areas. First, it helps explain apparent anomalies in the conduct of states. In an anarchic system, roles impose obligations on states and help shape their interests. Why would Canada, for example, cancel nearly half of Poland's debt between 1992 and 1994 when its external indebtedness relative to its gross domestic product (GDP) was twice that of Poland's? Why do states maintain military forces that are disproportionate to perceived threats, as does France? The idea that Canada should define for itself a military niche in peacekeeping, or France's concern for maintaining its overseas presence, illustrates the obligations that roles exert beyond mere considerations of the national interest. A role can even lead states to undertake actions that would contradict the national interest as in the French and English support to Finland in 1939–40, the extension of the American involvement in Vietnam, or the promotion of climate leadership in the face of immediate economic costs. In that regard, it can explain some shortcomings of the interest-based model, according to which the willingness to participate actively in regime building is related positively to ecological vulnerability and negatively to the estimated costs of solving environmental problems (Sprinz and Vaahtoranta 1994). In the case of the EU, for example, Hovi, Skodvin, and Andresen (2003) have argued that internal institutional support and the desire to play a leadership role in climate change have been more potent driving forces behind EU climate policy than rational cost-benefit calculations (Zhang 2013).

Capacities alone do not define a role. Structural realism cannot explain why Japan and Germany have chosen not to shoulder greater responsibilities through a leadership role commensurate with their power or why France and Great Britain have differed so much in their foreign policies. This does not mean that role definition should replace geopolitical analyses as a basis for the identification of threats that states must reduce. Foreign policy, however, is not simply about preventing what is unacceptable, and beyond that minimal imperative, role conceptions will matter. They expand the definition of the national interest beyond the basic geopolitical factors that are linked to national survival.

Second, role theory may offer a promising avenue for resolving one of IR theory's long-standing problems, namely the relationship between agents and structure, or actors and the system (Harnisch et al. 2011) "because it incorporates the presence of institutional factors and purposive action" (Cantir and Kaarbo 2011, 14). International structure, as Waltz (1979) said, "pushes and shoves," but states can make the wrong choices. "[It] does not give decision makers clear indications about what constitutes good foreign policy [(Breuning (1995, 237)]. Instead, leader perceptions enter into the equation" (Ibid.) The concept of role interfaces with the individual, society, and the system. It has the potential of reconciling different levels of analysis, and provides a means of assessing the interplay between individual (cognitive), internal (domestic), and external (structural) variables. That interface plays itself out through the representation that decision makers have of their identity and status (role conception and prescription), its implementation (role enactment and performance) and, of course, through the outcomes.[6] By bridging multiple levels of analysis and by drawing on the three dominant paradigms of IR, role theory holds the potential to illuminate foreign policy continuities as well as change and, more generally, the interplay among a variety of international actors interacting across levels in a complex governance system.

Finally, examining the evolution, origins, and contents of different roles that collective actors play on the international stage allows us to reflect upon the possibility of cooperation in the maintenance of international order. Studies can help identify the risks of conflicts rooted in clashing role conceptions masquerading as interests or in the contradictions between the internal conceptions and the external expectations of the role that a given state should play.

It is therefore surprising that role theory has not attracted the interest of more scholars. Following Holsti (1970), a first wave of research of fairly limited interest took place in the 1980s. It had already faded by the mid-1990s, and attempts to resurrect it at that time came to naught. But the concept has again found the support of several intellectual entrepreneurs who may be able to fill the conceptual, methodological, and empirical gaps so as to place it in the forefront of IR (Cantir and Kaarbo 2011; Harnisch 2012; McCourt 2012; Thies and Breuning 2012; Harnisch et al. 2011).

This perspective has not been devoid of criticisms. They pertain more to the way it has been operationalized than to fundamental epistemological flaws, or they question its ultimate usefulness. There is, for example, the tendency to consider National Role Conception (NRC) as somehow reflecting national consensus, which overlooks that foreign policy debates are also about roles. Most accounts of NRC formation also emphasize structure and material power (Wehner and Thies 2014) at the expense of other factors such as identity. Studies that look at the interplay between the two are few (e.g. Le Prestre 1997).

Another set of difficulties is methodological, starting with measurement. It is already problematic to ascertain the contents of a national role. Is it only expressed by its leaders? Through what actions? When applied to an organization such as the EU, who articulates its role? The presidency? The commission? The European parliament? Its members? The few articles that have used the concept to study EU foreign policy focus on the commission's outputs.

Further, there is the recurring issue of causal inference: how can we conclude that the role as expressed has favored certain policy directions over others (and not the other way around in this case), and how can we explain that it prevailed? The concept of role looks like one of those concepts (like political culture or the national interest) that at first seem to offer a promising avenue of research and a powerful analytical tool and then whose usefulness vanishes as one tries to go beyond the metaphor, with the result that it delivers less than what it promised. One could argue, however, that this criticism in part stems from a deterministic notion of theory building, whereas no single factor can explain a whole range of foreign policy behavior. Moreover, its potential usefulness depends on the definition of the dependent variable (what specific aspects of foreign policy behavior needs explaining). These reasons make it hazardous to venture into this minefield, although not impossible; the rewards, as seen above, could be substantial.

The role of the EU in international environmental affairs

Role theory and EU foreign policy

The concept of role has been applied to the EU since mid-2000, particularly in the context of security issues and relations with Eastern Europe. The role of the EU in international environmental governance has also led to numerous articles, but the concept has been used loosely to describe EU behavior and impact rather than as an attempt to uncover any relationship between role conceptions, behavior, and outcomes. Thus the term usually refers to the function of the EU or to its performance rather than to role conceptions. Nevertheless, a few authors have made reference to role theory in their analysis of the EU. Orbie (2008) raises the issue of role conflicts in the case of the EU. Several Scandinavian scholars have probed its usefulness, although the empirical foundation of these works appears limited (Elgström and Skovgaard 2014; Bengtsson and Elgström 2011; Kaya 2009; Aggestam 2006; Elgström and Smith 2004, 2006).

A thorough examination of the EU's role in environmental diplomacy should involve the following tasks:

1. Map out dominant and secondary roles.
2. Identify their origin. There is an ongoing debate regarding the factors shaping national roles that pits those who stress the actor's material or cognitive traits against those who grant more importance to language and social interactions (Harnisch et al. 2011, 7). Role theorists agree with Wendt (1999) that agent and structure are mutually constituted.
3. Examine the regulative and constitutive effects of the EU's roles. According to Harnisch et al. (2011, 253), "States, and to some extent also international organizations such as the European Union and NATO, now hold a host of national and international roles that constitute their identity, regulate their behavior, and shape the international social order."[7] To what extent and under what conditions this is so remains to be ascertained. This would also involve the identification of the existence of a consensus or of conflicts over these roles. In the case of the EU, role conflicts may reflect differences in role conceptions held by member states and the EC, or difference in those roles

enacted within the environment issue area, or between the latter and other issue areas (such as human rights).
4. Analyze the mechanisms of role change, that is learning and adaptation, that may have individual, domestic/social, or systemic causes (Wendt 1999, 227f.; quoted in Harnisch et al. 2011, 7).
5. Examine the impact of the EU role-set on international cooperation.

The origins of EU's roles

The EU, and before it the EEC, has not always been a leader in international environmental politics. If we consider those states that have been most active in this field and in climate change in particular, Denmark (1973) and the UK (1973) at the time of the 1972 Stockholm conference were not yet formal members. And at the time of the 1992 Rio "Conference on Environment and Development," neither were Austria (1995), Finland (1995), and Sweden (1995). Rather, it was the US, and to a lesser extent other countries such as Canada, which played a key role in the 1970s and into the 1980s in building international environmental governance.

In the 1970s, the US was the key source of innovative environmental policy on such issues as fisheries conservation, marine pollution, the Convention on International Trade in Endangered Species (CITES), and the restoration of the stratospheric ozone layer. Later several middle powers, such as Canada and Nordic countries, promoted cooperation in specific issue areas such as biodiversity, acid rain, and the climate (the first intergovernmental conference on climate was held in Toronto in 1988). However, by the early 1990s, it was becoming apparent that the US was fast abdicating this role, a process that was initiated at Rio 1992, that continued with the rejection of the Kyoto Protocol, and that was manifest in a desire to revisit some of the progress made in the previous decades and in a negative approach to other multilateral initiatives. Canada, not the US, was a key leader in the negotiation of a convention on persistent organic pollutants (POPs), for example.

At the same time, the European Council in 1988 singled out the strategic importance of environmental issues and pressured Europe to assume a leadership role in the policies needed to protect the global environment.[8] And in 1990, the council reaffirmed its position and reminded European institutions as well as member countries that their capacity to exercise leadership in this area was enormous.

Explanations of why the EU adopted this leadership role touch upon identity, integration dynamics, regulatory politics (domestic variables associated with international regulatory competition, see infra) (Kelemen and Vogel 2009), domestic factors (public opinion, economics), pressures from member states, and status. With a couple of exceptions (Schreurs and Tiberghien 2007), the literature emphasizes identity-related variables and the internal dynamics of the EU much more than status in explaining role conceptions.

In the case of the EU, identity is reflected in norms and process. Norms include peace, multilateralism, human security (development, basic needs, peace, human rights), and sustainable development, whereas process refers to multilevel governance, consensus (within limits), and networks (Elgström and Smith 2004). It is clear that "norm entrepreneur" corresponds to a basic EU role and that several forms of leadership are associated with either identity or status (a regional and economic power, for example).

Internal dynamics

This factor first points to the link between an activist EU international environmental policy and pressures from its more dynamic members. Indeed, several reasons might account for the desire of some members to push for a strong EU role in environmental matters, notably the desire to project their values onto the world, the ambition of some middle powers to play a traditional middle power role,[9] or the desire by some members, such as Scandinavian countries, to use international commitments to pressure EU laggards in these matters.

Climate negotiations have seen various countries take up the lead. Some sought in a strong EU environmental role a way to build their diplomatic image. For example, the Netherlands played a leadership role on climate change when it held the EU presidency in 1992 and 1997. The March 1997 Council decision on a common 15 percent reduction target as an opening bid for the upcoming Kyoto Protocol Conference of the Parties was engineered by the Dutch presidency (Bretherton and Vogler 1999, 93).

Germany and the UK have consistently pushed this issue, more visibly when they have held the council presidency (2005 for Britain and 2007 for Germany). No other country has been as important as Germany in establishing and achieving the EU burden-sharing goal with the closing of polluting factories in the former German Democratic Republic.[10] The UK went from being relatively skeptical about reducing its emissions in the early 1990s to being a strong supporter of action. This is explained by rising public concerns about global warming, the sharp drop in emissions from the switch to natural gas for electricity, and, in more recent years according to Schreurs and Tiberghien (2007), by considerations of status—that is, concern to show independence from the US and gain a degree of leadership in EU decision making. Other countries such as Austria, Belgium, Denmark, Finland, Luxembourg, and Sweden have often formed coalitions in support of aggressive action. And for strong internal reasons, France has also invested heavily in the success of COP-21.

Identity and integration dynamics

After the Cold War, at a time of great turbulence, major European powers (Germany, France, and the UK) tended to root the definition of their national identity in a concept of community, in this case an ideological and a geographical community (Le Prestre 1997). Clearly identity and status may be co-constituted (see Wendt 2003). This is precisely one of the main arguments regarding EU foreign policy, namely that it is about creating status through a redefinition of European identity around certain norms. In times of systemic turbulence and status uncertainty, identity becomes more important in guiding foreign policy roles.

Indeed, the most popular explanation for EU policy emphasizes identity building. The EU's environmental policy, it is said, should reflect its values and contribute to strengthen them as well as the union itself. The EU has articulated a vision of itself as a community of values and norms with the moral imperative of promoting them (Bengtsson and Elgström 2011). In particular, the commission has used climate change to build the EU's foreign identity, especially relative to the US's (Schreurs and Tiberghien 2007), and international negotiations as an identity-building process.

These dynamics combined with the leadership played by the European Parliament (EP) and the European Commission through, for example, the commission's promotion of carbon emissions trading. For the commission, climate policy was also a means to promote integration in new areas of competency and empower the commission with new regulatory tools and monitoring powers in the energy sector (Schreurs and Tiberghien 2007). From the commission's viewpoint, an active international environmental policy responded to public opinion thereby showing its relevance (Ibid.). Challenged in the 1990s for its supposed democratic deficit and the establishment of the single market, the EU, through the environment, could speak with one voice on a popular issue, and present itself as the defender of the welfare of all Europeans (Dahan and Aykut 2015).

Politics abhors a vacuum

According to Vogler (2011), the change in US international environmental policy in the 1980s, which became more pronounced in the run-up to 1992 and beyond, opened an "enormous" opportunity for the EU. This was illustrated by the rejection of the Law of the Sea Treaty; the cancellation (and subsequently limits to) the US contribution to UNEP; the initial refusal to sign on to the Convention on Biological Diversity (CBD) (of which the US was an early promoter) and later, the refusal of every US administration to put it up for ratification by the Senate; the difficult negotiations of the Cartagena Protocol; laggardly positions regarding the negotiation of new agreements; the questioning of some of the principles of the Stockholm and Rio Declarations (such as the principle of common but differentiated responsibility), etc. Members of the EU, especially Germany and the UK, stepped forward in support of UNEP. The EU strongly supported the CBD and the Cartagena Protocol as well as other international agreements and singled out the environment as an area where it could play a significant diplomatic role. Thus the EU's role after the US withdrawal from Kyoto has been seen as a way of demonstrating independence from the US in this area (see Lucarelli 2014) with the objective of responding to the expectations of other international actors and asserting its influence in the international system through multilateralism.

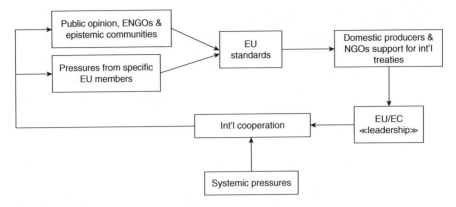

FIGURE 4.1. The regulatory politics model
Source: Philippe Le Prestre

Regulatory politics

Another explanation, less common in the European literature, that precisely mixes willingness and opportunity, emphasizes a combination of domestic politics and international regulatory competition (Schreurs and Tiberghien 2007).

The regulatory politics model applies equally well to member states and the EU. Once strict environmental standards have been adopted at the national or EU level (through a coalition of environmental groups, epistemic communities and, sometimes, segments of business and of local authorities), business (for competitive reasons) and environmentalists (for normative reasons) have an incentive to extend them internationally, supported by the state or the EU (see Vogel 1995). This model explains US promotion of the regulation of ozone-depleting substances in the 1980s in the face of European, especially British, doubts (DeSombre 2000) and, according to Kelemen (2010, 339), "fits well with the empirical record in the EU, explaining both the general shift toward a leadership position from the early 1990s and the specific positions taken by the EU on a number of important international environmental issues." Finally, multilevel governance also created numerous leadership points where competitive leadership was initiated. As Schreurs and Tiberghien (2007, 25) pointed out, "[t]he EU's governance structure opened numerous avenues by which advocates of climate change action have been able to inject their priorities and concerns into policy debate."

The bases of the EU's role

EU action in that area has a dual basis: its environmental and foreign policy. Surprisingly, the community's competency on environmental matters was not formally recognized until the adoption of the 1986 Single European Act which called for community actions in this area to "be based on the principles that preventive action should be taken, that environmental damage should be rectified at source, and that the polluter should pay" (art.130r). Subsequently, the Maastricht Treaty on European Union explicitly gave the community responsibility for "promoting measures at international level to deal with regional or worldwide environmental problems" (art.130r(1)) and added the precautionary principle as a principle of public policy (art.130r(2)).

Internationally, it is the European Community (EC) rather than the EU (established by the 1992 Treaty) that enjoys legal personality. As such, it can be a party to international treaties in its own right with the status of "Regional Economic Integration Organization" (REIO). The EC is now party to more than thirty conventions (including the United Nations Framework Convention on Climate Change [UNFCCC] and the CBD) (Bretherton and Vogler 1999). Finally, the 2007 Treaty of Lisbon made one of the objectives of the EU's external action to "help develop international measures to preserve and improve the quality of the environment and the sustainable management of global natural resources, in order to ensure sustainable development" (ch.I, art.10A(2f)), and, more specifically, "promoting measures at international level to deal with regional or worldwide environmental problems, and in particular combating climate change (143(a))."

Now fully part of the EU's external policy, the environment nevertheless remains a shared competency, "which subordinates the EU collective negotiation capacity to the prior development of ad hoc political compromises among Member States and between them and the Commission" (Petiteville 2006, 107). Though the EU has exclusive competency over fisheries,[11] member states maintain competence in other sectors such as fiscal and energy policy. Any community-wide energy tax designed to address climate change, for example, must enjoy unanimous support, which seriously constrains the EU's ability to coordinate its actions across sectors (Schreurs and Tiberghien 2007).[12]

Ultimately, the question of the legal status of the EU, a status that varies according to the issue area (party to a treaty or not; full member of an IGO such as the FAO, full participant or just an observer (Wouters et al. 2012, 4)), should affect more the international impact of the role (as opposed to its internal impact, such as harmonizing member states' climate policies) than role performance.

The role set of the EU

There is a large consensus among EU officials and academics that the EU has developed three basic and interrelated roles in the international environmental arena: norm entrepreneur, multilateral power, and leader (itself a set of several distinct subroles).

First, the EU likes to present itself as a union of values. European integration emphasizes the promotion of core values that it is perceived to embody, notably democracy, multilateralism, the promotion of human rights, and environmental protection.[13] Regarding environmental norms, the EU has strongly promoted the precautionary principle which is embedded in several national constitutions. In climate change, it has embraced the principle of common but differentiated responsibility (PCDR) and the notion of the historical responsibility of the industrialized states. And it has defined climate change action as a moral and ethical issue that must transcend narrow economic interests (Schreurs and Tiberghien 2007).

As a multilateral power, the main objective of the EU's foreign policy is to improve the effectiveness of multilateral institutions, predominantly the UN, and to support and promote those fundamental values. According to the former European commissioner for external relations Benita Ferrero-Waldner,

> The EU is convinced that only an effective multilateral system can adequately address the new and complex challenges the international community faces today. For that reason, the EU has made effective multilateralism with the UN at its core a central element of its external action.[14]

And according to the commission,

> An active commitment to an effective multilateralism means more than rhetorical professions of faith. It means taking global rules seriously, whether they concern the preservation of peace or the limitation of carbon emissions; it means helping other countries to implement and abide by these rules; it means engaging actively in multilateral forums, and promoting a forward-looking agenda that is not limited to a narrow defence of national interests.[15]

This translated into a strong preference for the Kyoto Protocol and keeping climate change negotiations in the UN forum, in the face of developing parallel arenas. The EU feels responsible to support and strengthen the UN in order to enable the latter to fulfill its role effectively in seeking multilateral solutions to global problems.

Moral suasion is not enough; cooperation also requires leadership, a role that is externally prescribed as well as internally developed.[16] One generally distinguishes among four broad kinds of leadership: structural, instrumental, intellectual, and directional (Gupta and Grubb 2000; Underdal 1994). EU leadership, so far, has essentially been intellectual and directional, although one could make the case for attempts at structural leadership (albeit outside the negotiation of regimes), and though the EU also claims some sort of instrumental leadership.

Structural leadership refers to the exercise of material power (military, economic, technological) in the promotion of the national interest in the context of a common good. For Gupta and Grubb (2000), the EU's structural power is insufficient to support leadership in the climate change area. What is true of climate change may not be so in other issue areas, though. As previously mentioned, the threat of unilateral action enabled the EU presidency to engineer the adoption of more stringent standards at the IMO (Van Leeuwen and Kern 2013).

Whereas norms backed by power are thought to be most effective, the EU's self-conception as a normative power may interfere with its aspiration to be a structural leader. To the gap between potential, usable, and effective power, one must add another between norms and power, as when the exercise of power in defense of norms is considered illegitimate. This may account for the gap between potential and actual leadership as perceived both by elites and the general public. And it may reflect a tension within the EU between a norms-based role conception arising from a middle power outlook (which dominates) and a power-based role conception more in tune with the experience of European great powers.

The second type of leadership, instrumental leadership, refers to the use of diplomacy in order to build coalitions and structure negotiations in pursuit of a common goal. Naturally, a distinction has to be made between the diplomatic power of the EC/EU and that of its members. One could argue that the limited diplomatic resources of the union (the establishment of the green diplomacy network notwithstanding) would render this type of leadership marginal. In international environmental negotiations, EU diplomats either emanate from or must work with relevant national diplomatic services, whose responsibility it is to build coalitions with their national counterparts within and outside the EU.

In some areas, such as international environmental governance, leadership was left to those EU states that wished strongly to promote the issue, such as France in the case of the United Nations Environment Organization (UNEO). France obtained the support of the EU (starting with Germany) and then enlisted the Francophonie and the EU. But it was not able to translate that support into a larger international coalition, and the scheme died.

The EU has also liked to present itself as a mediator between developed and developing countries. It was able to play the role of a "bridge builder" between developed and emergent countries on climate finance (Oberthür and Groen 2014). It also played this role after the rejection of the Kyoto Protocol by the US when it successfully brought back Russia and Australia into the game (although not for long).

Instrumental leadership also takes the form of attempts to mobilize a variety of actors, not just states. The EU and its richer members have played an active role in empowering civil society (to wit Aarhus convention) and in mobilizing it ahead of key negotiations, since its environmental agenda is in line with the preferences of environmental nongovernmental organizations (NGOs). This strategy, however, may backfire (see infra). Before the UNFCCC COP-21, France actively mobilized churches, NGOs, and local authorities, as well as the scientific and business communities.

Intellectual leadership, for its part, refers to the provision of information and the capacity to redefine the problems so as to move cooperation forward. This type of leadership is designed not only to convince but also to change the structure of the game by developing linkages with other issues, thereby also changing the nature of the players who should be legitimately involved.

This leadership was primarily performed by individual states, more than by the EU/EC as such. The Stern Review on the Economics of Climate Change (Stern 2006) was sponsored by the UK; The Economics of Ecosystems and Biodiversity (TEEB) by Germany and the European Commission. In the case of basic science, the

British and German governments have invested heavily in climate modelling (as they have in biodiversity). The EU and its member states together have contributed nearly as much to the IPCC as the US (around 40 million Swiss francs since 1988 out of a total of 135 million or so).

Germany and later the Netherlands played key roles in translating article 2 of the UNFCCC into a threshold that would constitute a tipping point.[17] These efforts reflected both the belief that effectiveness was linked to the adoption of international commitments in the form of targets, and to the intellectual leadership of boundary organizations (see chapter 3), such as the German Advisory Council on Global Change (WBGU). This ceiling was suggested by the EU Council in 1996 as a global goal, then endorsed by the international community in 2009, first by the G8 and then at COP-15 (Copenhagen). Remarkably, the definition of this "boundary object" originated neither within the IPCC nor the COP but through dynamics that were external to these forums (see Aykut and Dahan 2014).

In terms of directional or political leadership, the EU has primarily staked its leadership claim on leading by example (e.g. Parker and Karlsson 2010). The EU and its members have adopted policies and programs that have put it at the forefront of international efforts to address climate change. In so doing, it aimed to act as a policy entrepreneur, setting emission targets, goals, and measures designed to become benchmarks against which other states would have to react. This role was developed by the EU in response to initiatives from several of its members in the early 1990s,[18] and has been facilitated by the size and diversity of the European economy that allow for innovations in policies and technological development. Examples include:

a In 1997, in the run-up to the Kyoto Protocol negotiations, the commission argued strongly that in order to attain a global leadership role, the EU had to propose a politically credible target of no less than 10 percent reduction by 2005 (Vogler 2011; Ringius 1999). Subsequently it proposed that industrialized states commit to reducing their greenhouse gas (GHG) emissions by 15 percent of 1990 levels by 2010, which several developed countries, such as the US, Japan, and Australia, opposed. In the end, the EU committed to a far more modest 8 percent to the US 7 percent, but it put other countries on the defensive, pushing them to go farther than they had said they were willing or able to go.
b In 2007, the European Council adopted a proposal by the commission to limit global warming to 2 degrees and announced the 20–20–20 commitment: a cut of its CO_2 emissions by 20 percent of 1990 levels by 2020 (increasing this to 30 percent should other developed countries agree to take action within the framework of an international agreement); a binding target of 20 percent of renewables in the EU's overall total energy consumption with a subtarget of 10 percent for biofuels in the total mix of transportation fuel (petrol and diesel) consumption by 2020.
c The EU has also implemented the world's first international carbon emissions trading system (ETS). This was all the more remarkable given EU members'

early reluctance to support market-based instruments in the context of the negotiation of the Kyoto Protocol.
d   In the run-up to COP-21, the EU was the first to commit to an ambitious target: GHG reductions of at least 40 percent by 2030 (against 1990) and 85–90 percent by 2050.

In this as in the former examples, the aim is to show the way and encourage states to follow suit, as well as reinforce national individual commitments.[19]

The impact of role conceptions on performance

Explaining EU performance

The answer to our initial question (what explains the gap between the EU's aspirations and achievements?) obviously lies in a variety of internal and external factors. The concept of role allows us to touch upon some of them at both levels of analysis.

A first set of hypotheses pertains to "actorness," that is the characteristics of the EU itself (Elgström and Smith 2004; Bretherton and Vogler 1999, 38). Roles are hypothesized to vary with different combinations of policy coherence, divisions of competencies, access to policy instruments, and the clarity of EU goals.[20]

A second set of hypotheses would look into the nature, origins, and impacts of role conflicts. These conflicts pertain both to different role expectations held by the EU and its member states and to mismatches between the latter and role expectations and prescriptions stemming from an evolving foreign policy environment. These conflicts may take three forms: (i) with the EU enlargement and the change in the nature of issues, conflicts about the definition of the role may have increased (H_1); on a number of issues, the EU found itself opposed by the G77, as in its attempts to promote environmental norms in the face of US (and Australian and Canadian) opposition. As in the case of the tension between the role of norm entrepreneur and structural leadership (H_2), here we may have an example of another role conflict, in this case between norm entrepreneur and mediator (H_3); a mismatch between the EU's self-image and the one held by international actors.

The lack of progress in certain international environmental negotiations, such as climate change, has led to studies of the EU's perceptions by other actors as a leader and of its actual impact on solving the collective action problem, the issue being to reconcile role prescriptions/expectations as mediated by policy makers and role conceptions, that is how it sees itself (rooted both in status and identity).

The impact of various forms of leadership rests on how it is perceived by others. When addressing leadership, EU officials insist less on the economic than on "soft power," the power to attract. In that sense, soft power is akin to charisma insofar as it is granted to the state by others. Thus, the EU's soft power originates both within the union and through its interactions with other international actors (Fliegauf 2012). Hence to be a leader, one must not only claim to be a leader and act accordingly, but also one has to be perceived as such. There are no leaders without followers.[21]

Several studies have qualified the image of the EU as an environmental leader among foreign elites and the foreign media. The EU is perceived as an economic giant, a multilateral actor, an area of economic integration, and only rarely a norm promoter (Lucarelli 2014). Another study underscores that the environmental role of the EU was rarely mentioned by Pacific and East African elites (Chaban *et al.* 2013). On the other hand, positive perceptions of the EU as an environmental leader, particularly on climate change, were present in South Africa and Southeast Asia. But in the latter case, the union was often seen more as a broker than a leader in world diplomacy. "Only a few Thai, Malaysian and South African elites regarded the Union as a great power in environmental protection," in sharp contrast with the EU's self-perception (Chaban *et al.* 2013, 445).

When compared with other potential leaders,

> the EU is regarded as one leader among others, and not the only one: 62 percent of all respondents identified the EU as having a leading role in the climate change negotiations; almost half the respondents recognized China as a leader, and a quarter regarded the G-77 and the US as leaders. However, the percentages change if we only consider the responses of those directly involved in the negotiations, in which case more people see China as a leader.
>
> *(Lucarelli 2014, 9, citing Karlsson* et al. *2011)*

Finally, a third set of hypotheses pertain to what can be called "role entrapment," to which we shall turn after a few words about the perils of leadership.

The perils of leadership

Optimists might believe that all there is to do to improve EU effectiveness in negotiations is to clarify responsibilities within the EU and between the EU and EC, or ensure that all members support a given policy. The limited effectiveness of EU's leadership so far, in terms of engineering a comprehensive agreement to curb CO_2 emissions drastically, however, should lead us to reconsider certain role conceptions, starting with the virtues of directional leadership.

Directional leadership rests on unilateral action in the hope of boosting the credibility of commitments to a given collective action goal, and demonstrating the feasibility, value, and superiority of particular policy solutions (Gupta and Ringius 2001). Leadership is a necessary condition for reaching international agreements and overcoming collective action problems associated with global environmental problems. The strategy of leading by example can be effective in a negotiation context where mistrust dominates and where each country hesitates to make the first move. And as in domestic settings where actually there is no race to the bottom on environmental issues, one can hope that it will trigger new dynamics within other polities in favor of stricter norms. Presented as a virtue and inherently positive for individuals; when is it wise for collective actors to adopt a strategy of leading by example? On the one hand, there is the need to agree to commitments that will enable the international community to reach a given target (such as the 2-degree target for climate warming); on the other hand, states will commit based on relative positioning. In such a situation, does it make sense to start with an opening gambit as the EU has done? Only if that commitment is ambitious, credible, and coupled with the use of structural power.

First, success is more likely if the leader is the overwhelming power or contributor to the problem in a given issue area. Otherwise, the message is only moral or limited to showing that the benefits of adopting a similar policy outweigh its costs, which can take time.[22] And directional leadership must be coupled with the use of structural leadership (that is with the right incentives). The case of the control of acid rain in Europe is exemplary in that respect.[23]

Further, to be successful, directional leadership must show that such moves were the result of genuine choices in the context of collective action, rather than mere by-products of business as usual; or that the promotion of those norms was not just a manifestation of regulatory politics. Credibility also relies on subsequent action. In structural leadership, it means using one's resources at one's disposal; in intellectual leadership, it is putting forth visions and plans; in diplomatic leadership, it is building winning coalitions; and in distributional leadership, it is performance. If the internal performance of EU members relative to the pledges by the EU is found wanting, the credibility of this leadership strategy becomes open to question. In this context, the EU's ability to meet its commitments thanks to differentiated obligations (the European bubble) and the restructuring of the economies of some of the biggest polluters (UK, Germany, Italy), which made it easier for the EU to meet its emission reduction targets even under business-as-usual scenarios, weakens the credibility of that role, since international commitments were not associated with significant domestic efforts at mitigation (or financing for that matter). The lack of a common internal policy (in terms of a tax on carbon or energy-saving measures) to achieve the "bubble" targets was also damaging (Bretherton and Vogler 1999, 105).

The impact of this role also depends on how the EU is perceived (see above). Research on other countries' perceptions of EU leadership first shows that the US and China are also considered leaders,[24] and then stresses attributes other than leading by example (such as structural and intellectual leadership) (see Lucarelli 2014; Karlsson et al. 2012). In addition, its exercise may be misperceived. The ability of the EU to lead by example is challenged by the perception by external elites that in doing so, it adopts a patronizing negotiating style (Lucarelli 2014).

Role entrapment

Directional leadership creates expectations that may come back to bite you. The intellectual and directional leadership that the EU demonstrated in proposing and imposing the 2-degree ceiling may have had the perverse effect of forcing it to adopt much more ambitious reduction targets when the IPCC changed its estimate of allowable total concentrations from 550ppm down to 450ppm. This suggested the danger of "sanctuarizing" a specific value to operationalize UNFCCC's Art.2 reference to "dangerous anthropogenic interference with the climate system" (Aykut and Dahan 2014, 345). It runs also the risk of displacing the political debate to one over scientific estimates, thus threatening a wholesale questioning of the science underlying international climate policy.

Further, the optimism created by internal European agreements, such as the 2014 European commitment for emission reductions by 2030, can heighten expectations which, if they are not met, may lead to renewed criticisms. Heightened expectations may also lead to negative assessments of negotiations such as the so-called failure of UNFCCC COP-15 in Copenhagen. In the case of UNFCCC COP-21, the EU was accused by Friends of the Earth before the meeting of falling short of what it should do according to its avowed commitment to fight climate change. Likewise, there were pressures from environmental groups for the EU to "save Kyoto" after the US withdrawal in 2001.

A more significant problem is that this strategy means giving up negotiating cards (your opponents will pocket what could have been concessions). The EU attempted to overcome this difficulty by pledging to adopt even stricter commitments if other states would commit to making an extra effort, but it had already made significant concessions by moving ahead alone. Clearly, instead of making its commitments contingent and thus using them as bargaining chips, the EU commitment to a role of leading by example meant that it would go ahead with mitigation whatever the actions of other actors. In the absence of the capacity to force similar moves by using structural leadership (such as shutting off the EU market to goods from countries that did not pledge emission reductions), the EU in fact weakened its hand.

The role conception of norm entrepreneur can lead to other perverse effects. For example, it may entail adopting maximizing positions (couched in moral principles) that lead to failure. This may have been the case both at The Hague in December 2000, when EU intransigence prevented a significant agreement, and in Copenhagen nine years later. The failure of Copenhagen (from the EU's point of view but not necessarily from that of developing countries) can be explained by the adoption of a maximalist and moral position which found the EU isolated (Tiberghien 2013). In the case of biodiversity, the negotiations over the Cartagena Protocol were notably held up by the EU's insistence on the inclusion of the precautionary principle (which became the precautionary "approach"). Finally, one should not dismiss the impact of the EU's so-called successes that covered profound differences, for these successes later turned into failures.[25]

In the end, because of its role conceptions, the EU was inclined to define problems in moral terms (as when it opposed the CDM and later insisted on restrictions to their use), to making first moves, to stick to the Kyoto model, and to adopt a global perspective. This had two consequences: (i) it made its goals more elusive, and (ii) it significantly weakened the leading role it could have played in engineering another model of climate governance based on regional governance.

One could argue that the EU won a pyrrhic victory over the US when it successfully supported the Kyoto Protocol's eventual coming into force. First, it widened the split with the US and undermined the work of subsequent UNFCCC Conferences of the Parties, for delineating what fell under the UNFCCC or the Kyoto Protocol was often contentious. Second, it meant clinging to a model that may have been right for the EU but was clearly wrong for the world, and consequently delayed the search for a more realistic and flexible model by ten years. Third, by adopting the role of normative leadership and leading by example, the EU was weakening its negotiating position rather than stimulating concessions. And fourth, it entailed further concessions to Russia, such as support for Russia's admission to the WTO, in order to secure the coming into force of the Kyoto Protocol. These dynamics suggest that the EU became trapped in a role actually or potentially counterproductive.

Pyrrhic victories are not limited to climate change. Effective EU leadership at a time of US retreat from multilateralism has been hailed in the cases of the adoption of the 1989 Basel Convention on Hazardous Waste Disposal, the 1992 CBD, the 2000 Cartagena Protocol on Biosafety, and the 2001 Stockholm Convention on Persistent Organic Pollutants. In each case, the US failed to ratify these agreements.[26]

Role entrapment takes two forms. First, role enactment may undermine the national (or collective) interest, as when identity-forming roles lead to policies that are counterproductive since they diminish the actor's bargaining power, and even reduce the probability of cooperation. Moreover, equating negotiation success with identity building may backfire when the negotiating process fails. As mentioned previously, a classic example given by Morgenthau (1954) is the decision by Britain and France in the fall of 1939 to send troops in support of the Finns who had been attacked by the Soviet Union, when these two countries were already nominally at war with Germany. Morgenthau wanted to condemn "legal/idealism," but using the concept of role entrapment might provide a fruitful way of disentangling what lies behind this legalistic/moralistic approach.

A second manifestation of role entrapment is the inability to switch role even in the wake of information that suggest clinging to it is pernicious (what could be dubbed "role inertia"), in that it compromises the goal being pursued. In the case of the EU, it corresponds to clinging to Kyoto and to the role of leading by example which diminished its bargaining power and prevented the consideration of alternative arrangements (such as bottom-up regional arrangements).

The possible causes of role inertia in the EU, include:

1. the fear of breaking a fragile consensus and of triggering internal disagreements among EU members, leading to a failure to change or reverse course;
2. the importance of identity variables in the shaping of national roles, especially if interrogations about status are high and role conceptions are granted an identity-building function;
3. domestic pressures from public opinion and environmental nongovernmental organizations (ENGOs), or from business;
4. simple path dependency (sunken costs in the form of commitments having been made in the name of this role limit future diplomatic options), or what Thomas (2011, 17) calls "precedent."

Conclusion: The region as the building block of environmental governance

Theories need entrepreneurs who will attempt to flesh them out, probe their ramifications and test new propositions. It means carefully and slowly building their foundations, which in this case, as Walker has pointed out, starts with an examination of the nature, evolution, and origins of role conceptions before one can attempt to relate roles to behaviour. A "robust" theory of roles would: (i) clarify concepts, (ii) develop hypotheses regarding the sources of role conceptions, (iii) specify under what conditions various roles emerge, and (iv) relate roles to behavior again through a number of hypotheses (Walker 1987).

International environmental governance is a particularly appropriate field through which to study EU foreign policy roles, for the EU itself has heavily invested in it (see Wouters *et al.* 2012). Moreover, the turbulence and complexity of the international system open windows of opportunity to redefining the EU's roles. If role expectations (or role prescriptions) change or if these expectations are unclear or mixed, then internal variables should have a greater impact, and the EU's roles will change according to the opportunities that open externally combined with the internal willingness to use them. Clearly, leading by example is not enough and may, at times, be counterproductive. Its effectiveness rests on other kinds of leadership. In Durban, for example, rather than stressing its own example, the EU switched to an instrumental strategy that emphasized coalition building and network creation in order to advance its interests.

In order to understand the paradoxes that characterize the EU's action in international environmental diplomacy, scholars may thus explore a variety of research paths. Beyond precisely mapping the set of primary and secondary roles, one path is to examine the development and enactment of role conceptions by looking at the impact of individuals, the articulation between EU and national role conceptions (using, for example, social identity theories, Druckman 1994; Tajfel 1982), as well as models of bureaucratic and organizational politics that may explain under what conditions particular roles obtain. There is an assumption in the role theory literature that roles are not contested, yet much of the foreign policy debate revolves around different roles that a collective actor should play on the world stage (Cantir and Kaarbo 2011). Former great powers do not have the same vision as new Eastern European members. Although this is evident in the security field (where there is no consensus as to EU's role), one should not presume that the environment would display more unity in this regard. Indeed, as mentioned earlier, a more active role of the EU in international environmental governance coincides with the admission of new states, in addition to strong support from Germany and the UK and later from France.

Another path is to look at role performance and impact. This entails examining the links between internal cohesiveness and role performance, as well as identifying the manifestations of role conflicts (see Thies 2009) and role entrapment, and test for their effects. Role entrapment may not affect all issues in the same way for it is also linked to systemic dynamics that vary among issues.

Finally, role entrapment is failure to adapt. Because the EU could not redefine its role, it was excluded from Copenhagen. Thus, under what conditions do inertia and entrapment arise and can be overcome? In this regard, role change deserves greater scrutiny.[27] Roles are stable, which is why they make good candidates for explaining policy continuities; but they are not static. To what extent, for example, may COP-21 announce a reconfiguration of roles, with some secondary roles, such as instrumental or structural leadership, acquiring more importance, and new ones developing?

Change and foreign policy learning are again at the center of current work about role theory and foreign policy. The causes of role change are rooted in changes in identity and status. As EU domestic constituencies and polities turn inward, how does that turn affect role conception? What happens when public opinion or society contests the role conceptions promoted by elites?[28] Will it lead to a renewed use of foreign policy as a builder of the community through a reassertion of the norms that form its backbone, or to a change in this role?

Role change is hard. Even in times of profound systemic turbulence, or perhaps because of it, role conceptions change rarely. One way of avoiding entrapment might lie in divorcing environmental diplomacy from its community-building functions. If role change is perceived as endangering integration or community identity, then inertia will set in. And this question needs to be raised in the current context of a divorce between elites and opinions regarding a number of foreign policy actions and roles, ranging from the refugee crisis to trade relations.

Finally, it may be that we have been looking in the wrong place all along for evidence of effective leadership. Rather than during negotiations over a regime, EU leadership may be more in evidence within existing regimes in encouraging the implementation of its provisions and a deepening of global commitments. The case of the IMO (Van Leeuwen and Kern 2013) shows the EU's potential to be a leader outside the formal negotiations process by enforcing existing norms and pressuring for the development of new ones, which would tend to support a regional-based approach of which the EU could be a more effective promoter (it would also entail articulating a new role). In this context, more importance should be granted to the role of the EU as a regional model of cooperation. Its unique contribution to complex governance might lie in giving other regions the opportunity and capacity to learn from its experience and in articulating effective ways of linking regional and global levels of governance (chapter 6 also takes up this issue).

A regional approach is intuitively appealing in the case of biodiversity, but it also makes sense in the case of climate change and is a logical extension of the evolution of climate governance since Copenhagen. Its applicability to other issue areas must be examined on a case-by-case basis; thus it is not offered as a panacea.

Viewing the region as the main locus of international action against climate change seems to fly in the face of COP-21 only if one believes that COP-21 has legitimized a universalist approach. In reality, it allowed for the development of regional approaches, complemented by a global forum of coordination of regional initiatives, ensuring that all move in the same direction. Far from being a mere relay of international norms and policies, the region is the level where consensus can be constructed around the definition of problems and appropriate solutions. Although environmental problems and globalization may encourage a convergence of norms, they also give rise to a reassertion of local and regional perspectives, if only in their interpretation and in the development and implementation of policies designed to address their impacts. Several aspects justify building up from a regional level of cooperation:

- It allows for addressing problems at a more appropriate level (as in the cases of biodiversity or water, which are worldwide rather than global problems).
- It can enhance collective learning through the establishment of joint institutions for knowledge generation, discussion, and information sharing.
- It may constitute a level where peer pressure could have a significant influence and encourage a race to the top rather than to the bottom, be it for regional or national policies.
- It would allow for different norms to govern cooperation, different regions having different approaches toward conflict resolution, for example.[29]
- It can build on culturally and socially determined risk conceptions, which might facilitate reaching compromises at the regional level.
- Finally, regions are where new governance models adapted to regional needs and reflecting different notions of justice can be experimented (see for example, Adger et al. 2006), which should make agreements more viable and may lead to a "world federalism of [environmental] policies" (see Victor et al. 2005).

Institutionally, a framework convention could establish common norms and directions, much like the COP-21 Agreement, which regional protocols could then flesh out on the model of the CCD. The role of the UN would also be transformed into a coordination forum, one where initiatives that would benefit the entire community (such as scientific assessments, cross-regional learning, transparency, financial transfers, etc.) are developed, and where information is gathered and disseminated (such as in fulfillment of the transparency requirements of the UNFCCC COP-21 Agreement).

The development of a regional level of governance (which, in any case, would be a building block of a complex governance system), faces a number of potential difficulties. First, one could object that a regional approach would be inefficient and would not guarantee the resolution of the problem. Neither did previous agreements, however, such as Kyoto-II, that followed a more centralized model. Rather than a weakness, regional fragmentation represents forces that can be harnessed. The definition of the problem and the choice of solutions both environmentally appropriate and political feasible are not given but contextual. Not all countries and not all regions have to proceed at the same pace and in the same way, provided that they move in the same direction.

A second objection is ontological: The definition of a given region is often very subjective. As Smouts and Badie (1996, 16) underline, "this is such a moving notion that it has been considered a 'residual category' and is always being re-characterized." A general picture is nearly impossible to draw because of the diversity of regional configurations and governance structures. Imposing a precise definition could also be antithetical to the spirit of this perspective that emphasizes diversity. Various options exist, from more to less integrated across a large or a limited number of sectors. Regions are intersubjective understandings of common policy interests and/or identity and may overlap.

Third, one may fear that a regional approach might increase the likelihood of interregional conflicts or, at the very least, complicate policy coordination. Divergent climate change policies might widen the gap between large existing coalitions, such as North America and Europe. This potential danger heightens the need for a structure that fosters dialogue and coordination at the global level; the global level of governance complements rather than oversees the regional level, both being ultimately partly mutually constituted. A global institution capable of defining minimal common and noncontradictory norms and principles in support of a given direction is needed. We know that transnational firms generally prefer a universal governance model over a regional or national one, always sources of uncertainty (unless needed for marketing reasons). A regional approach does not contradict the need for a WTO or rules governing intellectual property rights. But it can also be a locus for experimenting new rules. Firms and networks act as lubricants just as do those states whose territory spans several continents (France, United Kingdom, United States, and Russia). Fragmentation is not chaos.

Fourth, not all states have the same capacities or the same propensity to develop the needed governance structures. Would adopting a regional approach mean abandoning some of them and reinforce inequalities in, say, adaptation to climate change since vulnerability and adaptation to climate change are linked to poverty? Here again, intergovernmental, transnational, transcontinental actors as well as networks, can play a role in minimizing this risk.

Fifth, one could raise doubts as to the feasibility of such an approach for various political reasons, ranging from a nationalistic turn at one opposite end, to the fear that it would reduce the bargaining power of developing countries now less able to link progress on global goals to progress on local ones (such as mitigation and adaptation for climate change, or wildlife trade and conservation for biodiversity), at the other. Many developing countries have an interest in a universal and centralized model of climate policy which allows them to benefit from the schemes designed to facilitate the attainment of individual emission targets through such instruments as the CDM or Reducing Emissions from Deforestation and Forest Degradation (REDD+).

In that case, they may fear that a regional approach would reduce the demand for emission credits, and thus their financial prospects. From their perspective, industrialized countries may worry about heightened outsourcing and industrial flight unless compensatory trade rules are adopted. Moreover, nothing ensures that regional cooperation would be easier. Intraregional differences are often large and difficult to overcome, so global dynamics would still be in evidence at the regional level. For example, India, as a developing country, was opposed to the Japanese proposal to use a sectoral approach on clean development and climate change that might have been acceptable to the members of ASEAN or the Asia-Pacific partnership. Naturally, these difficulties may not be worse than what happens at the global level either, and the existence of a regional hegemon could be beneficial. The conditions of such leadership, because of intra-regional rivalries, are not always present, however.

Finally, the development of a regional approach entails strengthening knowledge about the regional dimensions of global problems. Such data are often lacking and regional expertise might be very unevenly distributed. In the case of climate change, the IPCC has neglected these dimensions. International initiatives geared to develop targeted research are needed, with the aim of developing regional scientific networks able to interact fruitfully with decision makers.

These potential objections do not fundamental invalidate the benefits of looking seriously into ways of defining a model of complex governance around the notion of "pluralistic universalism" (Acharya 2014). Rather, they should be regarded as challenges to be overcome since the rise of regions reflects both new scholarship around global governance models as well as political trends.

Notes

1 Adopted in 2006, the EU policy came into force in 2007, with its provisions phased in over 11 years. REACH concerns nearly all chemical substances, old and new. Manufacturers and importers are required to gather information on the properties of their chemical substances, which will allow their safe handling, and to register the information in a central and public database managed by the European Chemicals Agency (ECHA).
2 The fallacy of composition means applying and generalizing from one concept designed to address individual behavior to a collective actor. It exists when we apply the sociological concept from the individual to the state in foreign policy analysis; it is compounded by applying it to a group of states or an IGO.
3 Quoted in Thies (2009, 13) who cites Holsti 1970; Walker 1979; and Breuning 1995.
4 The literature usually views role conceptions as encompassing both an actor's own considerations of its place, position, and appropriate behavior vis-à-vis others in a given social environment (cf. Wendt 1999; Harnisch, Frank, and Maull 2011) and the expectations, or role prescriptions, of other actors, as signaled through language and action (cf. Holsti 1970, 238–39; Kirste and Maull 1996). This separation seems only pertinent in case of a conflict between role performance and role expectations by other actors. In that case, role expectations might then subsequently inform national role conceptions (NRCs), through their appropriation by policy makers. Thus it makes greater sense to follow such authors as Bengtsson and Elgström (2011) and Thies (2009) and define NRCs as also encompassing role prescriptions as mediated by national policy makers. Accordingly, I shall use the term "role conception" to cover the actor's own definition of its role as well as its interpretation of other actor's expectations. "Role enactment" will refer to the translation of role conceptions into policy and "role performance" to actual behavior resulting from it.
5 National role conceptions "make [certain] interests and policy options intuitively implausible, categorically exclude them as wrong or unacceptable, or make them unthinkable" (Krotz 2002, 8).
6 Another confusion stems from the dual meaning of enactment in the literature, which can refer either to the institutionalization of a role in an official text (such as the Treaty of Lisbon) or to behavior adopted in fulfillment of the role. The latter will be called role performance, but both refer to implementation.

7 There is, however, a risk of tautology here if we also believe that roles are rooted in identity, although both may be self-reinforcing.
8 "The Community and the Member States are determined to play a leading role in the action required to protect the world's environment and will continue to strive for an effective international response, particularly to such global problems as depletion of the ozone layer, the greenhouse effect and the ever-growing threats to the natural environment…" (European Council, 1988, "Conclusions of the Presidency, Annex 1," Rhodes, December 2–3). See www.europarl.europa.eu/summits/rhodes /default_en.htm?textMode=on.
9 It is indeed striking to see how the articulation of EU's role closely resembles that of middle powers (Canada, Scandinavia).
10 Angela Merkel was Helmut Kohl's environment minister from 1994 to 1998 and helped negotiate the Berlin Mandate and the Kyoto Protocol.
11 Art. 3 and 4 TFUE (Treaty on the Functioning of the European Union).
12 This phenomenon is not unique to the EU. Even in national federations, such as Canada, the issue of exclusive and shared competencies plays out. Conflicts over international environmental policy have been high between Ottawa and provincial governments, for example. The big difference, of course, is that the Commission, as opposed to Canada, is not the only signatory to a treaty.
13 Multilateralism refers to "an institutional form that coordinates relations among three or more states on the basis of generalized principles of conduct" (Ruggie 1993, 11), although the actual contents of the concept (beyond a preference for collective action) may vary. It is a form of cooperation among states and/or nonstate actors that functions according to "principles which specify appropriate conduct for a class of actions, without regard to the particular interests of the parties or the strategic exigencies that may exist in any specific occurrence" (Ruggie 1993, 11; quoted in Wouters et al. 2012, 12).
14 Ferrero-Waldner, Benita. (2004). "The Future of the UN: Results of the Kofi Annan High Level Panel on Threats, Challenges, and Change." December 8, 2004. Brussels. See http://ec.europa.eu/external_relations/news/ferrero/2004/speech04_524_en.htm.
15 Commission of the European Communities. (2003). "The European Union and the United Nations: The Choice of Multilateralism," Communication from the Commission to the Council and the European Parliament, September 10, 2003. Brussels: European Commission, 3.
16 Leadership may be defined as "an asymmetrical relationship of influence in which one actor guides or directs the behavior of others towards a certain goal over a certain period of time" (Underdal 1998, 101).
17 "The ultimate objective of this Convention and any related legal instruments that the Conference of the Parties may adopt is to achieve, in accordance with the relevant provisions of the Convention, stabilization of greenhouse gas concentrations in the atmosphere at a level that would prevent dangerous anthropogenic interference with the climate system" (United Nations Framework Convention on Climate Change).
18 Reacting to these national developments, the European Ministers of Energy and the Environment announced that the European Community as a whole would seek to stabilize its joint carbon dioxide (CO_2) emissions at 1990 levels by the turn of the century, a goal that the EU was able to achieve.
19 It is likely that based on the experience of the Kyoto Protocol, these targets contain also a part of bluff.
20 This may explain different roles played in different issue areas, but it may be less relevant for our purpose since we are only dealing with the environment, unless these factors vary according to the environmental issue in question.
21 As noticed by Ole Elgström (2007b, 952), there is a close relationship between external images, legitimacy, effectiveness, and distinctiveness: "[w]hen the EU tries to lead in multilateral negotiations, it needs followers. The tendency to follow the EU increases if the Union's policies are seen as coherent and consistent and if they are considered legitimate […] Furthermore, an actor that is perceived to be legitimate has to use less

tangible power [and] base its support on normative consent, in line with advocacy [...] to act as a "different," "civilian power."

22 One could point to the difficulty of balancing long-term benefits against short-term costs as an impediment to cooperation, but (i) measures, such as mitigation funds, can be put in place to lower the short-term costs, and (ii) business tends to exaggerate the costs of change; actual dynamics may be different (in the stratospheric ozone case, companies benefited from adopting cleaner technologies; see Le Prestre et al. 1998).

23 The starting point was the discovery in Germany of a diseased forest in the 1980s accompanied by a significant change in German public opinion. Indeed, in 1981–83, this phenomenon triggered citizens' action supported by scientific data and benefiting from favorable press coverage. This prompted the German government to change its position and adopt a national policy to limit sulphur emissions. Germany subsequently pressured neighboring nations to do the same. In order to promote cooperation, Germany did not hesitate to threaten other countries with trade sanctions while providing the technologies that would reduce transborder pollution. At the same time, Sweden was also pushing in the same direction and advocating emission standards in line with those it had already adopted domestically. As a result, the Helsinki Protocol was signed in 1985. From this point on, the regime grew rapidly, leading to the signing and ratification of other agreements.

24 Subsequent to the Copenhagen meeting, UNFCCC insiders were more likely than the media to see the EU as a leader.

25 It may also have been the case of the compliance system of the Kyoto Protocol, which made it more difficult for laggard states to make up for the shortfall in their performance, and reduced the incentives to support a Kyoto Protocol II.

26 Which does not mean that the US fails to abide by the spirit of these agreements, although it may have worked actively to undermine them. The EU could hope that by agreeing to a set of multilateral rules in a given area, the conditions for further deepening and later accession were put in place, that is for a redefinition of the national interest (through demonstration of value, removal of fears—such as economic costs in the case of the Kyoto Protocol—and the build-up of domestic constituencies) even though the particular moment may have been unfavorable. Hence the care in some cases not to adopt rules that would make such future accession more difficult. This, of course, leads to the underdevelopment of the regime as well as implementation difficulties when the US attempts to undermine that very agreement nonetheless.

27 Here we must distinguish between role change and changes in the means to pursue a given role (tactics). The problem may be that means have become identified with ends. In the case of multilateralism, for example, a change in means rather than role conception would involve using forms of multilateralism other than the UN process.

28 See Cantir and Kaarbo 2011. It does not mean that identity does not matter; it is one thing to say that identity variables shape role conceptions, and another to ascribe roles with an identity-building function.

29 Florano (2007), for example, recalls the advantages of approaching problems "the Asian way" as illustrated by ASEAN's treatment of the 1997–98 Borneo forest fires. Avoiding defining the problem as one of identifying a culprit and imposing sanctions, this approach was based on volunteering, the absence of blaming or shaming (at least publicly), and on granting specific aid according to the means of each party. Subsequent improvements have been slow, however; 20 years later, the problem endures.

References

Acharya, A. (2014). "Global International Relations (IR) and Regional Worlds: A New Agenda for International Studies." *International Studies Quarterly* 58: 647–659.

Adger, W. N., et al., eds. (2006). *Fairness in Adaptation to Climate Change.* Cambridge: MIT Press.

Aggestam, L. (2006). "Role Theory and European Foreign Policy: A Framework of Analysis." In *The European Union's Roles in International Politics: Concepts and Analysis*, edited by O. Elgström and M. Smith. London: Routledge, 11–29.

Aykut, S. and A. Dahan. (2014). *Gouverner le climat? Vingt ans de négociations internationales.* Paris: Presses de Sciences Po.

Baker, J. (1989). "Moscow's New Thinking Should Be Tested: Address Before the Center for Strategic and International Studies." Washington, DC: US Information Service. USIS-Eur408; 5/4/89.

Baker, J. (1992). "A Summons to Leadership: Address before the Chicago Council on Foreign Relations." Washington, DC: US Information Service. USIS-Eur204; 4/21/92.

Bengtsson, R. and O. Elgström. (2011). "Conflicting Role Conceptions? The European Union in Global Politics." *Foreign Policy Analysis*: 1–16.

Bretherton, C. and J. Vogler. (1999). *The European Union as a Global Actor.* London & New York: Routledge.

Breuning, M. (1995). "Words and Deeds: Foreign Assistance Rhetoric and Policy Behavior in the Netherlands, Belgium, and the United Kingdom." *International Studies Quarterly* 39: 235–254.

Cantir, C. and J. Kaarbo. (2011). "Contested Roles and Domestic Politics: Reflections on Role Theory in Foreign Policy Analysis and IR Theory." *Foreign Policy Analysis*: 1–20.

Chaban, N., et al. (2013). "Images of the EU beyond its Borders: Issue-Specific and Regional Perceptions of European Union Power and Leadership." *Journal of Common Market Studies* 51 (3): 433–451.

Dahan, A. and S. C. Aykut. (2015). "De Rio 1992 à Rio 2012. Vingt années de négociations climatiques: quel bilan? Quel rôle pour l'Europe? Quels futurs?" Paris, Rapport pour le Centre d'analyse stratégique.

Department of Energy and Climate Change (DECC). (2014). *Article 2 of the United Nations Framework Convention on Climate Change.* London: DECC. Available online at http://unfccc.int/files/essential_background/background_publications_htmlpdf/application/pdf/conveng.pdf.

DeSombre, E. R. (2000). *Domestic Sources of International Environmental Policy: Industry, Environmentalists, and US Power.* Cambridge: MIT Press.

Druckman, D. (1994). "Nationalism, Patriotism, and Group Loyalty: A Social Psychological Perspective." *Mershon International Studies Review* 38 (1): 43–68.

Eagleburger, L. (1992). "Intervention before the CSCE." Stockholm.

Elgström, O. (2007). "Outsiders' Perceptions of the European Union in International Trade Negotiations." *Journal of Common Market Studies* 45 (4): 949–967.

Elgström, O. and J. Skovgaard. (2014). "Previewing Paris 2015: The EU's "Leadiator" Role in Future Climate Change Negotiations." Georgetown Journal of International Affairs Website. Available online at http://journal.georgetown.edu/previewing-paris-2015-the-eus-leadiator-role-in-future-climate-change-negotiations.

Elgström, O. and M. Smith. (2004). *New Roles for the European Union in International Politics: Frameworks for Analysis and Understanding.* ECPR Joint Sessions, University of Uppsala, April 13–18.

Elgström, O. and M. Smith. (2006). *The European Union's Roles in International Politics: Concepts and Analysis.* London: Routledge.

European Council. (1988). "Conclusions of the Presidency, Annex 1," Rhodes, December 2–3. Available online at www.europarl.europa.eu/summits.

Fliegauf, M. T. (2012). "Review of Joseph S Nye, The Future of Power, New York, Public Affairs, 2011." *Cambridge Review of International Affairs* 25 (1): 174–176.

Florano, E. R. (2007). "Regional Environmental Co-operation Without Tears or Fear: The Case of the Asean Regional Haze Action Plan." In *Towards Collective Action on International*

Environmental Governance. Proceedings of the Paris Workshop on International Environmental Governance, March 15–16, 2004, edited by P. Le Prestre and L. Tubiana. Québec & Paris: IHQEDS & IDDRI, 93–114.

Gupta, J. and M. Grubb. (2000). *Climate Change and European Leadership*. Springer Science & Business Media.

Gupta, J. and L. Ringius. (2001). "The EU's Climate Leadership: Reconciling Ambition and Reality." *International Environmental Agreements: Politics, Law and Economics* 1 (2): 281–299.

Harnisch, S. (2012). "Conceptualizing in the Minefield: Role Theory and Foreign Policy Learning." *Foreign Policy Analysis* 8: 47–69.

Harnisch, S., et al., eds. (2011). *Role Theory in International Relations Approaches and Analyses*. Abingdon: Routledge.

Holsti, K. J. (1970). "National Role Conceptions in the Study of Foreign Policy." *International Studies Quarterly* 4: 233–309.

Hovi, J., et al. (2003). "The Persistence of the Kyoto Protocol: Why Other Annex I Countries Move On without the United States." *Global Environmental Politics* 3 (4): 1–23.

Karlsson, C., et al. (2011). "Looking for Leaders: Perceptions of Climate Change Leadership among Climate Change Negotiation Participants." *Global Environmental Policy Sciences* 1: 89–107.

Karlsson, C., et al. (2012). "The Legitimacy of Leadership in International Climate Change Negotiations." *Ambio* 41: 46–55.

Kaya, T. Ö. (2009). "Identifying the EU's Foreign and Security Policy Roles." *Uluslararası Hukuk ve Politika* 5 (17): 107–131.

Kelemen, R. D. (2010). "Globalizing European Union Environmental Policy." *Journal of European Public Policy* 17 (3): 335–349.

Kelemen, R. D. and D. Vogel. (2009). "Trading Places: The Role of the United States and the European Union in International Environmental Politics." *Comparative Political Studies* XX (X): 1–30.

Kirste, K. and H. W. Maull. (1996). "Zivilmacht und Rollentheorie." *Zeitschrift für Internationale Beziehungen* 2: 283–312.

Kissinger, H. (1994). *Diplomacy*. New York: Simon & Schuster.

Krotz, U. (2002). "National Role Conceptions and Foreign Policies: France and Germany Compared." Harvard University, Program for the Study of Germany and Europe, Working Paper vol. 2, no. 1.

Le Prestre, P. G., ed. (1997). *Role Quests in the Post-Cold War Era, Foreign Policies in Transition*. Montreal & Kingston: McGill-Queens University Press.

Le Prestre, P., et al., ed. (1998). *Protecting the Ozone Layer: Lessons, Models and Prospects*. Boston/Dordrecht/London: Kluwer Academic Publishers.

Lucarelli, S. (2014). "Seen from the Outside: The State of the Art on the External Image of the EU." *Journal of European Integration* 36 (1): 1–16.

McCourt, D. (2012). "The Roles States Play: A Meadian Interactionist Approach." *Journal of International Relations and Development* 15 (3): 370–392.

Morgenthau, H. (1954). *Politics among Nations. The Struggle for Power and Peace*. New York: Knopf.

Oberthür, S. and L. Groen. (2014). "EU Performance in the International Climate Negotiations in 2013: Scope for Improvement," Institute for European Studies (IES) Policy Brief, 2014 (1), Brussels, Vrije Universiteit Brussel. Available online at www.ies.be/policy-brief/eu-performance-international-climate-negotiations-2013-scope-improvement.

Orbie, J., ed. (2008). *Europe's Global Role: External Policies of the European Union*. Farnham, UK: Ashgate.

Parker, C. F. and C. Karlsson. (2010). "Climate Change and the European Union's Leadership Moment: An Inconvenient Truth?" *Journal of Common Market Studies* 48: 923–943.

Petiteville, F. (2006). *La Politique internationale de L'union européenne*. Paris: Presses de Sciences Po.

Repetto, R. (1994). *Trade and Sustainable Development*. Geneva: PNUE.

Ringius, L. (1999). "Differentiation, Leaders, and Fairness: Negotiating Climate Commitments in the European Community." *International Negotiation* 4 (2): 133–166.

Ruggie, J. G., ed. (1993). *Multilateralism Matters: The Theory and Praxis of an Institutional Form*. New York: Columbia University Press.

Schreurs, M. A. and Y. Tiberghien. (2007). "Multi-Level Reinforcement: Explaining European Union Leadership in Climate Change Mitigation." *Global Environmental Politics* 7 (4): 19–46.

Schunz, S. (2012). "The EU in the United Nations Climate Change Regime." In *The European Union and Multilateral Governance. Assessing EU Participation in United Nations Human Rights and Environmental Fora*, edited by J. Wouters, et al. Basingstoke, UK: Palgrave Macmillan, 191–213.

Smouts, M.-C. and B. Badie. (1996). "Introduction." *Cultures & Conflits* 21–22: 9–18.

Sprinz, D. and T. Vaahtoranta. (1994). "The Interest-Based Explanation of International Environmental Policy." *International Organization* 481: 77–105.

Stern, S. N. (2006). *The Stern Review on the Economics of Climate Change*. Cambridge: Cambridge University Press.

Stryker, S. and A. Statham. (1985). *Symbolic Interaction and Role Theory. Handbook of Social Psychology*, edited by G. Lindzey and E. Aronson. New York: Random House: 311–378.

Tajfel, H. (1982). "Social Psychology of Intergroup Relations." *Annual Review of Psychology* 33: 1–39.

Thies, C. G. (2009). "Role Theory and Foreign Policy." International Studies Association Compendium Project, Foreign Policy Analysis section. Available online at www.isanet.org/compendium_sections/2007/06/foreign_policy_.html.

Thies, C. G. and M. Breuning. (2012). "Integrating Foreign Policy Analysis and International Relations through Role Theory." *Foreign Policy Analysis* 8 (1): 1–4.

Thomas, D. C. (2011). "Explaining EU Foreign Policy: Normative Institutionalism and Alternative Approaches." In *Making EU Foreign Policy*, edited by D. C. Thomas. Basingstoke, UK, Palgrave Macmillan: 10–28.

Tiberghien, Y. (2013). "Introduction: Minervian Actors and the Paradox of Post-1995 Institution Building." In *Leadership in Global Institution Building: Minerva's Rule*, edited by Y. Tiberghien. London: Palgrave Macmillan, 1–21.

Underdal, A. (1994). "Leadership Theory: Rediscovering the Arts of Management." In *International Multilateral Negotiation: Approaches to the Management of Complexity*, edited by W. I. Zartman. San Francisco: Jossey-Bass Publishers, 178–197.

Underdal, A. (1998). "Leadership in International Environmental Negotiations: Designing Feasible Solutions." In *The Politics of International Environmental Management*, edited by A. Underdal. Dordrecht: Kluwer Academic Publishers, 101–127.

Van Leeuwen, J. and K. Kern. (2013). "The External Dimension of European Union Marine Governance: Institutional Interplay between the EU and the International Maritime Organization." *Global Environmental Politics* 13 (1): 69–87.

Victor, D. G., et al. (2005). "A Madisonian Approach to Climate Policy." *Science* 309 (5742): 1820–1821.

Vogel, D. (1995) *Trading Up*. Cambridge: Harvard University Press.

Vogler, J. (2011). "EU Policy on Global Climate Change: The Negotiation of Burden-Sharing." In *Making EU Foreign Policy: National Preferences, European Norms and Common Policies*, edited by D. C. Thomas. Basingstoke, UK: Palgrave Macmillan: 150–173.

Walker, S. (1979). "National Role Conceptions and Systemic Outcomes." In *Psychological Models in International Politics*, edited by L. S. Falkowski. Boulder, CO: Westview Press.

Walker, S. (1987). "Role Theory and the Origins of Foreign Policy." In *New Directions in the Study of Foreign Policy*, edited by C. F. Hermann, C. W. Kegley Jr., and J. N. Rosenau. Boston: Allen & Unwin: 269–284.

Waltz, K. (1979). *Theory of International Politics*. Chicago: Addison-Wesley.

Wehner, L. E. and C. G. Thies. (2014). "Role Theory, Narratives, and Interpretation: The Domestic Contestation of Roles." *International Studies Review* 16: 411–436.

Wendt, A. (1999). *Social Theory of International Relations*. Cambridge: Cambridge University Press.

Wendt, A. (2003). "Why a World State is Inevitable." *European Journal of International Relations* 9 (4): 491–542.

Wouters, J., *et al.*, eds. (2012). *The European Union and Multilateral Governance: Assessing EU Participation in United Nations Human Rights and Environmental Fora*. Basingstoke, UK: Palgrave Macmillan.

Young, O. (1989). *International Cooperation: Building Regimes for Natural Resources and the Environment*. Ithaca, NY: Cornell University Press.

Zhang, H. (2013). "China and International Climate Change Negotiations." WeltTrends Online-Dossier, http://welttrends.de/res/uploads/Zhang_China-and-International-climate-change-negotiations.pdf.

5

THE POWER OF THE WEAK

Developing countries in the global governance of climate change and biodiversity

Introduction

The received wisdom is that developing countries have largely been "policy takers" rather than policy makers in international environmental negotiations and have struggled to avoid the imposition of an environmental agenda and of policy commitments that, in their view, threatened their economic prospects as well as their national autonomy; and this in the name of solving problems they had not created or the importance of which they deemed secondary to their primary objective of improving human security. In fact, many of the initial fears held by developing countries did not come to pass. Rather, they have successfully resisted obligations they rejected and managed to use the environmental issue to further their political and economic priorities, even though their hopes have sometimes been dashed. But the evolution of the international environmental politics and of the context in which it takes place points to a changing role for developing countries in international environmental governance (IEG).

This chapter first recalls briefly the enduring concerns of developing countries since 1971. The constancy of fears, mistrust, and demands is noteworthy although the evolution in their attitudes has been equally remarkable. It then outlines examples of resistance and influence, in spite of these countries' negotiating weaknesses. A third section looks into the nature and sometimes limits of several strategies for collective influence. The final part then tries to distill some implications of the above for the role that developed countries can play in a complex decentralized environmental governance system. The context of the discussion is international environmental governance (see chapter 2), not the domestic environmental policies of developing countries or the nature and conditions of development.

Enduring concerns

The Souths have expressed their concerns and priorities with remarkable consistency for the last 45 years, ever since the 1971 Founex meeting sketched the contours of a grand bargain.[1] Despite significant evolutions in developing countries' attitudes, the relative importance and the definition of environmental problems, their integration into larger concerns, the principles that should govern their resolution, and the choice of means to address them remain conflictual and addressing the consequences of such choices a major concern.

Until recently, the discourse of developed countries has been essentially reactive and emphasized a number of concerns among which three stand out. Foremost among those concerns is the primacy of development, which often lies at the heart of their attempts to build a nation-state (at least in states created after World War II). Development is considered both an individual (when defined as meeting people's basic needs) and a collective right (in terms of economic growth).[2] The discourse of developing countries is intended to protect states' prerogatives as well as improve the well-being of their population. Thus, the Preamble to the 1986 UN Declaration on the Right to Development maintains that "equality of opportunity for development is a prerogative both of nations and of individuals who make up nations."[3] This, in turn, entails the definition of different environmental priorities.[4]

Forty-five years after Founex, developing countries still fear that the environment might be used as a pretext for questioning the economic goals of development, reduce aid, or raise trade barriers. They denounce the culture of consumerism of industrialized countries that imposes a huge toll on global ecosystems as well as the past exploitation of their natural resources. Environmental protection, therefore, must serve development and growth. Timber exporters, such as Malaysia, have criticized what they deemed a biased discourse that, for example, condemned timber harvesting in tropical forests but ignored boreal forests.[5] Developing countries now recognize the importance of conserving natural resources but insist on the right to development and on the developed countries' responsibility, whether because of their wasteful consumption or their past behavior, to take the lead.

Equally important is the sovereignty principle. The Beijing Declaration, for example, states that "[i]nternational cooperation in the field of environmental protection should be based on the principle of equality among sovereign States." The globalizing ecological discourse, the global change problématique, the proclamation by some of a right of ecological intervention, and the imposition of global rules have led developing countries to reaffirm strongly the right to exploit national resources according to their own national priorities and needs. Controversies over conditionality are but one manifestation of this concern in limiting outside interference. Neo-colonialism is thus invoked to condemn attempts to impose a particular agenda or solutions that reflect Northern concerns or are biased in their favor. One example was the initial opposition to a complete ban of North-South trade in hazardous waste, which Southern countries saw as a form of exploitation (Miller 1995, 97). Similar fears arose following attempts to impose domestic norms on other nations. USAID pesticide policy all but stopped the exportation of such products to developing countries where, despite their toxicity, they were important weapons against pests (Tobin 1996). And a universal ban on such products is to the advantage of companies whose patents have expired.

Finally, the additionality and compensation principles, and later the Principle of Common but Differentiated Responsibility [PCDR] have been core demands ever since Founex. The first two principles mean that additional aid should be granted to developing countries to cover the cost of putting in place environmental measures, and to compensate for lost earnings due to environmental measures adopted in the North that affect the competitiveness of their products. Further, the special circumstances and needs of these countries must be factored into any obligation to which they might subscribe (see infra). This in turn also entails technology transfers.

This question is particularly important, for the capacity of developing countries to fulfill their international obligations often rests on the development or access to new technologies. From the South's viewpoint, this issue becomes more acute as they must accept or adapt to new production norms that render existing technologies obsolete.

During the negotiations of the Montreal Protocol on the ozone layer, India pointed out the irony of a situation in which, having purchased chlorofluorocarbon (CFC) production technology, it was asked to abandon it and acquire new ones in the name of environmental protection, and under threat of seeing its CFC export markets closed. In this context, it and other countries could not but demand new financial resources and guaranteed access to new technologies on preferential terms in order to support the reconversion of their industries. The interests and positions of emerging countries, however, can be at odds with those of poorer countries. The former are more open to policies that rely on market instruments rather than regulations and are all the more favorable to protecting intellectual property rights as their capacity for technological innovation increases.

Although the dominant discourse reflects fundamental constants, it also displays new features. Four major changes have occurred since 1972 and the Stockholm conference. First, developed countries no longer question the legitimacy of putting the environment on the international agenda, the potential impacts of environmental degradation on their development prospects and on human security, or the need to adopt national and collective measures to face them. In addition, there is a sense of urgency, which in the minds of many developing countries' leaders seemed to herald an era where they would be better able to press their concerns, and take an active part in IEG. As pointed out by the minister for the environment from Indonesia in 1990, environmental cooperation and development aid are no longer moved by some sort of altruism, if they ever were. Rather, they reflect one aspect of international relations based on new conceptions of the national interest and on the realization that the fate of all countries is now linked. The weak need to be strengthened lest we all perish together (Shabecoff 1996, 120). For many developing countries, the need for global cooperation for the protection of the global commons means that the Souths are no longer in a role of beggars or policy takers, provided they can develop constructive leadership to that end.

Second, a consensus has been constructed around a definition of the problem based on the notion of sustainable development and its links to poverty, considered both a cause and a consequence of environmental degradation.

Third, the global dimensions of environmental problems have led to the adoption of the PCDR, included in the Montreal Protocol, which has been at the heart of the negotiations on climate change. The adoption and implementation of this principle raised new hopes among developing countries that they could use the collective action problem to their advantage.

Finally, the instrumentalization of the environment has increased. The North has used it to justify drastic fiscal policies,[6] the maintenance of NATO, both protectionism and free trade,[7] changes in the political status of certain groups within states, birth control, structural political reforms, or a right to intervene in the internal affairs of states. The Souths tied it to aid, internal political struggles, or to the extension of the concept of sovereignty.

Resistance and influence

The South as policy taker

We know that developing countries suffer from a series of deep weaknesses in international environmental negotiations, keeping in mind, of course, that they are profoundly different, and that emergent countries possess extensive and significant diplomatic resources and experience. The Souths, as we know, suffer from multiple inequalities which, in turn, have an impact on the dynamics of international environmental governance. Inequalities in economic resources affect the capacity to implement international agreements, encourage the instrumentalization of the environment, and shape definitions of the environmental problem. Inequalities in scientific capabilities may be used to impose a solution, which in turn generates suspicions. The EU, for example, enters the Convention on Biological Diversity (CBD) negotiations with lots of scientific input, whereas representatives from small Latin American countries have no scientific studies on which to call. This increases the reticence of already suspicious Latino delegations to accept knowledge coming from Northern parties. For other countries, such as India, the environment is the domain of uncertainty and a space where various social and economic issues interact, which Western science will reflect. Who controls knowledge and the bases of its legitimacy is therefore important.

Differences in natural capital are also sources of inequalities among developed countries insofar as they affect their negotiating capacity for political recognition, the volume of financial transfers (contrast Madagascar's appeal to that of, say, Mauritania), or alliance formation. States can compete or cooperate according to their amount of natural capital (see, for example, the formation of the group of megadiverse countries within the CBD) and influence the negotiation agenda. Inequalities in political and administrative resources affect the definition of the national interest and the credibility of commitments. Finally, inequalities in diplomatic resources deserve particular attention.

Indeed, the probability of international cooperation and of the national implementation of international agreements will be higher if states: (i) hold a clear idea of their interests relative to the international agenda, (ii) are able to shape the latter, and (iii) are convinced of the legitimacy of the norms that drive the negotiations, and of the equitable character of their outcome. In order to participate meaningfully and effectively in international negotiations, one has to know what those national interests are and be able to articulate and pursue them.

Improving effective participation in international negotiation has been a long-standing concern of the international community.[8] The need to assess clearly the factors limiting developing countries' participation and the initiatives that might help overcome them is particularly acute at a time when traditional negotiation coalitions are fragmenting. These factors include:

- A poor definition of the national interest in light of the country's needs and experience; that is, the absence of a clear articulation between national experience and the international agenda. This means that in many cases, country delegates will lack clear instructions and thus tend to defer to the leader of the negotiating groups (such as the African Group) and repeat current mantras. They will also be inclined to instrumentalize the negotiations in terms of pursuing objectives other than environmental ones.
- Limited or no coordination among national agencies, focal points, and stakeholders, which, again, weakens the development of a negotiation strategy.
- Lack of resources, such as financial constraints, linguistic shortcomings (background documents in other UN official languages are usually available much later than documents in English), human resources shortcomings (in terms of expertise, for example). The poorest countries lack the means to send delegations large enough to be able to attend relevant meetings and participate meaningfully. The size of the delegation typically reflects the amount of external financing that was procured to that end.
- Self-censorship on the part of individual representatives because of a feeling of technical and linguistic inadequacy.
- Dependence on individuals' qualities and resources. It may be surprising to mention it as a limiting factor, but the idea is that lack of coordinated and coherent national policy and interest means that negotiating strategies and positions are more likely to be determined on the basis of the negotiator's personal views. The latter may even be influencing policy at the expense of participation, the democratic process, or policy coherence. The country's impact on the negotiations (within and outside coalitions, which are iterated games) will thus be uneven when individuals change. It also entails an absence of institutional memory.

Resistance and influence: Agenda setting and problem framing

The idea is not to reject developing countries' fears as unfounded. Neither is it to argue that developing countries have largely succeeded in obtaining what they sought and that current negotiations have become negotiations among equals. Rather my aim is only to show that developing countries have not been the victims of international negotiations to the extent it is often believed. Neither should we deny the existence of profound differences among developing countries in their ability to resist pressures and influence the international environmental agenda. There are clear differences and one could even argue that environmental politics have increased inequalities among Southern countries. It is also clear that the influence of the Least Developed Countries (LDCs) is minimal unless they are in a coalition with emerging powers or parts of the North (such as the EU).

True, most international environmental negotiations have been initiated by the North which has largely controlled the agenda. There are few exceptions, such as the Desertification Convention, which has remained the neglected child of Rio 1992. Agenda control includes the power to impose issues that the North wants discussed (such as the thinning of the ozone layer) as well as the power to prevent questions from being debated (such as the responsibility of wealthy countries and firms in the emergence of global problems).[9] Both the North and the South have been able to do so, however.

As mentioned previously, developing countries were able to redefine the environment problem into one rooted in poverty and of making development sustainable, an evolution symbolized by the transformation of large UN environmental conferences into sustainable development conferences. Beyond the link to development, the Souths have often managed to amend the agenda. In the case of the CBD, they broadened the objectives of the Convention to include sustainable development and benefit sharing, sovereignty over genetic resources, and technology transfers (which led to its rejection by the US). And they succeeded in placing adaptation at the heart of the Conference of Parties (COP-21) agreement on climate change, when it was barely mentioned in the Convention and largely overlooked in the early reports of the Intergovernmental Panel on Climate Change (IPCC). Control of the agenda is also tied to the control of information. The Souths often denounce the type of indicators used by the North in the context of the definition of global problems. For many Southern observers, the interpretation of data is contextual, influenced by politics and by the beliefs of the actors that perform it.

The redefinition of environmental protection as a sustainable development issue, adopted even by the United Nations Environment Programme (UNEP), leads to a fracture between sustainable development and the environment. Making sustainable development a priority entails emphasizing local development concerns at the expense of transnational environmental issues or the management of the global commons, (re)distributive considerations, and poverty reduction. This is one of the great hidden tensions of global ecopolitics. It reflects less a lack of concern for the environment than an agenda dominated by the concerns of developing countries, centered on the provision of goods and services, such as access to water, sustainable agriculture, or water- and sewerage-treatment facilities.

Resistance and influence: Principles

The second example worth mentioning pertains to principles. Issues never die. It would be naïve to believe that once embedded in a regime, norms and principles are widely accepted or do not evolve. This is so, first, because international declarations that embody them are additions rather than syntheses or compromises over the contents of norms and principles held dear by various groupings. Second, political battles do not end with the signing of a regime. States and other stakeholders attempt to shape the interpretation, operationalization, and implementation of the norms and principles it contains in order to further their interests and promote their concerns. Third, in an evolving political, scientific, technological, and cultural context, principles and norms have to be adaptive in order to respond to an evolving scientific, social, and political context.

Many of the principles advanced by the Souths have been adopted. While some are not questioned, such as the additionality principle (even though practice may be far below expectations),[10] many measures have been adopted in accordance with this principle. The creation of the Global Environment Facility (GEF) stands out in that regard. But other principles have been under sustained attack and their defense has become a key item of current negotiations, particularly in climate change. Consider two examples: sovereignty and the PCDR.

Although the sovereignty principle itself has never been in question, its scope and exercise are subject to intense conflicts.[11] All in all, international efforts aiming at protecting the environment have both limited and strengthened the concept of sovereignty. On the one hand, ever since the Trail Smelter case in the 1930s, the received wisdom has been that effective international environmental protection must entail a certain dilution of the strict interpretation of the concept of sovereignty.[12] Indeed, sovereignty, in the 1970s and 1980s, was thought to be one of the main obstacles to effective international environmental governance. The possible extension to genetic biodiversity of the concept of Common Heritage of Mankind first included in the Law of the Sea, the articulation of the notion of "ecocide" that would justify intervention in internal affairs, the extensive broadening of conditionality clauses in project lending, and the principle of not causing harm to neighbors appeared to question the very legitimacy of the concept.[13]

Yet global ecopolitics also offers a striking example of efforts by the Souths to assert sovereignty more effectively and even expand it. This trend took on four aspects: (i) the reaffirmation of the sacrosanct character of national sovereignty and of the right to develop natural resources on the sole basis of national priorities; (ii) the willingness of certain states to make this sovereignty effective by controlling the entirety of their territory; (iii) the extension of the geographic boundaries of territorial sovereignty to the oceans and space; and (iv) a broadening of the scope of sovereignty, for example, to genetic materials.

The PCDR is another principle that has been both key to international environmental cooperation and increasingly questioned along the way. Adopted as part of the Montreal Protocol and later included in the United Nations Framework

Convention on Climate Change (UNFCCC), the PCDR was the result of a bargain between the Souths and the Norths where (i) the Souths recognized that they and the Norths shared a common stake in addressing environmental problems and (ii) the Norths accepted that the obligations this recognition may entail could not be the same due to different historical responsibility, the current level of inequalities, and the development priorities of the Souths. It is a principle of international public policy that largely explains the massive ratification of the UNFCCC but also the tensions of the COP-21 agreement. It has also faced growing opposition.

Indeed, absent a common conception of equity, the PCDR has not solved political conflicts but created new ones over the relevant norms of equity. Questions of legitimacy and equity also arise when developed countries do not meet their commitments to increase financial and technological transfers. It has also been beset with conceptual uncertainties: responsibility for what? For causing the problem (past and present responsibility)? In addressing the sources of climate change? In addressing their impact?

Conflicts also occur around its implementation. There are political difficulties in calculating differentiated responsibilities. Why should emergent economies, wealthy oil-producing states, or rich trading states such as Singapore invoke this principle as much as the Least Advanced Countries? In addition, there are difficulties in maintaining a strict North/South dichotomy given changes in the evolution of environmental issues, such as the distribution of GHG emissions. It can be argued that rejecting any commitment to reduce emissions in the name of the PCDR has become both unfair and illegitimate in light of the evolution of scientific knowledge regarding, for example, the nature of the atmosphere (a finite resource) or the existence of planetary boundaries (see chapter 1).

Moreover, critics have charged that it had become counterproductive and an excuse for doing nothing (although one should distinguish between rejecting new binding international commitments, and domestic policy inertia). By creating categories of countries subject to different obligations, it created vested interests in the status quo. In the Copenhagen (2009) climate negotiations, emerging countries refused to constitute an intermediary category or to join Annex 1 countries (those countries subject to emission reductions), whereas the US wished to divide Non-Annex 1 countries and proposed that those contributing above a certain percentage of global emissions should join Annex 1 countries. One of the great achievements of the process leading to the conclusion of the 2015 COP-21 agreement on climate change was precisely the willingness of developing countries to recognize that they should make efforts to reduce their greenhouse gas (GHG) emissions as well.

Finally, it creates perverse incentives such as complicating technological transfers. The PCDR entails concessions toward emerging countries in terms of GHG emissions. But as the development of clean technologies is taking place mostly in Northern countries, the conditions of their transfer generate new disputes when the recipient countries reject any emission reduction obligations.

Resistance to these criticisms has taken several forms: appeals to equity, strict opposition to its questioning, and attempts to suggest ways its implementation might be amended. But the main form of resistance has been to use a moral argument. The PCDR is seen as an equity principle by the Souths, based not just on the level of development or wealth (as many developed countries would see it) but also on past responsibility for the problem and on the structure of international economic relations.

Splits within the Souths have arisen on this matter. On the one hand, many developing countries (such as China, Brazil, and Nicaragua) have reaffirmed the importance of the principle in the run-up to COP-21. On the other hand, an increasing number of Southern countries such as the members of the Association of Small Island States (AOSIS) and the Asociación Independiente de América Latina y el Caribe (AILAC) have explicitly called for abandoning the strict and rigid interpretation promoted by emerging countries. *De facto*, its operational contents have become negotiable, with individual commitments taking a variety of forms (e.g. industrial emission reduction, Reducing Emissions from Deforestation and Forest Degradation (REDD+), energy-intensity reduction, energy savings, the end of perverse subsidies, etc.).[14] The UNFCCC COP-21 agreement reaffirms the PCDR and imposes stricter obligations ("shall") on the Norths than on the Souths ("should").[15] But the price of saving the PCDR, in a somewhat diluted form (actions should "reflect" the principle), has been the universality of commitments through periodic review of Intended Nationally Determined Contributions (INDCs) that in effect amounts to a redefinition of equity or of the contents of responsibility. Principles advanced by developing countries have been useful, but they should be approached as tools rather than absolute norms. Their operationalization, meaning, and usefulness depend on the context of their application and on their impact. Still present in the COP-21 agreement, the PCDR clearly is being redefined.

Resistance and influence: Financing and programs

Southern countries have also been able to obtain the creation of new funds and programs in order to further their environmental and development priorities. As in other areas, these financial achievements are mixed. On the one hand, a great deal of the national budgets going to environmental protection measures in developing countries comes from the North (for administration, parks, training, or to fund the environmental components of development projects). Conventions and environmental intergovernmental organizations (IGOs) are largely funded by Northern countries. The volume of financial transfers has increased considerably. Funds have multiplied.

On the other hand, calculating the evolution of such transfers is difficult. There have been instances of a reallocation of funds from traditional aid to the environment, and many funds remain grossly underfunded. Furthermore, budgetary constraints have led Northern countries to emphasize stable convention and IGO budgets, cost accounting of decisions made by COPs, and the need for wealthier developing countries to raise their contributions.

An illustrative example of using the global agenda to further national objectives is found in REDD+, which can be seen as an avatar of the compensation principle. It followed earlier proposals for example by Malaysia, asking for compensation for the opportunity costs of not exploiting its tropical forests. Climate change provided a new and forceful opportunity to advance that claim. In 2005, the coalition of Rainforest Nations, represented by Papua New Guinea and Costa Rica, proposed the adoption of a market mechanism called "Reducing emissions from deforestation and forest degradation" (REDD) as a means of mitigating climate change by reducing net emissions of GHG through enhanced forest management in developing countries and trading them on the carbon market, thus complementing the existing Clean Development Mechanism. A consensus was finally found at UNFCCC COP-16 in 2010, after Brazil had changed its stand at COP-15 and no longer opposed the use of carbon markets to finance what then had become REDD+ (Akanle et al. 2010). Why, in general, were the Souths able to play such a significant role in shaping international environmental governance? Several distinct strategies were used to that end.

Strategies and the new conditions for collective influence

Unity and its limits

Historically, unity has been most important in furthering the respective concerns of the advanced and least developed countries through the grand bargain of the new international economic order (NIEO) of the 1970s and early 1980s (access to markets and reform of international institutions, on the one hand, and stable terms of trade and aid transfers on the other). Unity, today, is probably more important for the LDCs than for emerging countries, which places the former at a certain disadvantage since the latter's environmental priorities may differ.

The South in international environmental negotiations is highly fragmented, although the Group of 77 (G77) and China still provides a baseline for a common position and a forum where divergences are discussed. Interests differ considerably, as the location of these countries in the international economy, their vulnerability to environmental change, and their political circumstances evolve. The Souths, for example, have different approaches to intellectual property rights on living material, biotechnology, and agricultural trade (see Rosendal 2001).

The existence of centrifugal forces does not, by itself, imply less influence; only that the sources of influence change. Influence will emanate from smaller coalitions rather than from overall unity, with the G77 and China acting more as a coordinating mechanism. But it does raise the issue of the ability of the poorest or more vulnerable countries to express and pursue their interests when they differ from those of the more powerful. They then have to rely on different strategies to pursue them.

In the absence of Southern solidarity, the poorest countries have indeed a limited margin of maneuver when they are only in a position of claimant and when their concerns are not widely shared. For example, during the negotiations of the Convention to Combat Desertification (CCD), African countries attempted vainly to introduce issues pertaining to land productivity, the living conditions of local populations, food and energy security, employment, and financial transfers. Although the CCD is a sustainable development convention, it initially left aside socioeconomic issues in order to concentrate on desertification and drought, rather than poverty and growth (Chasek 1997).

Regarding climate change, the evolution of the dynamics within the G77 and between the latter and the North is illustrated by the emergence of Brazil, South Africa, India, China (BASIC) and AOSIS. In the CBD, one could point to the creation of the group of like-minded megadiverse countries. BASIC has typically opposed AOSIS proposals, with the G77 and China siding with BASIC.[16] In practice, the Organization of the Petroleum Exporting Countries' (OPEC) position is only supported insofar as it corresponds to the BASIC position. Because of a lack of support by the other G77 and China members, AOSIS has had difficulties achieving its goals (although see below). At the UNFCCC COP-21, however, several of its core demands have found their way into the Agreement in one form or another. We shall return to these groupings later.

South-South cooperation (SSC)[17]

In recent years, SSC has benefited from collaborative actions on issues related to climate change. For example, cooperation in the South Asia region is gradually deepening to include exchanges of information, expertise, and lessons. Such cooperation yielded results when the South Asia region came together to negotiate issues during UNFCCC COP-20 (Lima 2014).[18]

This, to be sure, is far from new. Such cooperation has been taking place in different forms and at different depths for a while. But it is taking on new dimensions under the leadership of China. It concerns not only trade, but also scientific and technical cooperation, financial loans, and development aid (China and Brazil), experiences in designing and implementing policy, technology transfer, technical and institutional capacity building, and access to data. The share of South-South exchanges in global trade doubled from 2002 to 2008.[19] Chinese banks loaned more to Latin American governments in 2005–11 than did either the World Bank or the Inter-American Development Bank (IDB), and they made infrastructure and industry loans to the global financial system's pariah states like Venezuela and Argentina, while other states financed the rule followers (Gallagher *et al.* 2012).

In July 2014, under Chinese leadership, as a counterpoint to the International Monetary Fund (IMF) and the World Bank Group, Brazil, Russia, India, China, and South Africa (BRICS) established the New Development Bank in Shanghai in order to foster greater financial and development cooperation among the five emerging markets. And in October 2014, 22 Asian countries, still under China's leadership, signed a Memorandum of Understanding (MOU) to establish the Asian infrastructure investment bank (AIIB). By July 2016, 57 countries (including 16

European countries) had signed its Articles of Agreement. Finally, in September 2015, China announced the establishment of an RMB20 billion ($3.1 billion) South-South Climate Cooperation Fund to help developing countries fight climate change.

These developments have the potential to make South-South cooperation a key element of the regional and global response to climate change and other environmental challenges. They also change the mechanisms and the details of the North-Souths relationship in ways likely to matter to local communities, local environments, and local conditions of resistance. Chinese loans, for example, do not come with the policy conditionalities imposed by international financial institutions and Western lenders. This, in turn, means a weakening of the linkage strategy used by the North to gain support for its environmental agenda, such as calls for internal reforms in terms of the adoption of national action plans or the promotion of certain norms (participation, gender equality, and "good" governance).

Linkages

Linkage is about changing the power balance. It depends on creating the belief on the part of other states, such as the North, that the participation of developing countries in the negotiated regime is necessary to combat an environmental problem (for example, by defining a given problem as a collective action problem), thereby allowing the latter to push for differentiation in norms and responsibilities and for side payments. Such was the case for the Montreal Protocol on stratospheric ozone followed, three years later, by the London agreement that created the ozone fund.

Linkages and grand bargains are at the heart of environmental negotiations. The Law of the Sea was based on balancing the recognition of the maritime rights of the great powers by the South, with the sharing in the benefits derived from the exploitation of the deep seabed by the North. This model was later picked up in other forums such as the UNFCCC and the CBD. It generally takes the form of linking agreement on a given question dear to one group to progress on another question that matters more to another group (for example, an agreement on forests linked to debt alleviation, access to genetic resources linked to benefit sharing from their use, or a CFC production ban in developing countries predicated on the establishment of an Ozone Fund to help developing countries' industry adapt). During negotiations, it is generally embodied in the saying that "nothing is agreed until everything is agreed."

At the CBD COP-10, for example, African countries explicitly conditioned the adoption of the Intergovernmental Platform on Biodiversity and Ecosystems Services (IPBES), which was being negotiated in another forum, a new strategic plan for the CBD, and the positive outcome to the negotiations on the Nagoya Protocol on Access and Benefit Sharing, to the mobilization of new sources of financing (Coolsaet and Pitseys 2015). Indeed, developing countries have long fought the tendency to pile up new obligations without new financial resources to carry them out. Efforts to overcome this situation have led to the adoption of innovative instruments, such as tri-partnerships, debt for nature swaps, the Clean Development Mechanism, and REDD under the Kyoto Protocol, or payments for ecosystem services. Moreover, the GEF has become an important source of financing for projects with global dimensions, and the financial instrument of an ever-increasing number of Multilateral Environmental Agreements (MEAs).

Moralism (equity, justice)

A strong aspect of the political game (between and within negotiating coalitions) has focused on framing environmental issues in moral terms and imposing one's conception of equity. In the context of the distribution of GHG emission rights, for example, it ranged from insisting on historical responsibilities (the meaning contained in the Kyoto Protocol) to the relative contributions to future climate change given the current definition of the problem (the atmosphere as a common good) and the evolving distribution of GHG emissions (such as the rise from China), through per capita emissions (see chapter 1).

The Souths have openly used equity and moral considerations to pressure the North. At COP-21, India talked about the need to grow, about survival emissions, and about the preemption of the ecological space by the North.[20] As India's Prime Minister put it eloquently:

> And climate justice demands that, with the little carbon space we still have, developing countries should have enough room to grow... The principles of equity and common but differentiated responsibilities must remain the bedrock of our collective enterprise across all areas – mitigation, adaptation and means for implementation. Anything else would be morally wrong... Equity means that national commitments must be consistent with the carbon space nations occupy.[21]

The increases in world trade and the relocation of firms, as well as the growth of the services sector in the economies of the North, coupled with the growth of the industrial sector in the South, exacerbate this aspect since it amounts to exporting pollution. Western virtue comes cheap. China has argued that its emissions should be reduced by 25 percent to account for this dimension. Moral considerations also underlie discussions around Loss and Damages due to the impacts of climate change. Finally, moral arguments are the basis of the AOSIS position on climate change.

Strictly environmental and economic reasoning clashes with this equity viewpoint, as evidenced by the polemics around consumption vs. survival emissions. And it is also on the basis of the equity principle that Agarwal and Narain (1991) condemn any allocation of emission rights that are based on criteria other than population (such as past emissions or the level of economic activity), which benefits the biggest polluters.

This attitude is not limited to governments. Southern nongovernmental organizations (NGOs) are not ready to cede to Northern NGOs a monopoly of virtue, when the latter are prompt to believe that their norms, values, and interests are shared by their Southern counterparts. They will criticize the hypocrisy of the latter that condemn Southern practices without questioning the policies of the North. Why do Northern NGOs oppose tropical deforestation in the name of the greenhouse effect instead of campaigning for higher gas prices?

While some of these arguments still hold water, the moral debate is no longer taboo. Although for a long time they refrained from directly questioning them, with the rise in emissions of the BASIC, developed countries can argue that now that we know about the effect of GHG emissions and that some emitters have either become (China) or will become (India) the largest emitters, these countries have a moral responsibility to limit their emissions and thus their impacts on the rest of the globe, as well as support the adaptation of the poorest and most vulnerable countries.[22] Some question the notion that Northern emissions are primarily consumption based, whereas emissions in the South would be survival emissions (e.g. Bompard and Godard 2015). Still others will condemn the sovereign claim to adopt policies or accept situations that encourage biodiversity loss. Moral arguments have been powerful frames and have probably played a large role in mobilizing NGOs which are particularly sensitive to them and use these arguments to mobilize public opinion in the North. But they are increasingly double-edged swords when used by actors that actually have options and can be made accountable.

Alliances

The power of developing countries also stemmed from their capacity to strike alliances not only among themselves but with a variety of actors. Suffice it to evoke the cases of AOSIS, Africa and BASIC for climate change, keeping in mind, that other alliances and groupings exist based on a variety of criteria, such as the like-minded megadiverse countries for the CBD.

Founded in 1990, AOSIS includes 44 members. It has been active in major environmental negotiations forums but particularly at the UNFCCC. Tuvalu has been at the forefront of the Group, portraying itself as the emblematic representative of vulnerable states. On the one hand, the discourse of AOSIS strengthens the pressure the G77 and China puts on the North for decisive action and financial and technical support for adaptation. On the other hand, AOSIS has broken with the G77 and China in asking for a universal commitment to mitigation and for an ambitious 1.5-degree warming target (Betzold et al. 2012, 594). Since the Johannesburg Summit of 2002, AOSIS has been remarkably successful in having its particular concerns and interests recognized in international agreements (see infra).[23] At COP-21, AOSIS obtained mention of the 1.5-degree target, as well as a separate section on Adaptation and Loss and Damages in the Paris Accord.

The African group has also been increasingly vocal. The activism of the group has served to compensate for the negotiating weaknesses of individual countries. In the case of the Nagoya Protocol, it was influential in getting its concerns across. Pooling resources has proven a challenge though. The Francophonie has done a lot in disseminating information and fostering dialogue among francophone countries, but many weaknesses remain (such as a failure to think about national interests anew, and the limited coordination with English-speaking countries). Further, the African group has tended to be dominated by individuals, lead negotiators who did not always share the notion of participation and transparency that this position requires. Finally, the investment of the African group varies across issues; they have concentrated on negotiations that are of a direct concern to them (such as the Nagoya Protocol) at the expense of others, which may overstate their overall influence (Coolsaet and Pitseys 2015). Nevertheless, Africa came out of COP-21 satisfied with the treatment of adaptation, the scope of the agreement, and references to the PCDR, Loss and Damages, the $100 billion as a floor for financial transfers, and technological transfer.

Finally, the rise of BASIC has shaken up negotiation practices. BASIC emerged plainly during the final stages of negotiations at COP-15, when the group struck a deal with the US that led to the Copenhagen Accord which reflected their will to act domestically as well as their reticence to accept international commitments. The same countries and the same measures (a bottom-up approach and national periodic communications), have lain the foundation of the COP-21 agreement.

It is a sign of how far we have come that BASIC, which was perceived as an obstacle to an ambitious accord in Copenhagen, has been considered a leader in the success of COP-21 where, as in Cancun in 2010 and Durban in 2011, they asserted their will to act together and with the international community. This importance is illustrated by the decision of French Foreign Minister Laurent Fabius to end his pre-COP-21 worldwide tour of capitals with visits to India, South Africa and Brazil, after earlier visits to China. This came in addition to the deal that China and the US had struck earlier and which largely framed the COP-21 agreement. This suggests: (i) that the fragmentation of the South into Souths may not entail a weakening of influence, and (ii) the emergence of a movement toward concert or club-based governance depending on the issues.

A universal model as embodied by the UN process is not always necessary. All collective action problems (and many environmental problems are not) do not require that all actors participate and be part of the solutions; only those that have the potential of furthering or preventing the achievement of the collective interest. In the security field, cooperation is more likely to occur when there is a concert among the great powers in a given issue area (see Drezner 2007), which may then be institutionalized in groups of like-minded states or in IGOs. When interests diverge and prevent the formation of a concert or threaten institutional deadlock, then club groups emerge.[24]

The greater role played by BASIC, the G20, and various other transcontinental groupings does not represent the progressive integration of developing countries into the existing international architecture of environmental governance but a new kind of governance. Issues related to the legitimacy of such arrangements, arising, for example, from the exclusion from all discussions (ranging from the definition of the problem to implementation and the evaluation of the outcomes) of those actors likely to be seriously affected by environmental change (such as, global warming) or by the solutions adopted at the local or regional level, can be addressed at the domestic level of both concert and nonconcert states through the enhancement of electoral and administrative accountability (elected governments, delegation of authority, and parliamentary oversight) as well as through other sources of accountability, such as the development of a public sphere (of which NGOs are but one aspect), professional norms and networks, or markets (see Keohane and Nye, 2000 for a discussion of these instruments).[25]

Mobilizing expertise and NGOs

Scientific and diplomatic inequalities beset the G77 and China. One effective strategy that least developed (such as most members of AOSIS) and smaller countries (such as Panama) have used successfully has been the mobilization of external expertise. AOSIS has relied on the legal advice and substantive input from the Foundation for International Environmental Law and Development (FIELD), which has prepared draft AOSIS submissions and acted as the delegation of some AOSIS members in climate change and biodiversity negotiations. AOSIS thus was able to define its interests as distinct from those of the G77, based on common vulnerability and innocence, putting pressure both on emergent and Northern countries. As a result, it became a potent negotiation force, representing what Zartman and Rubin (2000) have called a "structural paradox." This was seen in its influence on the agenda in the inclusion of special clauses for the small island developing states in certain agreements, such as the 2002 Johannesburg Declaration, and in its achievements at the UNFCCC COP-21.

The case of Panama and climate change shows that a small country, despite its diplomatic limitations, can play a catalytic and leading role. Desirous to be more active in international negotiations but wary of being instrumentalized by NGOs, Panama, which in the past had largely adopted a passive role in the CBD, in the early 2000s, successfully used a network of foreign academics to support a more active role in the negotiations and, at times, represent it. It was able to make submissions, enlist Central American countries, then several Latin American countries, and subsequently display diplomatic and intellectual leadership on key points regarding REDD, with Northern experts effectively acting as go-between between Panama and Northern delegations. Panama is now a pillar of AILAC, which has adopted positions more flexible than those of the G77 and China on certain issues (such as the PCDR).

More common have been alliances with NGOs and epistemic communities. Although suspicions abound, both NGOs and developing countries have found it in their interest to promote a common moral message. This alliance concerned access to information (for LDCs) or, more often, the enlistment of NGOs in public diplomacy. For example, by exaggerating the volume of hazardous waste exported to the Souths, and using television to document that trade, importing countries were able to exercise significant pressure on exporting industrialized countries in favor of a strict control of such transboundary movements. Through their alliance with domestic NGOs that relayed their discourse and preferences, they succeeded in promoting a more comprehensive regime.

The effectiveness of NGO support during negotiations, however, is more mixed. First, because the interests of NGOs and developing countries do not always coincide. Second, because that support is erratic. In the case of the Nagoya Protocol, while delegate capacity may have increased through active engagement with pre-Nagoya epistemic communities, the support provided by NGOs during the final negotiations may not have been regular and steady enough to guarantee effective strengthening of African capacity during the negotiations, which mirrors a situation found at the national level as well. This shows that creating epistemic communities, capacity-building platforms, and/or NGO networks is not sufficient to equalize the background conditions between the parties. Although they may reinforce capacity, research shows that these networks often fail to fully address knowledge gaps and diverging priorities between powerful and weaker actors. Transforming information resources available in civil society networks into effective negotiation strategies requires possessing a range of social resources, technical expertise, and logistics that African delegations did not hold individually. Moreover, rivalry between NGOs and scientists can also play to the detriment of developing countries, with the former trying to shut out access to non-NGO expertise. The field of Norths-Souths environmental relations is littered with the remnants of overblown expectations. One example has been benefit sharing in the context of the CBD. Another example has been the Yasuni initiative.

Transforming weakness into power: The fate of Ecuador's Yasuni initiative

On various occasions, developing countries have attempted to transform the value Western societies place on their resources into bargaining chips. In 2007, President Rafael Correa of Ecuador attempted to use this strategy most explicitly by tying the nonexploitation of the oil fields within the Yasuni National Park (a UNESCO Biosphere preserve since 1989) to the provision of around $3.6 billion over 13 years, which would compensate for 50 percent of the opportunity costs of not exploiting this field, prevent the emission of an estimated 400 million tons of CO_2, and reduce the threats to the rich biodiversity of the area. These revenues would then be invested in renewable energy and social development projects.[26] In 2010, UNDP set up a trust fund to receive international contributions.

Justified both on climate change and biodiversity grounds, this scheme could also be presented as an interpretation of the principle of compensation. It echoed earlier claims made regarding the protection of tropical forests, for example by Malaysia.[27] Yet on August 15, 2013, President Correa announced that the oil fields of Ishpingo, Tambococha, and Tiputini ("ITT") and their estimated 900 million barrels of oil, 20 percent of Ecuador's reserves, would be open to exploitation as a result of the failure of this strategy.

Why did it fail? At first glance, this project resembles REDD+. Yet it has been criticized on effectiveness, credibility, and logical grounds. In the first instance, for reasons of cost, it could not be replicated widely. Second, the credibility of the scheme was put into question since Ecuador, through this very initiative, announced that it was ready to violate its own laws. Indeed, the target zone lay inside a national park that later became a world heritage site. Furthermore, Ecuador's law grants Indians the right to reject the development of these lands. In this context, how could one be sure that the government would not change its mind again at some point? Third, in effect, it asked for guaranteed revenues based on the fixed price of the resource (whereas the price of a barrel of oil fluctuates), while keeping future exploitation options open. In addition, framing the issue in terms of CO_2 emissions mitigation (rather than biodiversity protection), although it appeared more politically potent and the UNDP used it to justify its involvement, led to a quandary: either pressures to exploit the resource will become insurmountable if world reserves dwindle and demand grows or the world decarbonizes. If so, why would one pay for keeping a resource rather than exploit it when cheaper (by definition) alternatives exist and this resource is subjected to little pressure? (On all these points, see Pirard and Billé 2012).

In practice, despite pledges amounting to US$116 million, by August 2013 the funds had received only $13 million (Ibid.), and President Correa insisted that Ecuador alone would decide how the donations would be spent, despite early arrangements. In the meantime, the state-owned oil company, Petroamazonas, continued to lay the groundwork for the exploitation of the area through the construction of access roads.[28] And as elsewhere, local populations want access to health and education. If the official discourse is convincing enough that oil exploitation could be done without too much harm to the environment, then they will support it. This often puts local communities at odds with international NGOs. Finally, the perception that it was blackmail (and a bad precedent) rather than compensation for opportunity costs impeded a strong endorsement by international actors.

The Souths as policy makers: Moving toward proactive strategies

Since the dawn of international environmental governance in the 1970s, the nature of the involvement of the South has profoundly changed. It has achieved many of its objectives in resisting pressures, redefining the agenda, and using the environment to further its development goals. The environment has largely led to new financial transfers, although there is significant donor fatigue and new financial instruments are needed, with the Yasuni initiative proving another false good idea. The South is now deeply fragmented, with power distribution varying across issue areas, but (i) such fragmentation does not necessarily entail a weakening in the bargaining power of specific coalitions composed of states, other actors, and networks, and (ii) that countries belong to overlapping groupings (e.g. G77 and China, Africa Group + Arab Group, megadiverse countries, etc.) may also promote coordination.

Clearly, international dynamics are becoming less North–South; rather they tend to pit coalitions composed of states from the North and the South supported by transnational links and networks (e.g. cities, business, various NGOs). Endowments in natural capital may create common interests,[29] and the nature of problems and the interests they define lead to a variety of alliances between the Norths and the Souths. Finally, several emerging countries are ready to take the lead, not simply by opposing Northern initiatives as before, but also by strengthening South–South cooperation. For example, we could witness a division of labor, with intellectual leadership coming from India and Brazil and financial leadership from China (although the latter is also investing heavily in scientific research).

Traditionally, the attitude of developing countries has been either to dispute the goals of environmental protection or, when their adoption was inevitable, to seek exemptions to the obligations that the North sought to impose. This attitude has long been denounced as short-sighted by critics who before 1992 saw in it the source of a lack of influence (for example, Banuri 1993). It prevented them from trying to redefine the problem and its solutions from their own perspective or from developing innovative national solutions to these problems. Clearly, not only have developing countries been able to resist and sometimes use the environment to further their goals, but this attitude has now changed in line with the evolution of power distributions, the existence of a network of institutions, and the dissemination of knowledge and norms. Some developing countries can act as policy makers in their own right, having moved from a role of blockers to that of leaders. But we probably need new theoretical tools and new approaches to explain the role of informal groups or individual countries from the South, including their roles as leaders in some negotiation items and in new funding initiatives under Chinese leadership.

Conclusion: The contours of new North-South power relationships in a decentralized governance system

For a long time, the North and the Souths have tended to see each other as much more united and rational than they were. It appears that the only forces that now keep the Souths together are (i) a lingering mistrust of the North, (ii) the hope of benefiting from linkage strategies, and (iii) the institutionalization of the North–South divide in past agreements. The question now is to what extent are the Souths' achievements and failures, their characteristics and evolving roles, as well as the changing context of environmental diplomacy, both ushering in and making more indispensable a new decentralized environmental diplomacy.

For developing countries to take part and contribute to the development of an effective decentralized governance system, four interrelated conditions must be met: (i) a change in self-image and images of the other actors, (ii) strengthening scientific and diplomatic capacities, (iii) adopting national policies, and (iv) promoting a regional approach.

The question of image has a dual aspect. First, developing countries must realize they are not powerless either individually (even when they are small) or as a group.

Second, images of a North-South split remain (together with deep suspicions toward the North) even though the picture has become far more complex. This "North-South picture still prevails in the minds of people (like representatives of NGOs and developing countries), even though the issue specific power of the South has changed over the last decades" (Batta Bjørnstad 2004).

Secondly, to be policy makers, the Souths cannot depend only on a few of them leading on certain issues, on public relation campaigns, or on shaming by defining all issues in terms of justice. One important key to influence lies in a greater intellectual engagement in environmental matters. Brazil, for example, has used scientific arguments during the Kyoto Protocol negotiations in order to advance the concept of the historical responsibility of developed countries.

A strategy of education and norm diffusion is important in framing the problem and in ensuring that all parties play the same game (that is, that they share similar norm hierarchies). As the science-policy interface is moving toward a co-construction model (see chapter 3), the development of national and regional capabilities should help give it concrete form. This development can take place through the creation of networks of research institutes and think tanks able to counteract the influence of Anglo-Saxon organizations that dominate the definition of problems, the identification of solutions, and the generation of policy concepts. Too many countries are "takers" of technical and research assistance (i.e. supply-driven rather than demand-driven information) and are thus hostage to providers (IGOs, NGOs, other governments) or are given advice on what interests the North (implementation, specific agenda items).

Further, the need to assess clearly the factors limiting developing countries' participation and the initiatives that might help overcome them is particularly acute at a time when traditional negotiation coalitions are fragmenting. Effective international negotiation begins at home. The cases of Panama, Mauritius, Costa Rica, or Tuvalu show that even small countries can have an impact. Solutions to these problems lie in part in developing reputation and moral leadership (Costa Rica in biodiversity, Panama in REDD), in coalition formation (AOSIS), in alliances with external expertise (Panama on REDD) or NGOs (Tuvalu and FIELD), and in specialization (Ethiopia and the Cartagena Protocol) in addition to more specific actions that countries can undertake on an individual basis.

Third, influence also relies on the adoption of strong national policies by emerging countries, which happens when they are forced to do so for domestic reasons. Clearly, climate negotiations started moving forward once China had decided to adopt ambitious domestic policies. The Souths can no longer hide behind the failure of the Norths to keep their financial promises. National policies then will shape the definition of a national interest on the international scene (a prerequisite for effective negotiations) where harmonization with other states can take place.

We thus come back to the usefulness of exploring more seriously the development of regionally based governance systems (see chapters 4 and 6). It does not mean that cross-regional coalitions could not arise (such as BASIC, AOSIS, or the group of megadiverse countries), only that the building blocks of a decentralized governance system could start at that level. Such an approach in fact partakes of the larger issue of how would developing countries help manage a regime complex. The answer might lie in clubs (Keohane and Nye 2000), regions, South–South cooperation, and transnational links, rather than in a universal cosmopolitan model (see chapter 1).

Notes

1 The success of the Stockholm Conference (UNCHE 1972) in the face of deep suspicions from developing countries was largely rooted in the intense preparatory work which allowed for the identification and resolution of political problems likely to ruin all hope of a final consensus, The 1971 Founex meeting in Switzerland, for example, led to the adoption of the additionality principle and to a compromise over the definition of the problem, according to which environmental problems were defined as threatening the economic and social well-being of nations and individuals, as well as stemming from a lack of development and from poverty.
2 See the Beijing Ministerial Declaration on Environment and Development. Adopted on June 19, 1991, by 41 developing countries, it lists their major and enduring concerns and reaffirms the primacy of the right to development. A/CONF.151/PC/85 (August 13, 1991).
3 UN (United Nations). General Assembly, 1986, "Declaration on the Right to Development" (A/RES/41/128). In United Nations (1986), "Resolutions and Decisions Adopted by the General Assembly during Its 41st Session" (A/41/53), 186–7.
4 The African position vis-à-vis Rio was articulated in the Bamako Commitment on Environment and Sustainable Development adopted by the Pan-African Conference on Environment and Sustainable Development, Bamako, Mali, January 23–30, 1991. It identifies five priority areas: food and energy security, sustainable enduring growth, improvement of the quality of life and of housing, and access to new and additional resources.
5 Hurtado, "Malaysia Turns the Tables on the North," *Crosscurrents, PrepCom 2, 3* (March 28–April 3, 1991), 6.
6 The World Bank uses the environment to legitimize political and economic conditions that borrowers may be inclined to oppose. For example, it promoted subsidies reductions, the end of price control of agricultural products, and fiscal reforms, arguing that these practices indirectly encouraged the overexploitation of natural resources.
7 In their attempts to expand the range of topics to be negotiated during the Uruguay round to the opening of the European agricultural market, the United States accused the European Union's (EU's) Common Agricultural Policy of harming the environment. Environmental arguments were used to justify demands to reduce production subsidies (see Bradsher 1991).
8 It is one of the goals of the Bali Strategic Plan on technological support and capacity building, adopted in 2005, which aims, *inter alia*, to build the capacity of developing countries and countries in transition to participate effectively in international environmental negotiations. It has been and remains one of the priorities of the EU, France, Canada, Scandinavian countries, and of the Francophonie organization in the sustainable development and environment fields.
9 Even in the case of the 1989 Basel Convention on the Control of the Transboundary Movements of Hazardous Wastes and Their Disposal, where efforts by developing countries to mobilize public opinion in the North played an important role in its adoption and subsequent strengthening, the North largely succeeded in imposing its definition of the problem (see Miller 1995).
10 The South's traditional approach has been to ask for the establishment of special funds designed to facilitate the implementation of international agreements and allow them to

influence the amount of aid as well as the criteria used to distribute it. Since the 1980s, the North has been increasingly reluctant to go that route (notwithstanding the various funds created for climate change). Donors have demanded to maintain control over the use of the funds and argued that the problem was less a lack of financial resources than their utilization, insufficient data on their actual impact and on the factors that contribute to policy success or failure, and the elimination of obstacles to their effectiveness. They preferred relying on a centralized source of financing, such as the GEF or on existing structures. Numerous funds have thus remained "paper funds" absent minimal funding.

11 Though the South has been most vocal in its defense of the sovereignty principle, the principle of the right to exploit one's own national resources according to national priorities is certainly shared by developed countries such as Australia, Canada, or the United States.
12 The Trail Smelter case of 1935, where the US government (on behalf of the State of Washington) sought reparations from Canada (representing British Columbia) for damages incurred from pollution stemming from the operation of a smelter in British Columbia, was arbitrated in favor of the plaintiff, thereby establishing the no-harm principle, later endorsed by the 1972 Stockholm Conference, whereby states must minimize harm to their neighbors and compensate them for losses incurred.
13 See the Bangkok Declaration adopted by the Economic and Social Commission for Asia and the Pacific (ESCAP) (A/CONF.151/PC/44: 8).
14 One way to implement the principle in a more "dynamic" way is to pay greater attention to the "common" side of the responsibility equation. Another is to create new categories (see AILAC proposals) that take into account past and future emissions. Alternatively, other instruments could be used in order to facilitate the inclusion of developing countries while taking inequalities into account (such as side-payments, which have the advantage of not diluting treaty obligations). One could also fine-tune the implementation of the PCDR according to the evolution of knowledge and the relative contribution of states to global emissions (as proposed by the UK).
15 Implicitly when the Agreement refers to the UNFCCC principles, and explicitly in the Preamble, in diluted form in Articles 2(2) and 4(3) (where implementation will "reflect" (rather than be "in accordance with" the principle).
16 The BASIC group was established shortly before COP-15, when representatives of Brazil, South Africa, India, and China met during a preparatory meeting in China and announced a joint strategy for the negotiations (Olsson et al. 2010).
17 According to the United Nations Office for South-South Cooperation (UNOSSC), South-South cooperation can be defined as "a broad framework for collaboration among countries of the South in the political, economic, social, cultural, environmental and technical domains. Involving two or more developing countries, it can take place on a bilateral, regional, subregional or interregional basis." See http://ssc.undp.org/content/ssc/about/what_is_ssc.html.
18 Based on agreement reached on common positioning during the South Asian Association for Regional Cooperation (SAARC) summit held in Kathmandu in November 2014.
19 Southern countries came to be responsible for 38 percent of global merchandise exports (Hochstetler 2012, 36).
20 Agarwal and Narain (1991) distinguish between "luxury" emissions arising from wasteful consumption (such as gas-guzzling automobiles) and "survival" emissions caused by activities designed to ensure the basic needs of people (such as the use of water buffaloes and rice cultivation).
21 Statement by Prime Minister of India at COP-21 Plenary, Paris, November 30, 2015.
22 China's emissions of CO_2 have increased at such speed that all reductions by the EU between 1990 and 2007 were cancelled out by only 16 weeks' worth of Chinese additional emissions in 2007 (Bailey et al. 2012).
23 See Barnett and Campbell 2010; Yamin and Depledge 2004; Luterbacher and Sprinz 2001. Several documents reflect the growing role of AOSIS in climate negotiations as a

distinct actor, such as the 1994 Barbados Program of Action (BPOA), BPOA+5 in 1999, the 2002 Johannesburg Plan of Implementation (JPOI), the 2005 Mauritius Strategy of Implementation (MSI), MSI+5 in 2010, etc. The final declaration ("The Future We Want") of the Rio+20 Summit mentions small island developing states respectively in the chapters on the oceans and financing. Recurrent issues pertain to the difficulties and vulnerabilities they face such as natural disasters, food insecurity, domestic financial crises, or the low levels of development aid.

24 Concerts assume a prior agreement on the definition of the problem and on the general direction to be pursued. When such prior agreement is more elusive, club groups may be formed. In their paper, Keohane and Nye (2000, 2) seem largely to equate regimes with clubs, although the latter's membership may be much more limited.

25 This is not to argue in favor of a strong centralized governance model. Rather, these groupings can be seen as emergent properties, institutions that enhance coordination and reduce uncertainty but do not substitute to rule making and, in fact, rely on the activities of a variety of actors at lower scales (see chapter 6). Note that one of the purposes of Keohane and Nye (2000) was to identify the limits of the club-like model of governance based on issues of legitimacy and accountability.

26 UNDP. See www.undp.org/content/undp/fr/home/presscenter/speeches/2010/09/01/helen-clark-statement-to-the-executive-board-of-undp-unfpa.html.

27 This viewpoint was strongly articulated by the prime minister from Malaysia, Mohamad Mahathir, at the 1992 Rio Conference: "The Poor are not asking for charity [but] for the need for us to co-operate on an equitable basis. Now the rich claim a right to regulate the development of the poor countries. And yet any suggestion that the rich compensate the poor adequately is regarded as outrageous" (Mahathir 1992, quoted in Okereke 2006, 726).

28 Road construction, as in Brazil, has been blamed for encouraging migration from outsiders and subsequent deforestation. But even when outsiders are prohibited from settling in (always a very difficult if not impossible task), it changes the internal dynamics of the area for it creates a new market. In the case of Yasuni, "When oil companies built the Maxus Road (named after Maxus Energy Corporation, a US oil exploration firm) into Yasuní in the 1990s, measures were taken to block access to outsiders, but natives living within the park moved their villages to the road and began hunting animals to sell on the black market" (see Wallace 2013).

29 See, for example, the emergence of the "Miami Group" as a key coalition during the negotiations of the Cartagena Protocol on Biosafety of the CBD. Composed of Argentina, Australia, Canada, Chile, the United States, and Uruguay, it represented GMO-exporting countries' concerns with minimizing obligations regarding the transboundary movement of living modified organisms. Large timber and pulp-and-paper producers, such as Canada or Malaysia, have entered into diplomatic alliances against the imposition of conditions restricting their activities. Canada, Norway, Japan, and Zimbabwe have united against proposed regulations under the Convention on International Trade in Endangered Species (CITES). See also the alliance between the G77 and the United States against the EU's proposals on energy at the 2002 Johannesburg Summit.

References

Agarwal, A. and S. Narain. (1991). "Global Warming in an Unequal World: A Case of Environmental Colonialism." *Earth Island Journal*: 39–40.

Akanle, T., et al. (2010). "Summary of the Cancun Climate Change Conference: November 29–December 11, 2010." *Earth Negotiations Bulletin* 12 (498).

Bailey, I., et al. (2012). *Feeling the Heat: The Politics of Climate Policy in Rapidly Industrializing Countries*. Basingstoke, UK: Palgrave.

Banuri, T. (1993). "The Landscape of Diplomatic Conflicts." In *Global Ecology: A New Arena of Political Conflict*, edited by W. Sachs. London: Zed Books, 49–67.

Barnett, J. and J. Campbell. (2010). *Climate Change and Small Islands States: Power, Knowledge and the South Pacific.* Washington, DC: Earthscan.

Batta Bjørnstad, S.-I. (2004). *Breakthrough for "the South"? An Analysis of the Recognition of Farmers' Rights in the International Treaty on Plant Genetic Resources for Food and Agriculture.* Oslo: Fridtjof Nansen Institute.

Betzold, C., et al. (2012). "AOSIS in the UNFCCC Negotiations: From Unity to Fragmentation?" *Climate Policy* 12 (5): 591–613.

Bompard, J.-P. and O. Godard. (2015). "En matière de «justice climatique», attention aux faux arguments!" *Le Monde–Economie.* Available online at http://abonnes.lemonde.fr/economie/article/2015/12/10/en-matiere-de-justice-climatique-attention-aux-faux-arguments_4829059_3234.html?xtmc=olivier_godard&xtcr=5.

Bradsher, K. (1991). "Trade Official Assails Europe over Ecology." *The New York Times*, section D: 2.

Chasek, P. S. (1997). "The Convention to Combat Desertification: Lessons Learned for Sustainable Development." *Journal of Environment and Development* 6: 147–169.

Coolsaet, B. and J. Pitseys. (2015). "Fair and Equitable Negotiations? African Influence and the International Access and Benefit-Sharing Regime." *Global Environmental Politics* 15 (2): 38–56.

Drezner, D. W. (2007). *All Politics Is Global: Explaining International Regulatory Regimes.* Princeton: Princeton University Press.

Gallagher, K. P., et al. (2012). *The New Banks in Town: Chinese Finance in Latin America.* Somerville, MA: Global Development and Environment Institute, Tufts University.

Hochstetler, K. (2012). "South-South Trade and the Environment: A Brazilian Case Study." *Global Environmental Politics* 13 (1): 30–48.

Hurtado, M. (1991). "Malaysia Turns the Tables on the North." *Crosscurrents*, PrepCom 2, 3 (March 28–April 3, 1991), 6.

Keohane, R. O. and J. S. Nye, Jr. (2000). "Between Centralization and Fragmentation: The Club Model of Multilateral Cooperation and Problems of Democratic Legitimacy." American Political Science Convention. Washington, DC.

Luterbacher, U. and D. F. Sprinz. (2001). *International Relations and Global Climate Change.* Cambridge: MIT Press.

Miller, M. A. L. (1995). *The Third World in Global Environmental Politics.* Boulder & London: Lynne Rienner.

Okereke, C. (2006). "Global Environmental Sustainability: Intragenerational Equity and Conceptions of Justice in Multilateral Environmental Regimes." *Geoforum* 37: 725–738.

Olsson, M., et al. (2010). "Together Alone? Brazil, South Africa, India, China (BASIC) and the Climate Change Conundrum." Policy Brief. Stockholm: Stockholm Environment Institute.

Pirard, R. and R. Billé. (2012) "Ne pas exploiter le pétrole contre une rente: la fausse bonne idée du projet Yasuni ITT." *Slate.fr*. Available online at www.slate.fr/tribune/52279/projet-yasuni-itt-petrole-rente.

Rosendal, G. K. (2001). "Impacts of Overlapping International Regimes: the Case of Biodiversity." *Global Governance* 7 (1): 95–117.

Shabecoff, P. (1996). *A New Name for Peace: International Environmentalism, Sustainable Development and Democracy.* Hanover & London: University Press of New England.

Tobin, R. J. (1996). "Pesticides, the Environment, and U.S. Foreign Assistance." *International Environmental Affairs* 8 (3): 244–266.

UN (United Nations). (1986). General Assembly, 1986, "Declaration on the Right to Development" (A/RES/41/128). In United Nations (1986), "Resolutions and Decisions Adopted by the General Assembly during Its 41st Session" (A/41/53), 186–187.

UN (United Nations). (1991). "Summary of Recommendations of Regional Preparatory Meetings for UNCED: Report of the Secretary General of the Conference, A/Conf.151/PC/44." Summary, Preparatory Committee for the United Nations Conference on Environment and Development, Third Session, Geneva, August 12–September 4, 1991, July 5, 1991, 8.

UN (United Nations). (1991). "Beijing Ministerial Declaration on Environment and Development (adopted on June 19, 1991)." Declaration, Preparatory Committee for the United Nations Conference on Environment and Development, United Nations, A/CONF.151/PC/85, August 13, 1991.

UNCHE (United Nations Conference on the Human Environment). (1972). Stockholm.

Wallace, S. (2013). "Rainforest for Sale." *National Geographic* (January). Available online at http://ngm.nationalgeographic.com/2013/01/125-yasuni-national-park/wallace-text.

Yamin, F. and J. Depledge. (2004). *The International Climate Change Regime. A Guide to Rules, Institutions and Procedures*. Cambridge: Cambridge University Press.

Zartman, I. W. and J. Z. Rubin, eds. (2000). "Symmetry and Asymmetry in Negotiation." In *Power and Negotiation*. Ann Arbor, MA: University of Michigan, 271–293.

6

TOWARD FRACTAL GOVERNANCE

Introduction

That we live in an age of complexity and transition is hardly news. In some ways, humanity has always felt it did. Religion, philosophy, and the analytical method have been three ways of dealing with the difficulty of comprehending and acting in a complex world. Ours is one of interconnections (illustrated by globalization), ambiguity over the meaning of events and uncertainty over the consequences of one's actions; of the diffusion of authority and of various kinds of revolutions (military, technological, social economic, and philosophic)—regarding the place of the individual or our relationship to the environment and the planet, for example—rather than of incremental change.

Talks of the changing nature of international relations abound with the development of terrorism, failed states, the diffusion of technology and authority, the fusion between the internal and the external, linkage politics, the rise of the social media, the changing nature of force, the "securitization" (Waever 1995) of new issue areas, and apparent examples of the butterfly effect of chaos theory. We strive to explain 1914, the end of the Cold War, the Arab Spring, financial crises, or global environmental change.

What springs from these developments is the feeling of a lack of control. Decision makers either believe that they have no option but to act as they do or are paralyzed by the uncertainties and conflicting pressures they face. The usual solution is to try and reassert control, which leads to new problems. Paradoxically, as our tools to make sense and control societies and our environment increase, our ability to do so diminishes.

One major reason for this state of affairs lies in the difficulty of going beyond the analytical thinking approach that has served us so well. As Boulton *et al.* (2015, 230) have observed,

> we have increasingly been indoctrinated in the West with this idea that the world works like a machine and that to improve things we need to define

things better, we need to have better processes, we need to have tighter control. Machines have served us well and this type of thinking has its uses; but also its limits and perversity.

International environmental governance is a case in point. Previous chapters have attempted to show the limits of current thinking and the need to go beyond the prevailing doxa that confuses coordination with control and ignores whole developments in the study of international relations that point to different dynamics. Kavalski (2007) is therefore right to call for the emergence of a fifth debate, thus echoing a spate of books, special issues, and articles that have eloquently made the case for embracing complexity (Boulton et al. 2015). Yet students of international relations (IR) have been slow to do so. Jervis (1997) already bemoaned this inability to fully take into account the intellectual implications of system thinking. The profession uses the vocabulary but either forgets the supporting reasoning or rejects it outright as a potential theory of international relations (e.g. Earnest and Rosenau 2006).

Although agent-based modelling remains marginal, scholars have nevertheless increasingly turned their attention to the problems raised by the behavior of complex systems, notably through models of cooperation (Axelrod 1997), network analysis (Maoz 2011; Hafner-Burton et al. 2009), regime complexes (Orsini et al. 2013; Keohane and Victor, 2011; Alter and Meunier 2009; Raustiala and Victor 2004), boundary organizations (Miller 2001; Guston 2001), and multiscalar governance (Padt et al. 2014). Although research largely follows the development of instruments of governance that *de facto* respond to the challenge of steering a complex system, the prevailing discourse, both in academia and politics, remains steeped in analytical linear thinking that emphasizes centralized authority and prediction. Nowhere was this schizophrenia more evident than in the analyses and comments surrounding the United Nations Framework Convention on Climate Change (UNFCCC) COP-21, compared to the actual model that it put in place. Here again, actual dynamics overcame prevailing representations, such as those regarding multilateralism.

How are we to "embrace complexity"? Although complexity theory has been applied to socioecological systems (Wells 2009), its potential for rethinking governance has not been extensively probed. It deserves much more sustained attention. My purpose, therefore, is to try and see what embracing complexity would mean for global environmental governance in general, and global biodiversity governance in particular. After a brief overview of the etiology of complexity in the study of international relations, the chapter discusses the main features of complex systems in light of that concern, with illustrations from biodiversity or international environmental governance (IEG), and then suggests what it means to look at global biodiversity governance as a complex system.

The etiology of complexity in IR studies

Although system analysis has a long and distinguished history in IR, the integration of a complex systems approach into IR analysis has been slow.[1] Indeed, it has largely been confined to discussing its appropriateness rather than how it could be operationalized so as to help define and approach governance problems anew.

We could start with Gulick (1955) and Kaplan (1957), both of whom attempted to identify rules of behavior at the unit level. Then, with a detour by Steinbruner (2002) and the cybernetic theory of decision making, on to Waltz (1979) who used some ideas from complex systems and, famously against Kaplan, adopted a holistic systems approach rather than a unit-based (which he called reductionist) one. In *Turbulence in World Politics*, Rosenau (1990) developed a model that used many concepts and ideas either derived from or associated with chaos and complexity theories such as micro-macro feedbacks, complex adaptive systems, adaptive and decentralized actors, competing authorities, transnational links, rapid change, unpredictability, and ambiguity. In that book, however, Rosenau largely offered descriptive insights without probing the explanatory usefulness of a complex adaptive systems approach. Indeed, he later rejected complex systems theory as inapplicable for developing causal and predictive theories (Earnest and Rosenau 2006). Yet much in his writings remains relevant. Jervis (1997), however, showed what systemic reasoning really entailed through an appealing presentation of concepts illustrated with historical anecdotes. One of his main concerns was to point out the gap that exists between the common use of the vocabulary of systems and the failure to think through the very implications of system thinking.

At the same time, coming from game theory, Axelrod (1997) was focusing on the development of agent-based models (ABM) of politics, relying on sophisticated computational techniques. Lin Ostrom's work (1990) is also relevant here insofar as she focused on polycentrism, which speaks to the idea that cooperation and order do not have to depend on central control. The agent-structure debate only added to the relevance of this approach as complexity theory combines these two levels of analysis.

While complex system theory (CST) was expanding using agent-based models, primarily in math and physics, scholars in the UK became very active in reflecting on the application of CST to the social sciences, starting with Byrne's 1998 book. Many others followed (Chandler 2014; Bousquet and Geyer 2011; Cudworth and Hobden 2011) and it was in Britain that special issues were devoted to this approach. These scholars are interested in application to the social sciences, in general, and in its implications for the philosophy of the social sciences in particular (contra US scholars often more interested in applying physics model based on ABM). In North America, Harrison (2006) did raise squarely the issue of the application of CST to IR, and although it convinced Kavalski (2007), who announced the coming of a fifth debate the following year, no such debate ensued. Indeed, his subsequent edited book (Kavalski 2015) largely remains hortatory and even retreats from the ambition of proposing a new paradigm.

On the one hand, the lack of integration of complex system thinking into IR appears surprising, and this point appears repeatedly in Kavalski (2015). References to systems and their properties abound, but practitioners and academics (not to mention pundits) have found it difficult integrating such thinking into their analysis. This was apparent in the context of the end of the Cold War and the disintegration of the Soviet Union. Linear thinking was evident in the general belief that the removal of the obstacles to international cooperation rooted in the dynamics of a bipolar system would announce an era of unprecedented cooperation and progress. At the very least, it overlooked the simple observation that bipolarity spawned its own kind of cooperation and that when parts of a system change (and, *a fortiori*, the rules governing agents' behavior as was the case), then so do the behavior rules of all other agents. This blindness is puzzling, for ecology, for example, with its concept of niches and its predator-prey models has long shown what happens when you remove one species from an ecosystem, add new ones, or change their distribution.

Be that as it may, complexity is clearly raising the interest of an increasing number of scholars in all disciplines. It is in the air; although we fail to fully breathe it through our analytical gas masks. It has become a buzzword, and the characteristics and properties of complex systems have invaded the discourse in a variety of fields, notably the environment where complex socioecological systems have become the focus of the scientific production of many research centers and scientific subsidiary bodies of Multilateral Environmental Agreements (MEAs).

In this context, two features stand out. First, although system analysis has a long and distinguished history in IR, the integration of a complex systems approach into IR analysis has been slow. Nevertheless, the building blocks of such an approach, in particular of decentralized governance systems, are being put in place, such as agent-structure models, regime complexes, network theory, agent-based models, or multiscalar governance. Thus although we are in practice inching toward a complex system perspective, we have failed to integrate these evolving objects of inquiry into a coherent whole.

The development of a nascent "complex international relations theory" (Ibid.) and the adoption of this perspective as a sustained object of inquiry in IR have remained largely elusive. Going beyond the analytical perspective which typically emphasizes one feature of the system in order to highlight the whole (rather than focusing on relationships and their contribution to the expression of system properties) remains a challenge. What may explain the reluctance to embrace this perspective?

First, the nature of the approach itself is somewhat confusing. Complexity theory is not a single coherent theory but a collection of overlapping and complementary approaches from a variety of sciences from physics, to biology, to anthropology. This means that its application to international politics cannot be modelled after that of other disciplines (although anthropology and sociology would surely help) but has to develop idiosyncratically based on the discipline's ontology and epistemology.

Second is the mistaken belief that it is not all that new. After all, system thinking and the notion of feedbacks have been around for a while. Thus we think that because we understand the concepts, we also understand their implications.

Third come difficulties in defining and applying key concepts of complex systems to international relations. What are the units and boundaries of the system? What could be considered an emergent property or self-organization? How should we conceive hierarchy and governance, or the role of power, knowledge, and technology?

A related challenge is transforming a metaphor into a theory, even though, as Byrne and Callaghan (2014) remind us, all theories are rooted in metaphors. What new questions does it ask? Which new facts does it help uncover? What enigma and surprises does it explain? What does it add to analytical and mechanistic research programs? As Boulton *et al.* (2015, 3 and 5) ask,

> how can we really get to grips with what it means to say the world is complex and what that implies we should do? How can we understand it well enough to make sound judgements as to how to apply complexity ideas and respond to complex situations?... What does being in a complex world mean to individuals, to organizations, and more globally to issues of economics, climate change, and engaging with the developing world? What do you do differently? How do we engage empirically with a complex, interconnected, co-evolving, emerging world?

The difficulty of moving from metaphor to theory is the crux of Earnest and Rosenau's (2006) objections. Beyond its usefulness as a metaphor, a complex system perspective would be inappropriate "because social systems have structures of authority that may be inconsistent with the definition of complex adaptive systems" since these authority structures serve to minimize complexity.[2] The main criticism rests on the inability of the approach to become a theory in the positivist sense, and to specify the nature and bases of new knowledge claims. Their argument, though, reduces complexity theory to difficulties associated with the development and simulation of ABM models; methodology is one thing, theory development another, however.

Finally, there is the assumption that fragmentation weakens effectiveness through a waste of resources, conflicts over resources and policy domains, and normative contradictions (a strong element of the prevailing doxa, as related in chapter 2). Yet are conflicts so numerous? And when they exist, what are they about and how have they been managed? One should distinguish among different types of conflicts. Case studies, for example, suggest that normative conflicts among MEAs may be relatively few (Van Asselt 2014; Kim 2013). Conflicts over resources and turf, on the other hand, are real, but again, studies other than anecdotes looking at the impact of these conflicts remain few. In fact, the system has evolved tools to manage them and synergies are possible, such as the potential synergies between Reducing Emissions from Deforestation and Forest Degradation (REDD) and the Convention on Biological Diversity (CBD) (Van Asselt 2014). Conflicts over values, however, are real among different types of actors (market, nongovernmental organizations, states, business, science).

We have nonetheless *de facto* entered the complexity era; the issue now is how governance should be conceived in a decentralized context. Contemporary research focuses on several of its features, with many approaches reflecting the need to enhance the capacity to adapt to complexity, such as insisting on local participation in order to address potential nonlinear effects, promoting a dialectical construction of the science-policy interface (see chapter 3), or designing multiscalar models of policy. The very notion of governance, as articulated in IR, addresses the need to cooperate in solving common problems in the context of a fragmentation of authority and multiplication of actors. Complexity provides conceptual tools that enable us to identify the contours of global decentralized international governance despite recurrent assumptions that central control is the key to addressing uncertainty effectively or an inevitable outcome of current trends (as expressed by theories of unipolar stability, world order, world systems, etc.).

These developments, however, are conceived outside a complex intellectual framework. Rather, they seek to respond to local problems and are appended to linear frameworks. The remainder of this chapter, therefore, addresses the basic elements and properties of a complex systems approach as applied to IR, and sketches out the contours of a global biodiversity governance system. What would be its building blocks? What questions would we ask? What directions should we emphasize?

The world is not a machine

In a way, we are all M. Jourdains of complexity thinking. Features of complexity theory, like in most other realms of human thought, can be found among the ancients, in pre-Socratic philosophers and in Daoism: "Complexity thinking presents a vision, a view of the world as organic, adapting, becoming, and emerging. It contrasts with a mechanical worldview of a world that is or should be predictable, where actions have intended consequences, and in which the cogs in the machine, the variety of institutions and individuals (the agents) are unchanging (or slowly change) and controllable" (Boulton *et al.* 2015, 106).

Complexity science, then, lies in opposition to classical analytical thinking. It eschews simplification and reductionism, which, although hugely successful, also lead to models that have difficulties describing and accounting for observed reality. To illustrate this shift of perspective, complexity scholars distinguish between the "complex" and the merely "complicated" (Morin 1990). A jet engine, which can be disassembled and reassembled at will, will work as intended if the engineers have calculated properly the characteristics of its thousands of parts and if the mechanics have assembled it right. It is very complicated. Something "complicated" can be solved by cutting it down into manageable parts, following the Cartesian Method which invites "to divide each of the difficulties under examination into as many parts as possible, and as might be necessary for its adequate solution" (Descartes 1909 [1637], part II). Complex problems, on the other hand, cannot be reduced or simplified without being strongly altered or "mutilated" and their behavior is not predictable from the study of their parts (Morin 1990). The world is not a machine.

The distinction between complication and complexity lies at the heart of the impasse of current attempts at global environmental governance reform. Indeed, the dominant organizational approach, essentially centered on United Nations Environment Programme (UNEP) reform, constitutes conspicuous reductionism and a mutilation of the global environmental governance (GEG) problem. From a complex perspective, the right question is not how to make the current system less complicated (as evidenced by its fragmentation) by reforming UNEP or centralizing authority, but how to "harness" (Axelrod and Cohen 1999) the complexity of the GEG system in order to heighten its effectiveness. How do we recognize complex systems, then?

One difficulty lies in separating the characteristics of a complex system (how do we recognize it?) from its properties (how does it behave and with what consequences?). For example, defining a complex system as "a system in which large networks of components with no central control and simple rules of operation give rise to complex collective behavior, sophisticated information processing, and adaptation via learning or evolution" (Mitchell 2009, 318–19) confuses causes (the characteristics) and consequences (the properties) and prevents us from asking questions regarding which characteristics of the system lead to what kind of properties (such as learning and adaptation).

"Complex systems are open systems composed of multiple actors, operating at different spatial scales, which interact according to nonlinear and networked patterns" (Bousquet and Curtis 2011, 51).[3] Thus a system is complex when it has the following features:

- multiple elements (agents or units) of various types;
- intricately interconnected with one another (thus forming networks) which leads to...
- nonlinearity and feedback loops;
- hierarchy (the world is multiscalar);
- openness (it exchanges energy and information with its environment).

What makes complex systems interesting are their properties that include:

- self-organization and self-regulation;
- emergence;
- multilevel dynamics, stemming from hierarchy (requiring interscalar governance);
- unintended consequences;
- irreversibility (tipping points toward new regimes) and nonrenewability (such as depletion of resources);
- adaptability;
- surprises and catastrophes; multiple futures;
- path dependency (history); the behavior of a complex system is contingent on the local context and on the sequence of events;
- robustness, resilience, and sustainability.

The following section defines these features more extensively with illustrations from global ecopolitics.

The characteristics of complex systems

Multiple elements (agents)

Proponents of environmental governance reform see in the proliferation of institutions and actors the main reason for their perceived inefficiencies. As mentioned in chapter 2, the abundance and diversity of such actors are well documented. Regimes, MEA secretariats, nongovernmental organizations (NGOs), and ministries have multiplied, while existing intergovernmental organizations (IGOs) (most prominently development banks) and national aid agencies have added environmental concerns to their mission. Business has become part of the solution; scientific networks have coalesced (such as Future Earth) alongside individuals as potent forces of mobilization; new actors (indigenous populations, cities, substate entities, etc.) have come to the fore. The picture becomes even more complex when environmental concerns are considered intrinsic to sustainable development.

Several commentators have noted a shift from government to governance in which the roles of the public, private, and voluntary sectors are being restructured. The development of a governance perspective involves recognizing the roles of supranational and subnational state and nonstate actors, and the complex interactions among them, in the process of governing. Thus Rosenau and Durfee (2000, 57) suggest that we are now witnessing a "bifurcation of authority" in which the state-centric paradigm is no longer predominant (bifurcations are tipping points leading to new arrangements). Global governance features a "complex multi-centric world of diverse actors… replete with structures, processes, and decision rules of its own" (Ibid.). This growing number of "sovereignty-free actors" all claiming to share legitimacy leads to a world of turbulence, complexity, multiple causalities, and dynamic change.

Ever since Rio 1992, the United Nations (UN) has given civil society a legitimate role to play, although its status and actual privileges vary and depend on the willingness of states to allow them to assume a specific role. In the case of biodiversity, indigenous groups co-chair working groups of the Biodiversity Convention. The elements of the Global Biodiversity Governance System (GBGS), for example, might include nation-states, IGOs (United Nations Educational, Scientific, and Cultural Organization [UNESCO], FAO [Food and Agriculture Organization], Development Banks, etc.), hybrid IGOs (such as the International Union for Conservation of Nature [IUCN]), international programs (UNEP, United Nations Development Programme [UNDP]), and MEA secretariats (CBD, Convention on International Trade in Endangered Species [CITES], Convention on Migratory Species [CMS], Ramsar, Convention on World Cultural and Natural Heritage [WHC], International Treaty on Plant Genetic Resources for Food and Agriculture [ITPGRFA]), boundary organizations (such as Intergovernmental Platform on

Biodiversity and Ecosystems Services [IPBES], Intergovernmental Panel on Climate Change [IPCC]), networks (such as Group on Earth Observation Biodiversity Observation Network [GEOBON]), states and substate authorities (e.g. states/provinces, municipalities), international civil society as categorized by the UN (farmers, local government, science and technology organizations, indigenous people, youth, women, workers [unions], business, NGOs, foundations), regions (groups of states linked geographically), and regime and regime complexes.

One of the major challenges of global governance research is to understand better the dynamics of power and influence among this diversity of stakeholders. In a complex system, where uncertainty regarding the behavior of other agents, the nature of the problem, and the consequences of one's actions prevail, agents adopt strategies designed to ensure access to needed resources, maximize future flexibility, and minimize immediate losses. They may pursue a well-defined common good (i.e. a clear notion of desirable equilibria), but each class of agent will conceive and approach it differently.

Diversity, measured as a function of abundance and types of units as per the Shannon-Wiener index (Pielou 1975), may be positively related to stability (resilience) and adaptability (enabling change). The relationship between diversity and stability, however, is a matter of debate. Likewise, diversity should not be thought only in terms of the type of agents and their relative abundance and specialization, but also in terms of the links that exist among them.

Connections and networks

Connections define systems, of course, but in complex systems, the variety, density, and strength of connections define networks, which in turn become new types of units that comprise both agents and specific ways of apprehending the world (Wells 2009, 149). The field of IR has turned relatively late to social networks theory. The literature, however, has increased steadily since mid-2000 (Maoz 2011; Hafner-Burton *et al.* 2009) and forms one of the main bases of a complex analysis of IR.

Agents form networks based on their nature (such as the MEA biodiversity network, International Council for Local Environmental Initiatives [ICLEI], the indigenous peoples networks, or the clubs formed by states (Keohane and Nye, 2000),[4] or on their purpose (conservation, development, intellectual property rights, specific transnational campaigns, biodiversity science, ecosystem services). The diversity of interactions among the different agents of global environmental governance is illustrated by the variety of hybrid networks that "bring together public and private actors which interact to shape new forms of governance" (Dubash and Florini 2011, 13).

Indeed, one of the remarkable developments of the last two decades has been the emergence of new forms of collaborations between various types of authorities (public, private, and market), giving rise to a multiplicity of decentralized governance strategies (Lemos and Agrawal 2006): co-management (between state and community) and outright delegation of authority (as in the management of protected areas delegated to NGOs);[5] public–private partnerships (between state and market); private–social partnerships (between community and market); or private authority (between firms and NGOs, as in the case of certification programs such as the Forest (FSC) and Marine (MSC) Stewardship Councils). These new forms of collaborations, with "uncertain accountability mechanisms" (Dubash and Florini 2011, 13; Smouts 2003), are complemented by intranetworks governance strategies such as the development of industry-wide guidelines.

Future international relations will increasingly involve the interplay of agents and their networks (e.g. states) with hybrid networks of coalitions. Policy networks are particularly interesting in the context of global environmental governance. Examples are the Consultative Group on International Agricultural Research (CGIAR), the World Commission on Dams, the Global Water Partnership, the Roll Back Malaria Campaign, and the International NGO Desertification Network (RIOD).

Nonlinearity and feedback loops

Nonlinear systems are systems that display disproportionality between cause and effect, input and output, because their components interact with one another via feedback loops (a property of networks). When these loops are positive, the system undergoes exponential expansion where small influences result in unpredictable and large effects. Chaos theory is precisely the study of small causes leading to large effects or high dependence on initial conditions. Moreover, since these are open systems, agents interact or react to their environment (agents and processes), which enhances nonlinearity and uncertainty.

Since feedbacks can also be negative, nonlinearity may also result in a return to the initial state (resilience) following a disturbance. In both cases of positive and negative feedbacks, the result cannot be deduced from the behavior of the units. Thus in IR, nonlinearity refers to the gap between intentions, outputs, and outcomes. Examples of nonlinearity in international politics abound (see Jervis 1997). They can be illustrated by the fall of the Iron Curtain and regimes of Eastern Europe, the "Arab Spring," or the diffusion of Islamist terrorists and military networks. As Bousquet and Curtis (2011: 48) point out, "The turn toward complexity in the social sciences has thus been partly driven by the growing realization that nonlinear and networked social relationships characterize much of the contemporary world. In this sense, complexity offers the conceptual language and methodological tools for understanding the dynamics engendered by global flows and the interpenetration of societies."

Nonlinearity is also apparent in international negotiations. "Strange loops" occur during the negotiation process, as in Putnam's two-level games, which we could expand to multiple-level games (if we include civil society, other administrations, and substate authorities). More generally, one knows when and where a negotiation starts but not when and where it will end. The negotiation history of the Biodiversity Convention illustrates these dynamics, as the objective of the convention widened to produce an outcome that proved unacceptable to the US, which had been one of its early proponents.

Ever since the advent of general systems theory and cybernetics in the 1950s and 1960s and, in political science, Steinbruner's work on decision making in the 1970s, feedbacks have been acknowledged as a fundamental dimension of policy. Feedbacks are part and parcel of ecosystems and of critical significance in climate change. They are found in the natural and social worlds, but reflexivity, the ability of social agents to modify their behavior through learning, is tied to humans and some animal societies.

Biodiversity is full of these nonlinear effects. Numerous examples come from the introduction of new species. In the conservation realm, a classic anecdote is the ban on the exportation of endangered parrots from South America under CITES. Far from reducing the threat to the species, it increased it as traffickers caught more birds to make up for custom seizures and packed them into tighter packages so as to avoid detection, thus increasing their overall death rate (Pearce and Warford 1993). Another example comes from Madagascar where a policy of reducing the number of rats (to protect food and fight the plague) through economic incentives in the form of payment per dead animal, led to an increase in the rat population as people started raising rats in order to get the reward.

Some feedbacks are predictable; others are not. A complex system perspective says that one's best hope is to narrow down the range of possible feedbacks, not determine which one will actually come into play. A mechanical approach will try to use feedbacks to promote policy goals. A complex system approach will assume such actions will have unintended consequences. One should therefore strive to devise policies that take into account the possibility of massive, unpredictable positive feedbacks (as illustrated by the precautionary principle).

Finally, our concern for controlling for positive feedbacks is rooted in Janian assumptions. One favors stability and resilience, hence negative feedbacks; which overlooks the possibility that the latter may impede adaptation. The other considers positive feedbacks as inherently destabilizing or, in the case of resources, threatening to create a tragedy of the commons. Yet as Resnick (1997, 134) pointed out "[p]ositive feedback isn't always negative." Indeed, biodiversity policy aims at creating synergies (or positive feedbacks) among sectoral policies and policy instruments. The diffusion of new values regarding humans' relationship to the natural world will, it is hoped, benefit from similar dynamics.

Hierarchy

In a complex system, entities exist in a hierarchy of interrelated organizational levels:

> At each different level of complexity within a system a new set of patterns or properties emerge that are specific to that domain of interaction and that generally cannot be deduced from the individual behavior or character of its constituent parts but may subsequently come to act back upon these parts.
>
> *(Bousquet and Curtis 2011, 47)*

through "strange loops" ("situations in which the activities of entities interacting at a lower level give rise to higher–level constructs, the existence of which affects the dynamics of the lower–level entities that created them" [Parrott 2002, 2]).

> Thus, whereas in conventional approaches, systems are described at only one level of organization (e.g., community or nation, but not both simultaneously), complexity theory provides a framework in which the relationships between constructs at different hierarchical levels can be accommodated.
>
> *(Ibid.)*

These strange loops are evident in multiscalar dynamics (Bulkeley 2005), such as the Cities for Climate Protection program that features a combination of top-down and bottom-up dynamics (Betsill and Bulkeley 2004), which raises the issue of governing across scales and levels. Edgar Morin makes the need to consider the global-local link one of the main differences between his notions of general and restricted complexity: "in opposition to restricted complexity, general complexity requires that one tries to comprehend the relationship between the whole and the parts" (see Byrne and Callaghan 2014, 39). The challenge for governance is not only to understand the interaction mechanisms between different levels (Rosenau 1990, 153) but also to allow for the construction of an intersubjective world among them, one that enables the mobilization of actors engaged in the definition and the implementation of various institutions that define the regime complex. This interdependence among the different levels of the complex system means that one cannot escape governance issues (such as implementation) by merely switching levels or bypassing a particular level: the global is no substitute for the local or the national nor the global-local link for the national-local one (Le Prestre 2010). In this regard, networks have a key role to play in linking various governance levels, from the local to the global.[6]

At any level of analysis, order is an emergent property of individual interactions at a lower level of aggregation rather than explained by causal drivers at the same level of analysis. Complex models ask how changes in the agents' decision rules (through norm diffusion, for example), the interconnections among agents, or the strategies that agents employ produce different aggregate outcomes. Since each agent and each system is nested within other systems, all evolving and interacting, a single entity cannot be understood without considering the others. To model an outcome at a particular level of analysis, one assumes that the outcome is produced by a dynamic system comprised of agents at a lower level of aggregation (Holland and Miller 1991). For example, a liberal theory of foreign policy is conceived as a function of domestic politics and values rather than of structural forces at the international level such as the distribution of power in the system.

In this context, a model that places the region at the heart of biodiversity governance is worth serious consideration (see chapters 4 and 5 for observations on a general regional perspective). Regarding biodiversity, a better fit between governance and ecosystems through a regional ecosystem-based management approach (akin to regional emissions markets in climate change) deserves scrutiny.[7] Since networks crisscross regions, a regional focus does not have to lead to the emergence of competing closed systems, and make global governance more difficult. Although states form the basis of regional cooperation, they also belong to transcontinental networks. In addition, progress at the regional level may seep up to the global one (as when the EU disseminates its norms among its international trade partners) (see chapter 4).

Open system

Finally, complex systems are open systems:

> Open systems have boundaries that are porous and shifting, and exchange information and energy with their environment. It means that behavior is also constrained or at least influenced by the environment. This allows for the entry of contingency and evolution, and thus the introduction of the 'arrow of time', into systemic theorizing.
>
> *(Bousquet and Curtis 2011, 47)*

It raises the importance of history (path dependency) and leads to the notion of complex adaptive systems.

The properties of complex systems

Self-organization

Self-organization refers to order emerging naturally from unpredictable nonlinear interactions among agents.

> After a system has gone through a radical shift, a tipping point, new patterns of relationships and features will eventually emerge and the new situation will eventually settle down with a new underlying form. This building of new patterns is self-organization.
>
> *(Boulton et al. 2015, 44)*

These patterns are not centrally designed. Rather they result from a bottom-up process rooted in the interactions of the agents "as they react to the flow of resources through the system" (Bousquet and Curtis 2011, 47). One analogy might be the distinction between formal and informal organizational charts in organization theory. The form these patterns take cannot be predicted, and they may or may not accord with an overarching principle such as maintaining stability and control, maximizing profits, or minimizing energy consumption (Boulton *et al.* 2015, 17).

Self-organization (such as regimes) is a response to uncertainty. This means that the system has the ability to change its internal structure in order to interact with its environment better, that is, to learn and adapt (Wells 2009). Usually, self-organization is achieved and maintained by a dynamic system so long as there is a continual flow of some resources (in the form of political support, projects, financial resources, or information) across the system boundary. Examples include flocking birds where flocking patterns emerge as part of the system's self-organizing behavior.[8] This is evident in the multiplication of clubs, in governance partnerships, in the rise of regimes and the diffusion of norms or in the delegation of authority granted to NGOs in implementation and surveillance.

The establishment of specific regimes dealing with biodiversity can be approached as example of self-organization. Although interests matter, MEAs cannot be deduced from the aggregation of "states' ... conceptions of their own interests" (Mitchell 2003, 97) when preferences can be unclear and unstable in environmental arenas in which knowledge is uncertain, issues are complex, and material interests are "weakly or ambiguously affected." The timing and content of MEAs are influenced by the strength of states' interests in environmental protection relative to other concerns and by their power to promote those interests, the knowledge and discourse that structure perceptions of environmental problems and their solutions, and the efforts of individuals and groups in proposing solutions and pressing governments to reach a given agreement (Ibid.). Every regime symbolizing a combination of specific standards, interests, power, and knowledge, forming a specific governance system, is evidence of self-organization.

Although self-organization may be expected, the probability of a given one varies according to dimensions whose relative importance depends on context (the environment of the system, as it were). As Mitchell (2003, 442) underscores, neither scientific consensus about the nature of the problem (see chapter 3) nor public mobilization are sufficient to produce international action. Many facilitative conditions have been identified, but few, if any, are sufficient. For example,

> [h]igh levels of uncertainty can make interests and preferences hard to identify, sometimes hindering and sometimes facilitating agreement. Bargaining persuades as well as communicates interests, threats, and promises, and it alters perceived interests and whether and what type of regimes form.
>
> *(Ibid.)*

Emergence

Emergence refers to the rise of unexpected and complex structures, patterns, properties, or processes from simple interactions in a self-organizing system (Wells 2009; Jervis 1997). An emergent property is a property of the system as a whole which does not exist at the individual level (agents). Examples are water, the sweetness of sugar, the social ordering of bee colonies, or consciousness. It does not depend on any centralized control and is not planned. It implies that one cannot simply infer higher-level organizational structures and properties from knowledge about the individual elements and their interactions. Systems have to be approached as a whole.

Emergence is at the core of the notion of complex systems and what makes them interesting. It is usually referred to as "the whole is greater than the sum of its parts," but this expression is misleading for, as Jervis (1997) points out, the sum is not just greater but different. Emergence refers to second-order properties arising from the interactions of elements. In the case of sugar, a first-order property is the compound itself, whereas a second-order property would be sweetness (although this property is not intrinsic to sugar but to the one who tastes it). Emergence, in social systems stems from the feedback mechanisms at work: the existence of a system (defined by the number and types of agents and their interactions) changes the preferences or behavior of the agents (as in a crowd in a stadium or demonstration).

Whereas self-organization is a structural property of the system, emergence is a functional one. Cooperation and regime effectiveness, then, can be approached as an emergent property of interactions between agency and structure.[9] The use of the term "global environmental governance" instead of "international environmental governance" is emblematic of this emergence phenomenon. The adjective "global" reflects the sense that the density of the emerging network of international regimes and transnational relations amounts to something more than just direct or indirect links among states.

Whether governance is self-organization or an emergent property of the system is unclear so long as one does not, in fact, disentangle two uses of the term "governance": governance as an output (the arrangements put in place so as to pursue a common goal) and governance as an outcome (the results of these attempts). The first meaning could be thought of as self-organization, the second as emergence. When Najam *et al.* (2004) approach GEG as *de facto* a complex system, they have in mind the first acceptance. Identifying actors, their strategies, and their interactions is of course a necessary first step. But what interests us is the result of these dynamics in terms of cooperation and effectiveness.

In its second meaning, therefore, the global governance of biodiversity is not the outcome of centralized control (that is, norms, rules, and procedures edicted at the global level that guide the behavior of entities), but of what happens at lower and across levels (regions, states, communities, networks) and of feedback mechanisms between structure and agency. It is the (meta) emergent process of (sub) emergent processes, i.e. a result of a cascade of emergent dynamics. New networks of MEAs governance systems could be approached from this perspective, with emergence at the subsystem level leading to emergence at the system level. This description of a process does not assume a predetermined end point, which would be contrary to a complex system perspective. It might generate arrangements in favor of a decentralized governance system, but, ironically, an emergent property in the form of a more centralized system could not be ruled out.[10]

Adaptation

Linear thinking is hard to shed, even when one is convinced of the need for complex analysis and the vocabulary of complex systems is used. It is the case when Najam *et al.* (2006), for example, argue that

> The [GEG] system needs reform not because it has "failed," but because it has outgrown its own original design. Much like children who outgrow their clothes as they mature, or small towns that need new infrastructure as they blossom into large cities, the GEG system needs to be rethought so that it can meet the challenges of its own growth.

This raises the question of adaptation and the notion of complex adaptive systems (CAS).

A CAS is a special case of complex systems: it has the capacity to learn from and adapt – i.e. "cope" and "transform" (co-evolve) – to its environment over time, especially when this environment also consists of other such systems (Holland 1995). Examples include economies, ecologies, weather, traffic, social organizations, and cultures, to name but a few (Gell-Mann 1994). It is because the system is populated with agents that seek to better adapt to their environment that we can speak about an "adaptive system." The biodiversity regime complex is an example of a CAS.

The traditional perspective, as in evolutionary theory, is to locate the unit of evolution at the species level (and/or the gene), that is the agent. Governance systems are composed of organizations that attempt to reduce the uncertainty attached to their access to resources on which they depend (Le Prestre 1999). To that end, they use different strategies (called schema in agent-based models [ABM] complex systems theory). This understanding of system adaptability leads to two major points (Axelrod and Cohen 1999). First, CAS theory is used in cases where agents are capable of selecting adaptation strategies: agents select strategies, not outcomes (changes in behavior can lead to no real advantage or payoff for the agents). Second, adaptability is first of all an attribute of the agent, not of the system as a whole (strictly speaking, the outcome is adaptive, but the system does not adapt per se). It means that even if the agents are successful in their individual adaptation, by no means can we infer that the global performance of the system will tend to cooperation and effectiveness. On the other hand, only if agents adapt can the system be adaptive.

Although adaptation is neither automatic nor universal (indeed, one is interested in studying its determinants and nature), examples of it can be found in each class of actors. For example, as autonomous agents, IGOs active in environmental matters have repeatedly proven capable of adaptation, such as the World Bank (changes in goals, norms, procedures, and policies), Ramsar (transformation of its mission), the Convention to Combat Desertification (CCD) (institutional innovations), or the International Whaling Commission (IWC) (changes in norms and rules). One example is the emergence of compliance governance systems at the convention level; the CBD has gradually evolved such a system which was not foreseen by the convention. The evolving reporting system and various means of evaluating the national implementation of international agreements hold the potential for regime learning, for modifying the MEA's programs of work, and for devising new policies in order to improve the implementation record. States have changed or reversed policies. NGOs have formed transnational (Keck and Sikkink 1998) and transactor advocacy coalitions (such as the World Commission on Dams).

Business provides a good illustration of this adaptation. Historically, business actors have tended to oppose national and international environmental regulations, seen as limiting their competitiveness. To prevent adoption of constraining international regulations in new global environmental regimes, they first favored acting at the national level. It was the dominant political strategy used by the private sector at the Stockholm Conference on Human Environment in 1972. The 1992 Rio Conference on Environment and Development marked the beginning of a corporate strategic change that took two forms: (i) an increased and more direct participation of the private sector in international environmental negotiations, and (ii) the development of innovative forms of governance, such as voluntary guidelines or certification schemes. Examples include the International Organization for Standardization (ISO 14000), the Forest and Marine Stewardship Councils, as well as various codes of conduct (Coalition for Environmentally Responsible Economics [CERES] Principles; Responsible Care, etc.). From being an opponent, the private sector has gradually become a major partner in the development of a global governance of the environment. By promoting the idea of a partnership among the private sector, environmentalists, and the international community, the private sector has moved from laggard to "rule taker" to "rule maker." The CBD and states (such as Germany, Canada, and France) have adopted a strategy of engagement of the private sector, where business is seen as part of the solution.[11]

However fecund this unit-based traditional perspective can be (and it has a long history in international relations), another approach again mirrors debates in the biological sciences. Indeed this is what borrowing from ecosystem ecology and evolutionary theory, rather than physics and genetics, would suggest we explore. ABM is but one approach of complexity theory. Instead of looking at the institutional evolution of the governance system as the result of variation and selection at the unit level, one would emphasize the relationships among these units and the functions that the system performs. In ecology, what survives is not the single species, but the ecology or community of flora and fauna that are adapted to the prevailing conditions (Boulton et al. 2015, 62). In anthropology, it is the function it performs, not the rite, the tradition or the taboo itself that matters. Likewise, one would emphasize co-evolution dynamics among actors (referring to institutional and policy diffusion, or to the emergence of co-dependence) and the evolution of their interactions.

Path dependency and tipping points

Global environmental governance has a history, and this history matters. Although distinct phases can be distinguished, each phase retains characteristics of the former to which it adds new ones, thus becoming more complex. Complexity increases with the number of agents, the links among issues, the evolution of norms, knowledge, and technology, etc. Each of these periods is distinguished by the type of actors, new rules or schema (such as legal norms and policy principles), and different definitions of the nature of the problems that are addressed.

At the subsystem level, that of the governance of specific issue areas, such as biodiversity, similar dynamics are at work. An initial period, until the 1960s, is represented by the development of national parks and the conclusion of treaties designed to protect single species, usually in connection with a specific economic sector (such as agriculture or whaling). A second period followed the notion that the earth was itself a system (the biosphere) and that biodiversity protection was a socio-economic problem. A third period saw the development of the ecosystem perspective on the one hand and the need to take into account the dimensions and consequences of the genetic revolution (property rights, GMOs, biosynthesis) on the other. The last phase emphasizes the preeminence of the sustainable development paradigm, the fragmentation and further diversification of actors, the development of private authority, new links between science and policy (see chapter 3), and the consequent needs to improve knowledge, promote coordination, and change behavior.

Path dependency means that current institutions will shape future governance systems. One never starts from scratch. UNEP's weak resources bear that out to the point where global environmental governance has often been equated with merely strengthening UNEP or replacing it with a new World Environment Organization (WEO). And the very existence of UNEP has triggered new arrangements designed to bypass it, with states preferring to create new entities (such as the CSD) or to marginalize it (as in climate change). The creation of the IPCC, followed by the negotiations of the UNFCCC and the establishment of its secretariat, represent a string of conscious decisions not to give it more executive authority (Moltke 2001). This was to some extent motivated by the fear of creating a powerful international environmental agency, a recurrent fear in the history of UNEP (Ivanova 2007, 2005). States have been reluctant to provide UNEP, created when UN agencies were already involved in developing the environment as an issue area where they claimed leadership, with the resources that would be required to do what they claim it ought to be doing (Najam 2003). Several biodiversity-related conventions are administratively under UNEP, although they are politically and financially independent from it. Relations between UNEP and several of them have been tense over the years, however, further encouraging MEAs to form coalitions of their own, such as the Liaison Group of Biodiversity-Related Conventions.[12]

When catastrophes strike, analysts typically blame some rare set of circumstances or some combination of powerful mechanisms. But many

> [l]arge interactive systems perpetually organize themselves to a critical state in which minor events start a chain reaction that can lead to a catastrophe; complex systems (such as the biosphere, the stock market or an ecosystem) can break down not only under the force of a mighty blow but also at the drop of a pin.
> (Bak and Chen 1991, 46)

Hence the idea of tipping points.

Tipping points are a particular type of catastrophe (another is external pressure) and the product of history. "[H]istory is path-dependent in the sense that the character of current institutions depends not only on current conditions but also on the historical path of institutional development" (March and Olsen 1998). This means not only that what has happened before matters, but that the order of events in which it occurred is important in shaping the current governance system (Boulton et al. 2015, 41). The system has a history, what Prigogine referred to as the "arrow of time."

The issue of sensitivity to initial conditions highlights a very different understanding of the role of history (path dependency) to that displayed by structural realism, which has tended to develop ahistorical accounts of the international system. This is the notion that the state of a system at time t is dependent on the state of the system at $t-1$ and in particular stresses the system's dependence on initial conditions. Biodiversity-related IGOs, for example, embody the norms, technology, and political relationships that prevailed at the time of their creation, and these will continue to inform their behavior as long as the nature of the membership and of the human resources remains the same. But because of other properties of the complex systems that allow for nonincremental change, the behavior of the elements of the system (agents) at time $t+1$ is not predictable, although the structural state may be (as in a warming liquid: we can predict the future state of the system (evaporation) but not the individual behavior of the molecules). The point between predictability and unpredictability of the elements is a "bifurcation" (Prigogine 1997) where the system may go different ways. The future becomes structurally different from the past.

Species extinctions and the loss of whole ecosystems are the ultimate examples of irreversibility, and ecologists have long strived to identify the nature of tipping points and the processes leading up to them (with the notions of minimum sustainable gene pool, keystone species, etc.). The notion of critical boundaries (see chapter 1) is predicated on the need to identify potential tipping points before the earth system enters a new phase state with devastating consequences on societies.

Equilibrium, resilience, and stability

Governance refers to the development of stable rules governing relationships among agents. A state of equilibrium is then found when no agent has an incentive to change those rules, and system stability then is defined as the maintenance of these rules over time in the face of disruption (internal or external). Effectiveness, on the other hand, refers to the achievement of cooperation (that is, behavioral changes in the units of the system) in support of the common good.

There is some confusion in the literature over the notion of equilibrium in complex systems, which affects the identification of the location of stability and resilience. This is in part linked to the assumption of self-similarity used in nonsocial sciences—the idea that the same rules apply at different levels of the system, which clearly is not the case in social systems. It then makes more sense to view the global biodiversity governance system as a composite system without equilibrium (only attractors),[13] composed of subelements (sets of agents) that tend to equilibrium. As Prigogine and Stengers (1984) have shown, simple systems usually are static and tend to equilibrium; complex systems are always dynamic and dissipative. Although composite systems (such as the global biodiversity governance system composed of units of different kinds) produce more minor events than catastrophes, chain reactions of all sizes are an integral part of the dynamics of large interactive systems. Composite systems never reach equilibrium; rather, they evolve from one metastable state to the next.

Seeing as a complex system

Global biodiversity governance can be conceived as a constellation of regime complexes, a hierarchic, self-organizing, and open complex system with multiple entities interacting in nonlinear ways. Because entities and the environment of the system change, relationships among entities change also, which leads to the evolution of the system.

Seen through this prism, one may fear being face with a Panglossian view of global biodiversity governance. Far from it. The existing governance complex may not be the most effective for reconciling different conceptions of the relationship between societies and nature (the political problem) as well as protecting the natural conditions that enable societies to pursue their current and future goals (the biodiversity problem). Looking at global biodiversity governance as the emergent property of a complex system does not mean we cannot influence its dynamics.

Seeing biodiversity governance as the product of a complex system does not mean that governance itself is complex. Simple policies can be adopted to deal with complex problems, and one issue is to investigate how best to govern biodiversity in terms of effectiveness (whose definition must include features of complex systems, such as adaptation and learning). As shown previously, however, the international governance of biodiversity forms a complex system that should be approached as such. Thus, it means adopting a perspective from which new questions emerge. It leads to a redefinition of what is meant by science away from the modernist tradition (see Boulton *et al.* 2015 and chapter 3) that thinks about the social and natural world and their interrelationships in dichotomous and linear terms, and assumes the future is predictable (it is only a matter of knowledge) and that causes and effects are clearly related and measurable (Boulton *et al.* 2015, 52). In particular, it requires to think in terms of relationships among a diversity of agents and fractals, identifying rules that govern agents' behavior, accept that prediction is impossible (all one can hope for is predicting a range of possible states, rather than a specific one), think in terms of adaptive management rather than control, and rethink the bases of political action.

Think in terms of relationships among a diversity of agents and fractals

As in ecosystems, one should build upon diversity (rather than try and reduce it) and thus favor decentralized authority. In this view, MEAs of the biodiversity cluster are not a problem of institutional fragmentation, but adaptive features that may encourage effective governance through experimentation (Harrison 2006; Haas 2004). Moreover, rather than focusing strictly on MEA secretariats, the more appropriate unit of analysis should be the convention governance system itself, that is, the system of institutions, norms, and interrelationships created by international regimes, of which secretariats constitute the administrative and coordinating unit. These units of evolution and adaptation are mission-oriented, as opposed to management-oriented, institutions: more flexible (depending on their relationship with UNEP) and better able to learn, thus fostering the adaptiveness of the system.

As has been noted by others, distributing authority, resources, and capacities across multiple institutions may enhance relevance, flexibility, and legitimacy in dealing with complex biodiversity governance (Koetz et al. 2012). In this context, although chaos theory is a particular case of complex system theory, fractals, building on Thomas Frey, can be thought of as narrow spectra of global authority managed by networks, coalitions or a regime outside of the direct control of individual nations, although the latter will participate in them. Politics becomes the struggle over the range and limits of fractal authority, as well as the search for self-organization in order for cooperation and effectiveness to emerge.

Identify rules that govern agents' behavior

In some instances (such as flocking birds, market economies, ant colonies), understanding and managing complex systems may largely rest on identifying the rules that govern agents' behavior that give rise to their properties. We do not have to understand the complexity of the agents itself, only the rules that govern their interactions with other agents and in the face of evolving systemic variables. Biodiversity conservation is determined by local interactions among decentralized units. The rules they follow are only in part imposed by central coordination mechanisms. Within their respective mandate, IGOs and NGOs, as organizations, wish to secure access to the resources on which they depend (finance, expertise, projects, political, etc.). Firms are moved first by survival, then by profits. States seek to minimize uncertainty in the maintenance of their security (defined broadly) through "sovereignty bargains" or power politics. Organizations create and maintain boundaries; agents develop roles (that is, meta rules) that may even conflict (see chapter 4).

Note that the identification of such rules is a heuristics that should not be confused with the development of ABM. Identifying these rules may not always be feasible or appropriate, for agents may also be moved by ideas, develop networks, and act reflexively in their attempts to reconcile their twin quest for autonomy and uncertainty reduction, aspects that simple rules may not encompass. In addition, one should be weary of the fallacy of composition. To say that lower levels give rise to higher-level dynamics (see previous section on hierarchy) does not mean that we can confuse levels of analysis and assume that what is true of individual units is true for groups of such units (such as networks).

Accept that simple prediction is impossible

The notion of unintended consequences, of course, is a direct implication of nonlinearity. Ecologists have long integrated the possibility and even the certainty of surprises into their models. Policy analysts have more difficulty doing so.

Linear thinking is present when one looks at the new IPBES as a way of improving existing performance through the coordination of a scientific consensus around the protection of biodiversity (see chapter 3). But IPBES also represents a disruptive innovation as it tries to define for itself a new niche, thereby forcing units to adapt (such as MEA subsidiary scientific bodies) and changing the relationships within and between regimes and system attractors.

A complex system approach allows us to anticipate rather than predict. For example, we could anticipate several distinct developments or effects from one course of action but be unable to say which one will come to pass. The specific future state of a complex system cannot be predicted (because different causes can produce the same effect and conversely, similar causes, different effects), but possible states can be. This is the stuff of scenario exercises that have been popular. The issue is not predicting the future state of the system per se, but whether the functions it fulfills will last or expand, basically what the notion of ecosystem services encompasses. Which raises the issue of management.

Dissociate management from control

Complex systems cannot be controlled, because, as mentioned, in a complex system, the same causes do not always produce the same effects; context matters. Rather, we should opt for a reconceptualization of management in terms of adaptive management (Holling 1978). Adaptive management is characterized by flexible policies and the plurality of views that inform it; no particular epistemic community can possess all the necessary knowledge to form policy. Science, models, expert knowledge, and the policies based on them are not interpreted as ultimate answers but merely as a means to guide a cautious process of intervention in complex ecosystems. The goal of management shifts from achieving a single target to an integrated view of maintaining ecosystem resilience, avoiding for example, catastrophic and irreversible "flips" to other equilibrium states (that is, tipping points) (Holling 2001).

Approaching global biodiversity governance as a complex system allows us to incorporate much of current research in order to construct a coherent whole. Rather than being seen as the advent of chaos, paralysis, and effectiveness, the evolution of the global environmental governance system provides a set of tools for handling complex governance systems that take advantage of their properties and facilitate adaptation.

Rethink the bases of political action

Complex systems require to think anew about power, authority, accountability, and legitimacy. Earnest and Rosenau (2006) have argued that power posed a problem for complexity thinking. But in a complex system, the issue is not to determine which units or agents are dominant and able to resist change, impose policy directions, or affect outcomes; nor does it stem from asymmetric relationships as in complex interdependence. Rather, power is distributed and resides in the capacity to mobilize and form coalitions. Future international relations will increasingly involve the interplay of agents and their networks (e.g. states) with hybrid networks of coalitions. According to the US Intelligence Council (2012), power will disseminate among a variety of networks and coalitions nested in a multipolar world. Policy networks are particularly interesting in the context of global environmental governance. Examples are the CGIAR, the World Commission on Dams, the Global Water Partnership, the Roll Back Malaria Campaign, and RIOD.

Likewise, although authority can indeed be a simplifying force (Earnest and Rosenau 2006) through which agents reduce uncertainty at the cost of some autonomy, the contemporary foundations of authority are diverse and embedded in a variety of actors that claim and sometimes enjoy authority in their respective spheres. In addition, formal authority and power may not coincide, as organization theorists have shown. The function of boundary organizations, then, is to manage the interactions among these different spheres of authority and power (see chapter 3).

If authority is fragmented and power based on process and interactions rather than status or capabilities, what happens to accountability (see chapter 1)? Can any actor be held responsible for the observed outcomes if the latter are the fruits of nonlinear processes? Already, coalitions among private actors (such as the Forest Stewardship Council) have raised the issue of the democratic deficit of private governance (Smouts 2003). More specifically, how to ensure that nonstate actors are held accountable, and to whom? Does it mean that business and substate actors should be brought more fully into dialogues with governments around climate change, for example? Indeed, with participation comes responsibility.

Conclusion: Fleshing out a new method

The study of complex systems is the science of change and transitions, not equilibrium. Thus it constitutes an alternative paradigm that mirrors many debates in the biological sciences. The fundamental challenge is to develop a theory and practice of adaptive governance of complex systems. At the very least, this approach forces us to rethink the notion and value of equilibrium (systems are dynamic), the role of uncertainty, the relationship between agents and structure, the nature of learning (actors' coping and transforming strategies lead to adaptation and transformation, or decay), the notion of resilience and its links to diversity, the conception of power legitimacy, or the nature of change. Governance is the product of self-organization. The question then is what affects the emergence of various properties, how stable are these properties, and under what conditions does change take place.

At this point, we face two queries. The first one is easily handled: how useful could a complexity approach be in analyzing international politics, particularly surrounding issues such as the environment that cut across numerous actors, values, and knowledge bases? This chapter has shown (i) what it means to think in terms of a complex system in the case of biodiversity and (ii) how desirable it might be to do so in order to go beyond the current stalemates in thinking about international environmental governance. Complexity is more than a metaphor. As Boulton et al. (2015, 11) emphasize, complexity science is "much more than modelling. It provides ontology, a worldview, a generic insight into dynamics." The second issue is a much harder challenge: how do we go from a metaphor to a theory? As a general approach and as a heuristic policy tool, it holds much promise. As a theory, or school of theories, much remains to be done.

One can think of three ways of tackling that question. The first one is to reject theory building as a vain enterprise along with the positivist epistemology that goes with it. Perhaps, if we follow Earnest and Rosenau (2006), complex systems theory is nothing more than a conceptual framework that makes the world intelligible rather than predictable, much like the theory of evolution (see Byrne and Callaghan 2014). However, it would still be incumbent on those proponents to specify the bases of any knowledge claim. A second and more difficult way is to posit that a nonanalytical perspective can be positivist, and in that case, to see what its development would entail. Finally, one could sidestep the issue.

First, following Edgard Morin, Byrne and Callaghan (2014, 5) urge in the case of social systems to take up the distinction between restricted (the emergent product of "interactions among simple agents") and general complexity, that is systems with properties that are not just the product of simple interactions, but systems where the rules that govern agents' behavior may change through learning, and agents and structure are mutually constituted. Second, the fundamental concern behind a closer look at complexity remains the need to find how interdependent and self-interested entities can cooperate on solving problems that affect their survival as a whole. Complexity theory provides a way of conceptualizing the problem; it does not a priori exclude the generation of partial causal theories. Thus existing partial theories remain useful but have to be rethought in that light (for example regime and regime complex theory, game theory). Role theory, which already transcends the agent-structure debate, provides another avenue of theory building (see chapter 4).

Difficulties abound in seeing as a complex system because of our ties to linear thinking and positivism, because of the confusions in the literature on complex systems, and because of the domination of mathematical and physics approaches and corresponding attempts to ignore the specifics of social complex systems. As Byrne and Callaghan (2014) argue, complex system theory has to be adapted to social systems, which means amending, expanding, and discarding some notions, perhaps going as far as rejecting an ABM approach.

Intellectual schizophrenia looms large between the familiarity of linear thinking and the confusion of complex thinking, between developing predictive or heuristic models, or between an ABM and a holistic approach (unit-level rules of behavior as opposed to system-level connections and functions). The issue may be not to generate confirmable propositions, but whether this way of thinking helps uncover new avenues of empirical investigation and is thus generative as well as structural (see Clarke and Primo 2007). As Barkin (2015) recently argued convincingly, heuristic models are not designed to accurately describe or predict. Hence our frustrations with complex systems should be put in context. We are not developing a global biodiversity model similar to climate change models. Concern with developing testable hypotheses may therefore be misplaced. It would not be the purpose of a complex theory of international environmental governance. Thus evaluating the usefulness of such a model, when sufficiently developed, will mean evaluating its internal logic and its ability to make sense of particular situations in confrontation with reality (Ibid.).

Rather than a methodology that could produce law-like statements, complexity is a method (Morin 1990), a memento or reminder of how one should think about phenomena, and pragmatism may very well constitute its philosophy. It is already the case that, in truth, policy makers "muddle through" and that economic decisions are the result of rules of thumb or of a trial-and-error approach (Harrison 2016). Moreover, it would be a welcome return to the notion that knowledge is contextual, in opposition to efforts by IGOs and NGOs alike to discover rules of governance that quickly morph into universal principles of public policy. As we have seen throughout, and especially in chapter 2, this gives rise to a questionable doxa bound to disappoint for it may not be easily translated across time, space, and social systems.

Pragmatism is rooted in learning, conceived as "an on-going process of problem-solving, deliberation, experimentation, sedimented over time as experience, identity, habit, skill, and knowledge" (Geyer and Ansell 2016). It recognizes that problems are not given (see chapter 1), that values are contextual and that they spring from deliberation, and that experimentation is the only way of dealing with the inherent uncertainty of the world (Ibid.).

At best, a complex systems approach aims to supersede rather than replace the Cartesian model, just as relativity theory superseded Newtonian physics which nevertheless retains considerable usefulness. It represents the point of departure of stimulating research programs dedicated to finding new models of global governance.

Notes

1 For an overview on the emergence of complexity thinking in IR, see Kavalski (2007) and Bousquet and Curtis (2011).
2 Rosenau himself published an article the following year about the deliquescence of international authority. Indeed, having in place structures designed to deal with complexity does not logically imply that the system is not complex. Further, although the

distribution of power and authority among international actors is uneven, (i) the system is anarchic, (ii) there are competing loci of authority (state, market, civil society, knowledge, etc.), and (iii) these actors all claim legitimacy and possess a capacity to mobilize resources and form coalitions (albeit in different degrees).
3 "Generally speaking, "complexity" describes systems composed of elements in dynamic interaction engaged in emergent, self-organizing processes" (Wells 2009, 25).
4 The group of megadiverse countries might be one example in the biodiversity realm.
5 As in the management of the Aldabra Islands of Seychelles.
6 Levels should not be confused with scales. Scales are "the spatial, temporal, quantitative, or analytical dimensions used to measure and study any phenomenon," whereas levels are "units of analysis that are located at the same position on a scale" and that may be ordered hierarchically (Gibson et al. 2000, 218). Within the jurisdictional scale, for example, we may distinguish at least four levels (local, national, regional, and global). Other scales include time, space, institutions, management, networks, or knowledge. Managing across scales poses a number of challenges that co-management structures and boundary management attempt to meet (see Cash et al. 2006).
7 I.e. benefits and drawbacks of a regional ecosystem-based management of environmental issues.
8 Individual birds behave according to simple rules enacted based on local information. Any individual bird determines speed and direction by flying toward the center of the flock, mimicking the velocity of the neighboring birds and staying a safe distance away from them.
9 "One of the great mysteries of large distributed systems – from communities and organizations to brains and ecosystems – is how globally coherent activity can emerge in the absence of centralized authority or control" (Watts 2003, 51).
10 For example, Wendt (2003), reasoning from an apparent complex system perspective (which he calls self-organization theory), sees a world state as an emergent property. The basic underlying issue is whether complex systems tend to an end state and, if so, how the latter is defined. Although Wendt seems to view it as an institution possessing the monopoly of force, enjoying legitimacy, exercising sovereignty, and demonstrating corporate agency, he acknowledges that a world state might look very different and be much more decentralized, provided it respects these attributes.
11 Four main factors may account for this evolution: i) the emergence of a "green industry" which considers new international environmental regulations an opportunity for growth and profit; ii) the progressive awakening by some companies of the risk which environmental problems could represent to their legitimacy and competitiveness; iii) the perception that a strong, effective and efficient GEG is central to the development of the business world since it guarantees a clear and stable institutional environment; and iv) incentives given by IGOs and states for a more active role of private actors in finding solutions to global environmental issues (Le Prestre 2005).
12 This "biodiversity cluster" includes the Convention on the Conservation of Migratory Species of Wild Animals (CMS), the Convention on International Trade in Endangered Species of Wild Fauna and Flora (CITES), the Convention on Wetlands of International Importance (Ramsar Convention), the Convention concerning the protection of the World Cultural and Natural Heritage (WHC), the International Treaty on Plant Genetic Resources for Food and Agriculture (ITPGRFA) and the CBD.
13 Concerts are attractors. The notion of concert may also have to be redefined beyond involving only states.

References

Alter, K. J. and S. Meunier. (2009). "The Politics of International Regime Complexity." *Perspectives on Politics* 7 (1): 13–24.

Axelrod, R. (1997). *The Complexity of Cooperation: Agent-Based Models of Competition and Collaboration*. Princeton: Princeton University Press.

Axelrod, R. and M. D. Cohen. (1999). *Harnessing Complexity: Organizational Implications of a Scientific Frontier*. New York: Free Press.

Bak, P. and K. Chen. (1991). "Self-Organized Criticality." *Scientific American* 264 (1): 46–53.

Barkin, J. S. (2015). "On the Heuristic Use of Formal Models in International Relations Theory." *International Studies Review* 17 (4): 617–634.

Betsill, M. M. and H. Bulkeley. (2004). "Transnational Networks and Global Environmental Governance: The Cities for Climate Protection Program." *International Studies Quarterly* 48: 471–493.

Boulton, J. G., et al. (2015). *Embracing Complexity: Strategic Perspectives for an Age of Turbulence*. Oxford: Oxford University Press.

Bousquet, A. and S. Curtis. (2011). "Beyond Models and Metaphors: Complexity Theory, Systems Thinking and International Relations." *Cambridge Review of International Affairs* 24 (1): 43–62.

Bousquet, A. and R. Geyer. (2011). "Introduction: Complexity and the International Arena." *Cambridge Review of International Affairs* 24 (1): 1–3.

Bulkeley, H. (2005). "Reconfiguring Environmental Governance: Towards a Politics of Scales and Networks." *Political Geography* 24: 875–902.

Byrne, D. (1998). *Complexity Theory and the Social Sciences: An Introduction*. London: Routledge.

Byrne, D. and G. Callaghan. (2014). *Complexity Theory and the Social Sciences: The State of the Art*. Abingdon: Routledge.

Cash, D., et al. (2006). "Scale and Cross-Scale Dynamics: Governance and Information in a Multilevel World." *Ecology and Society* 11 (2): 8.

Chandler, D., ed. (2014). *Resilience: The Governance of Complexity*. London: Routledge.

Clarke, K. A. and D. M. Primo. (2007). "Modernizing Political Science: A Model-Based Approach." *Perspectives on Politics* 5 (4): 741–753.

Cudworth, E. and S. Hobden. (2011). *Posthuman International Relations: Complexity, Ecologism and Global Politics*. London: Zed Books.

Descartes, R. (1909 [1637]). *Discourse on the Method of Rightly Conducting the Reason and Seeking the Truth in the Sciences*. New York: Collier & Son.

Dubash, N. K. and A. Florini. (2011). "Mapping the Global Energy Governance." *Global Policy* 2 (Special issue): 6–18.

Earnest, D. C. and J. N. Rosenau. (2006). "Signifying Nothing? Why Complex Systems Theory Tells Us So Little About Global Politics." In *Complexity in World Politics: Concepts and Methods for a New Paradigm*, edited by N. E. Harrison. Albany, NY: SUNY Press.

Gell-Mann, M. (1994). *The Quark and the Jaguar: Adventures in the Simple and the Complex*. New York: WH Freeman.

Geyer, R. and C. K. Ansell. (2016). "Pragmatic Complexity and Its Implications for Policy and IR." 9th WIRE Workshop. Brussels: Université Saint-Louis.

Gibson, C., et al. (2000). "The Concept of Scale and the Human Dimensions of Global Change: A Survey." *Ecological Economics* (32): 217–239.

Gulick, E. V. (1955). *Europe's Classical Balance of Power*. Ithaca: Cornell.

Guston, D. H. (2001). "Boundary Organizations in Environmental Policy and Science: An Introduction." *Science, Technology, & Human Values* 26 (4): 399–408.

Haas, P. M. (2004). "Addressing the Global Governance Deficit." *Global Environmental Politics* 4 (4): 1–16.

Hafner-Burton, E. M., et al. (2009). "Network Analysis for International Relations." *International Organization* 63 (03): 559–592.

Harrison, N. E. (2006). *Complexity in World Politics: Concepts and Methods of a New Paradigm.* Albany, NY: State University of New York Press.

Harrison, N. E. (2016). "World Politics as Process: Toward a Complexity Paradigm of International Relations." 9th WIRE Workshop. Brussels: Université Saint-Louis.

Holland, J. (1995). *Hidden Order: How Adaptation Builds Complexity.* New York: Addison-Wesley.

Holland, J. H. and J. H. Miller. (1991). "Artificial Adaptive Agents in Economic Theory." *The American Economic Review* 81 (2): 365–370.

Holling, C. S. (1978). *Adaptive Environmental Assessment and Management.* Chichester, UK: Wiley.

Holling, C. S. (2001). "Understanding the complexity of economic, ecological and social systems." *Ecosystems* 4: 390–405.

Ivanova, M. (2005). *Can the Anchor Hold? Rethinking the United Nations Environment Programme for the 21st Century.* New Haven, CT: Yale School of Forestry & Environmental Studies.

Ivanova, M. (2007). "Moving Forward By Looking Back: Learning from UNEP's History." In *Global Environmental Governance: Perspectives on the Current Debate.* Introduction by L. Swart and E. Perry. New York: Center for UN Reform Education: 26–47.

Jervis, R. (1997). *System Effects: Complexity in Political and Social Life.* Princeton: Princeton University Press.

Kaplan, M. A. (1975 [1957]). *System and Process in International Politics.* New York: Krieger.

Kavalski, E. (2007). "The Fifth Debate and the Emergence of Complex International Relations Theory: Notes on the Application of Complexity Theory to the Study of International Life." *Cambridge Review of International Affairs* 20 (3): 435–454.

Kavalski, E., ed. (2015). *World Politics at the Edge of Chaos: Reflections on Complexity and Global Life.* Albany, NY: State University of New York Press.

Keck, M. E. and K. Sikkink. (1998). *Activists Beyond Borders: Advocacy Networks in International Politics.* Ithaca, NY: Cornell University Press.

Keohane, R. O. and J. S. Nye, Jr. (2000). "Between Centralization and Fragmentation: The Club Model of Multilateral Cooperation and Problems of Democratic Legitimacy." American Political Science Convention. Washington, DC.

Keohane, R. O. and D. G. Victor. (2011). "The Regime Complex for Climate Change." *Perspectives on Politics* 9 (1).

Kim, R. E. (2013). "The Emergent Network Structure of the Multilateral Environmental Agreement System." *Global Environmental Change* 23: 980–991.

Koetz, T., *et al.* (2012). "Building Better Science-Policy Interfaces for International Environmental Governance: Assessing Potential within the Intergovernmental Platform for Biodiversity and Ecosystem Services." *International Environmental Agreements: Politics, Law and Economics* 12 (1), 1–21, DOI: 10.1007/s10784–10011–9152-z.

Lemos, M. C. and A. Agrawal. (2006). "Environmental Governance." *Annual Review of Environment and Resources* 31: 297–325.

Le Prestre, P. (1999). "Adapting to Environmental Insecurities: A Conceptual Model." In *Environmental Change, Adaptation and Security,* edited by S. Lonergan. Dordrecht: Kluwer Academic Publishers: 57–74.

Le Prestre, P. (2005). *Protection de l'environnement et relations internationales: les défis de l'écopolitique mondiale.* Paris: Armand Colin.

Le Prestre, P. (2010). "La nécessité d'une gouvernance interscalaire de la biodiversité." In *La convention internationale sur la biodiversité: enjeux de la mise en œuvre,* edited by C. Nègre. Paris: La documentation française: 77–88.

Maoz, Z. (2011). *Networks of Nations: The Formation, Evolution, and Impact of International Networks, 1816–2001.* New York: Cambridge University Press.

March, J. G. and J. P. Olsen. (1998). "The Institutional Dynamics of International Political Orders." *International Organization* 52: 943–969.

Miller, C. (2001). "Hybrid Management: Boundary Organizations, Science Policy, and Environmental Governance in the Climate Regime." *Science, Technology, & Human Values* 26 (4): 478–500.

Mitchell, M. (2009). *Complexity: A Guided Tour*. Oxford: Oxford University Press.

Mitchell, R. B. (2003). "International Environmental Agreements: A Survey of Their Features, Formation, and Effects." *Annual Review of Environmental Resources* 28: 429–461.

Moltke, K. (2001). "The Organization of the Impossible." *Global Environmental Politics* 1 (1): 23–28.

Morin, E. (1990). *Introduction à la complexité*. Paris: Le Seuil.

Najam, A. (2003). "The Case Against a New International Environmental Organization." *Global Governance* 9: 367–384.

Najam, A., et al. (2004). "The Emergent 'System' of Global Environmental Governance." *Global Environmental Politics* 4 (4): 23–35.

Najam, A., M. Papa, and N. Taiyab. (2006). *Global Environmental Governance: A Reform Agenda*. Winnipeg, International Institute for Sustainable Development.

Orsini, A., et al. (2013). "Regime Complexes: A Buzz, a Boom, or a Boost for Global Governance?" *Global Governance: A Review of Multilateralism and International Organizations* 19 (1): 27–39.

Ostrom, E. (1990). *Governing the Commons: The Evolution of Institutions for Collective Action*. New York: Cambridge University Press.

Padt, F., et al., eds. (2014). *Scale-Sensitive Governance of the Environment*. Oxford: John Wiley & Sons.

Parrott, L. (2002). "Complexity and the Limits of Ecological Engineering." *Transactions of the American Society of Agricultural Engineers* 45 (5).

Pearce, D. and J. Warford. (1993). *World without End: Economics, Environment, and Sustainable Development*. New York: Oxford University Press.

Pielou, E. C. (1975). *Ecological Diversity*. London: Wiley.

Prigogine, I. (1997). *The End of Certainty*. New York: Simon & Schuster.

Prigogine, I. and I. Stengers. (1984). *Order Out of Chaos: Man's New Dialogue with Nature*. New York: Bantam Books.

Raustiala, K. and D. G. Victor. (2004). "The Regime Complex for Plant Genetic Resources." *International Organization* 58 (2): 277–309.

Resnick, M. (1997). *Turtles, Termites, and Traffic Jams: Explorations in Massive Parallel Microworlds*. Cambridge: MIT Press.

Rosenau, J. N. (1990). *Turbulence in World Politics*. Princeton: Princeton University Press.

Rosenau, J. N. and M. Durfee. (2000). *Thinking Theory Thoroughly: Coherent Approaches to an Incoherent World*. Boulder, CO: Westview Press.

Smouts, M.-C. (2003). *Tropical Forests, International Jungle: The Underside of Global Ecopolitics*. Basingstoke, UK: Palgrave Macmillan.

Steinbruner, J. D. (2002). *The Cybernetic Theory of Decision: New Dimensions of Political Analysis*. Princeton: Princeton University Press.

United States Intelligence Council. (2012). *Global Trends 2030 Report*. Washington, DC: Intelligence Council.

Van Asselt, H. (2014). *The Fragmentation of Global Climate Governance: Consequences and Management of Regime Interactions*. London: Edward Elgar.

Waever, O. (1995). "Securitization and Desecuritization." In *On Security*, edited by R. Lipschutz. New York: Columbia University Press: 46–86.

Waltz, K. (1979). *Theory of International Politics*. Chicago: Addison-Wesley.

Watts, D. J. (2003). *Six Degrees: The Science of a Connected Age*. New York: W. W. Norton.
Wells, J. L. (2009). "Complexity and Climate Change: An Epistemological Study of Transdisciplinary Complexity Theories and Their Contribution to Socio-Ecological phenomena." PhD Dissertation. Berkeley, CA: University of California–Berkeley.
Wendt, A. (2003). "Why a World State Is Inevitable." *European Journal of International Relations* 9 (4): 491–542.

INDEX

Aarhus convention 17
Access and Benefit Sharing 46
accountability 23, 119, 151
Acharya, A. 97
acid rain, 99n23
actors: actorness 88; and ecopolitics 30; see also business actors, cities, networks
adaptation 19, 143–5
African Group 108, 114, 117–8, 124n4
Agarwal, A. and S. Narain 63, 125n20
agenda-setting, 9, 108–9; see also issue–framing
agent-based modelling 130, 149
agent-structure 77–8
analytical approach 129, 132
anthropocene 10
Arctic Monitoring and Assessment Programme 60
Asociación Independiente de América Latina y el Caribe (AILAC) 112
assessments 60–1, 65, 66; conditions of influence 61, 65, 69n8; Global Biodiversity Assessment (GBA) 65, 66; Ozone Trends Panel 60, 66; see also IPCC
Association of Small Island States (AOSIS) 112, 114, 117, 119, 125n23
Association of South-East Asian Nations (ASEAN) 99n29
Austria 80, 81
authority 151, 153n2
Aykut, S. and A. Dahan 91

Bak, P. and K. Chen 146
Bali Box 57–58
Bali Strategic Plan 124n8
Ban Ki-moon 21, 53
Basel Convention on the Control of the Transboundary Movements of Hazardous Wastes and Their Disposal 17, 124n9
BASIC (Brazil, South Africa, India, China) 114, 117, 118, 125n16
Beijing Declaration 105
Belgium 81
bifurcations 136, 147
biodiversity: actors 58; business 145; global governance 140–1, 143, 146, 148, 150; governance system 136–7; regime complex 144; see also Convention on Biological Diversity
Boulton, J. G. 129, 133, 152
boundary organizations 58, 68, 69, 69n6, 151; see also Intergovernmental Panel on Biodiversity and Ecosystems Services, Intergovernmental Panel on Climate Change
Bousquet, A. and S. Curtis 135, 138, 139, 140, 141
Bretherton, C. and J. Vogler 88, 90
Breuning, M. 77–8
British Columbia 30
business actors 145, 154n11
Byrnes, D. and G. Callaghan 140, 152

Canada, 30, 98n12; role 37, 77, 80, 98n9
Cantir, C. and J. Kaarbo 77

Cartagena Protocol 34, 91, 126n29
Cash, D. 69n8
centralization 43–7, 49, 130
China, 18, 90, 114, 125n22
churches: and the environment, 14–6, 48
civil society 46, 136
cities: climate change 30, 49n2, 140; International Council for Local Environmental Initiatives (ICLEI) 137
climate change 14, 20, 80, 114; adaptation, 16, 19; ethics and justice, 16–17, 19; mitigation, 16; two-degree target, 56, 69n4, 87, 90
clustering 47
collective action problem 13, 20
Commission on Sustainable Development (CSD) 146
complex systems 30, 132, 152; adaptation 31–2; definition 135; knowledge 59, 68; theory 131, 132, 134–5
complexity 4, 44, 130, 153; complication 134–5; definition 154n3; general vs restricted 140, 152; international relations 132–4
compliance 42–3, 49n6, 144
concert diplomacy 38, 41, 118, 126n24, 126n25, 154n13
conferences (UN), see UN Summits
Consultative Group on International Agricultural Research (CGIAR) 138, 151
convention governance system 149
Convention on Biological Diversity (CBD) 17, 34, 36, 46, 58, 63, 136, 138, 144; COP-10 (2010), 35, 115; developing countries 109; indigenous knowledge 59; rights 17, 18; see also Access and Benefit-Sharing, Cartagena Protocol, Nagoya Protocol
Convention on International Trade in Endangered Species of Wild Fauna and Flora (CITES) 36, 80, 126n29
Convention on Persistent Organic Pollutants 80
conventions, see Treaties and individual conventions
cooperation 18, 36, 78, 143
cosmopolitanism 48
Costa Rica 113
courage 20–3

decentralization 149
decision making 34–35
Denmark 81
developing countries: agenda-setting 38, 104, 108–9; changing role 121–3;
environmental discourse 106–7; expert representation 66; participation 108; South-South Cooperation 114–5, 125n17; Stockholm conference 124; strategies of influence 113–23; unity 113–4; weaknesses 107–8; *see also* North-South
Development Assistance Committee (DAC) 38
dichlorodiphenyltrichloroethane (DDT) 18
diversity 137
Dubash, N. K. and A. Florini 137, 138

Earnest, D. C. and J. N. Rosenau 133
ecological imperialism 105
ecopolitics 21; definition 6n1; doxa 1–4; International Relations 27
ecosystems approach 34
ecosystems services 150
Ecuador 120–121
education 22
effectiveness 38, 47, 42, 143, 148
Elgström, O. 98n21
emergence 133, 140, 142–3
emergent countries 37, 107, 111
environmental non-governmental organization (ENGOs) 14
environmental issues: civic dimensions 13–4; ethical dimensions 14–6; instrumentalization 13, 107, 124n6, 124n7; political dimensions 12–3; scientific dimensions 9–12
environmental progress 34–36
epistemic community 56, 59, 70, 120
equilibrium 147–8, 154n10
equity 17, 116–7; *see also* Fairness, Justice, Principles, Common but differentiated responsibility
ethics 14–8; *see also* Justice
European Union (EU) 42; climate change 73, 98n18; commission 82; COP-15 (Copenhagen, 2009) 33; global environmental problems 82; identity 82; institutional foundations 83–4; Kyoto Protocol 18, 73, 91–2; Maastricht Treaty 84; perception 88–89; performance 73–5, 88; presidency 75; role 37, 73, 74, 79–82, 84–5; soft power 88, 99n21; subsidiarity principle 31
evolution, 145; *see also* Adaptation and Learning

fairness 18, 43
fallacy of composition 75, 97n2
Farrell, A. 60

feedback loops 138–9, 140
Ferrero-Waldner, Benita 85
financing 35, 112–3, 124n10; instruments 35; Monterrey consensus 34
Finland 80, 81
fisheries 80
footprint 10
foreign policy 77
Forest Stewardship Council (FSC) 145, 151
Foundation for International Environment Law and Development (FIELD) 119
fractals 149
fragmentation 46, 50n14, 113, 122, 133, 149
France, 18, 32n7, 47, 77, 81
Francophonie organization 117–118
free trade 28
Future Earth 11, 55, 69n2

genetically-modified organisms (GMOs) 65
Germany 77, 81, 82, 87, 99n23
Geyer, R. and C. K. Ansell 153
Global Environment Facility (GEF) 35, 38, 116
global-local links 42, 50n11, 140; see also Governance
global problems 41–2
globalization 28, 29
goods 10; common property resources 10; public goods 10, 23n3
governance 31; adaptive 151; decentralized 4; definition 50n13; global, 48; levels 42; multiscale 83, 140; new model 37–8, 130, 134; private 31, 137–8, 145; reform 45–7; see also REACH
green economy 74
green imperialism 18
Group of 20 (G20) 118
Group of 77 (G77) 49, 73, 88, 113, 114, 117, 119, 126n29
Group of megadiverse countries 107, 117, 154n4

Haas, P. 63, 66
Harnisch, S. 79
Hardin, G. 39
Harrison, N. 131
Holsti, K. 76
Hulme, M. 42

implementation 108
India 106, 116
Indonesia 106

interdependence, 28, 29
Intergovernmental Panel on Biodiversity and Ecosystems Services (IPBES), 44, 55, 59, 60, 61, 62, 63, 67, 68, 115, 150
Intergovernmental Panel on Climate Change (IPCC) 53, 55, 57, 60, 61, 66, 90, 109, 146
intermestic issues 28
International Maritime Organization (IMO) 73, 75, 85, 94
International Organization for Standardization (ISO) 145
international relations: new features 48–9, 129
International Whaling Commission (IWC) 144
interplay 146
issue-framing 3, 10; see also agenda–setting

Jankelevitch, V. 22
Japan 23n7, 36, 77
Jervis, R. 29, 131, 143
Juma, C. 45
justice 14–9, 63; biodiversity 17; climate change 16–7; international relations 17; see also ethics

Kavalski, E. 131
Kelemen, R. D. 83
Kennedy, J. 22
knowledge 62–3

Laudato Si Encyclical 15–16; see also churches, Pope Francis
leadership 36, 85–93, 98n16
learning 36, 68–9, 153
legitimacy 38, 151
linkages 11–2, 29, 115
Lucarelli, S. 89
Luxemburg 81

Malaysia 113, 120
management 150
March, J. G. and J. P. Olsen 147
marine conservation 80
Marine Stewardship Council (MSC) 145
Meadows, D. 11
Millennium Declaration 34
Millennium Development Goals 33, 38
Millenium Ecosystem Assessment 60, 66–7
Miller, C. 64
Mitchell, M. 135
Mitchell, R. 142

Montreal Protocol on Substances that Deplete the Ozone Layer, 35, 37, 44, 59, 63, 106
moralism, 17
Morin, E. 134, 140
multilateralism 49, 98n13, 130

Nagoya Protocol, 115, 120
Najam, A. 143, 144
national interest 77
Netherlands, 81, 87
networks 137, 138, 140, 151
non-governmental organization (NGOs) 29–30, 67, 116–7, 119
nonlinearity 138
Nordhaus, W. 11
nordic countries 80
norms 35; *see also* principles
North–South 37, 126n29

Ophuls, W. 23
order 140
Organization of Petroleum Exporting Countries (OPEC) 114

Palme, O. 33
Panama 119
Papua New Guinea 113
Parrott, L. 140
participation 67–8, 108; *see also* Developing countries
path-dependency 145–7
planetary boundaries 11
Plato 54
political will 20
Pope: Benedict XVI 44; Francis 9, 15–6, 22, 42, 44; John-Paul II 15
power 29, 41, 43, 75, 85–6, 88, 151
pragmatism 153
prediction 150
Prigogine, I. 147
principles 110–2; common but differentiated responsibility 18, 34, 37, 85, 91, 106, 107, 110–2, 125n14; no-harm 125n12; participation 35; precautionary 34, 35, 57, 139
prudence, 21, 23
pyrrhic victories 91, 99n25

Quebec 30

Ramsar convention 144
REACH 73, 75, 97n1
Reducing Emissions from Deforestation and Forest Degradation (REDD+) 93, 112, 113, 119, 123, 133

regime: complex 17; effectiveness 34; interplay 38; learning 144; self-organization 142
region 94–6, 123–4
regulatory politics 13, 83
Réseau international des organisations non gouvernementales sur la désertification (RIOD) 138, 151
Resnick, M. 139
Responsible Care 145
responsible economics principles 145
Rockström, J. 11
role: change 94, 99n27; conception 76, 78, 93, 97n4, 97n5; conflicts, 78, 88, 93; definition, 75–6; developing countries, 37; entrapment, 90–4; expectation, 97; limits 78–9; power 75; prescription, 76, 97n4; status v identity, 81–82, 99n28; theory 78; *see also* Canada, European Union, United States
Roll Back Malaria Campaign 138, 151
Rosenau, J. N. 28, 131
Rosenau, J. N. and M. Durfee 136

scales 154n6
Schreurs, M. and Y. Tiberghien 83
science-policy interface 64–5; co-production model 59, 67; linear model 53, 55–6
self-organization 141–2
Shue, H. 16–7
Smouts, M-C. and B. Badie 95
Solzhenitsyn A. 21
South(s), *see* developing countries
sovereignty 40–1, 105, 110, 125n11
stability 137, 147
states, 39–41, 50n9
Stengers, I. 68
Stern Review on the Economics of Climate Change 3, 12, 18
Sundqvist, G. and B. Lahn 57–8
sustainable development, 17, 38, 109
Sweden, 80, 81, 99n23
synergies 11, 29
systems: analysis 130–1; complex adaptive systems 144; open 141; stability 50n15; *see also* complex systems

The Economics of Ecosystems and Biodiversity (TEEB) 3, 12
Thies, C. G. 75
tipping points 11, 141, 147
trade-offs 11, 23n6, 30
trade-related environmental measures (TREMs) 44

trade-related intellectual property rights (TRIPs) 46
treaties: framework convention – protocol technique 36; legally-binding, 42–3; *see also* individual treaties and conventions
two-level games 28

uncertainty 29, 65, 137, 142
United Kingdom 23n7; climate change 13, 80, 81, 82; role 77, 87
United Nations Conference on Sustainable Development (UNCSD) 74
United Nations Convention to Combat Desertification (UNCCD) 49, 114, 144
United Nations Development Programme (UNDP) 34, 120, 121
United Nations Environment Organization (UNEO) 49, 86
United Nations Environment Programme (UNEP) 45, 46, 47, 63, 74, 82, 109, 135, 146
United Nations Framework Convention on Climate Change (UNFCCC) 17, 18, 36, 37, 58, 146; COP–6 (2000) 73; COP–14 (2008) 30; COP–15 (2009) 33, 38, 74, 91, 111; COP–16 (2010) 74, 113, 118; COP–17 (2011) 74, 93, 118; COP–21 (2015) 19, 50n8, 91, 109, 111, 112, 114, 117, 118, 130; Kyoto Protocol, 18, 35, 43, 49n6, 73, 74, 80, 85, 86, 87, 91, 92, 99n25, 116, 123; *see also* climate change
United Nations Summits: Johannesburg (2002) 33–4, 46; Rio (1992) 33, 34, 145; Rio+20 (2012) 32, 46; Stockholm (1972) 145; success and failure 33–4; usefulness 32, 34
United States 13, 23n7, 50n9, 124n7; AID 18, 105; biodiversity convention 13, 138; churches 15; global environmental problems 82, 99n26; international environmental governance reform 47; President Carter 13; President Obama 13; role 37, 80, 82, 90
universal model 118; *see also* cosmopolitanism
Universal Declaration on the Right to Development 18

van Leeuwen, J. and K. Kern 75
Victor, D. 95
Vitousek, P. 10
Vogel, D. 40, 83
Vogler, J. 82

Walker, S. 93
water issues 35, 38, 43, 46; Global Water Partnership 138, 151
Wehner, L. and C.Thies 75
Wendt, A. 154n10
Western Climate Initiative 30
World Bank 124n6, 144
World Commission on Dams 138, 145, 151
World Environment Organization 44–5, 47, 48, 74, 146
World Government 48
World Trade Organization (WTO) 34, 44, 57

Zartman, I. W. and J. Z. Rubin 119

Taylor & Francis eBooks

Helping you to choose the right eBooks for your Library

Add Routledge titles to your library's digital collection today. Taylor and Francis ebooks contains over 50,000 titles in the Humanities, Social Sciences, Behavioural Sciences, Built Environment and Law.

Choose from a range of subject packages or create your own!

Benefits for you
- Free MARC records
- COUNTER-compliant usage statistics
- Flexible purchase and pricing options
- All titles DRM-free.

Benefits for your user
- Off-site, anytime access via Athens or referring URL
- Print or copy pages or chapters
- Full content search
- Bookmark, highlight and annotate text
- Access to thousands of pages of quality research at the click of a button.

REQUEST YOUR FREE INSTITUTIONAL TRIAL TODAY — **Free Trials Available** We offer free trials to qualifying academic, corporate and government customers.

eCollections – Choose from over 30 subject eCollections, including:

Archaeology	Language Learning
Architecture	Law
Asian Studies	Literature
Business & Management	Media & Communication
Classical Studies	Middle East Studies
Construction	Music
Creative & Media Arts	Philosophy
Criminology & Criminal Justice	Planning
Economics	Politics
Education	Psychology & Mental Health
Energy	Religion
Engineering	Security
English Language & Linguistics	Social Work
Environment & Sustainability	Sociology
Geography	Sport
Health Studies	Theatre & Performance
History	Tourism, Hospitality & Events

For more information, pricing enquiries or to order a free trial, please contact your local sales team: www.tandfebooks.com/page/sales

 The home of Routledge books

www.tandfebooks.com